LOUISE WRIGHT studied at the Birmingham College of Art and trained as a stage designer at the Birmingham Repertory Theatre. She worked for several years as a freelance writer and illustrator before returning to the theatre. As a production manager, she was responsible for many London productions, including well-known musicals, pantomimes and straight plays.

When work permitted, she escaped to her remote Warwickshire cottage and became a keen walker and bird-watcher, one of the best ways to enjoy the gentle countryside to be found in the Midlands.

Her work in the theatre developed her knowledge and love of period architecture, furnishings and landscaping and she was interior decorator for the Lord Chamberlain's architect, designing colour schemes for theatres, cinemas and factories.

She has written several books for children.

JAMES PRIDDEY was widely known in the Midlands, particularly through his drawings, many of which have appeared in the *Birmingham Post*. He was born at Handsworth, Birmingham, and knew the area intimately all his life. He trained at Moseley School of Art and Birmingham College of Art, and later worked as a designer for silversmiths, producing designs for domestic plate, civic regalia and presentation plate. During this time he became interested in etching and aquatint engraving.

Mr Priddey became a freelance artist and his work has been exhibited at the Royal Academy, Royal Society of Painter Etchers and Engravers, Royal Society of British Artists, Royal Scottish Academy and most provincial galleries. He is very proud to include the Print Collectors Guild of America among his commissioned drawings and also a mural which he produced for the Ministry of Works.

Mr Priddey had many connections with local art activities including the Birmingham Easel Club, Birmingham Art Circle, Royal Birmingham Society of Artists and the Birmingham Water Colour Society.

The surprising beauty to be found in machine-made landscapes.

HEART OF ENGLAND

by *LOUISE WRIGHT*

with drawings by JAMES PRIDDEY

ROBERT HALE • LONDON

© *Louise Wright and James Priddey 1973*
First published in Great Britain 1973
Reprinted 1977
Paperback edition 1993

ISBN 0 7090 5274 X

Robert Hale Limited
Clerkenwell House
Clerkenwell Green
London EC1R 0HT

Printed and bound in Malta by Interprint Ltd.

Contents

Maps

Illustrations

Acknowledgements

Louise Wright wishes to thank the following individuals and organisations for their help and kindness:

In particular James Corbett and Richard Traves, and also William Bannister, the Earl of Bradford, John Denis, Charles Gibbs, Frank Hayes, Ian Langford, Miss Judy Littler, Philip Lloyd, Richard Luck, Philip Mander, Miss Dorothy McCulla, Mrs Bushill-Matthews, Mrs Pauline Norton, Ian Paul, Ernest Pee, E. J. Schatz, Mrs Esther Seager, Harry Seager, Arthur Smith, Mrs Sybil Stone.

The Librarians of Bilston, Dudley, Stratford-upon-Avon, Warwick and West Bromwich;

The Town Planning Departments at Birmingham, Dudley, Halesowen, Leamington, Stafford, Stourbridge, Stratford, Walsall, Warley, Warwick, West Bromwich, Wolverhampton and Worcester, and the Calthorpe Estate Office;

The Museums at Bantock, Bilston, Brierley Hill, Dudley and York;

The Black Country Society, The Council for the Preservation of Rural England, The Upper Avon Navigation Trust;

The Town Clerks of Bewdley, Bridgnorth, Bromsgrove, Droitwich and Tamworth;

Messrs Guest, Keen and Nettlefold, Chance Brothers, and Copper Enamels;

Mrs Barbara Ellis and the publishers of *Country Life* for permission to quote from the poem 'A Bus Ride in the Country'.

For permission to reproduce some drawings thanks are due to:

The Director, City Museum and Art Gallery, Birmingham (for the drawings of Lee Crescent, Harborne and Handsworth); Mr Martin Hedges (Halesowen) and Mrs M. G. Maher (Warwick and Leamington).

Introduction

James Priddey and I have lived in and around the Midlands most of our lives—and this book is our personal salute to its variety, charm and energy.

We have seen the devastation caused by the last war, the boom in motor-car production, the traffic jams, the new roads, the decline of familiar industries and the demand for new and better housing.

Together, we re-explored an area within a radius of 25 miles from the Bull Ring, Birmingham. We travelled east as far as Arbury, north to Abbots Bromley, west to Bridgnorth and south to Coventry. Wherever we went, we found a familiar but changing scene, which challenged our individual responses as artist and writer.

The result of our review is not a statistical Domesday survey, but an affectionate look at the heart of England, in a time of rapid change. More often than not, we found the changes achieved an overdue visual and social impro-

Clent village, at the foot of the Clent Hills. Five miles of walking country between Wychbury Hill and Waseley Hill. Highest point 1,000 feet.

vement in an area which has long borne the brunt of profound industrial upheaval.

In some areas, we saw there had been neglect and sometimes a stupid disregard of our past heritage—in others, the past is controlling the future. But old or new, the present scene in the Midlands has much to offer.

13

For readers who may wish to follow our steps more closely than they can from the maps in this book, we give particulars of the maps we used in our journeys. For Chapters 1 to 3 we used Geographia, Greater Birmingham; for Chapters 4 to 6: Geographia, West Midlands; and for Chapters 7 to 12: One-inch Ordnance Survey Maps, Sheets 119 (Stafford), 120 (Burton-on-Trent), 130 (Kidderminster), 131 (Birmingham), 132 (Coventry and Rugby), and 144 (Cheltenham and Evesham).

L.W.

TO 'OLD HERBACIOUS'

CHAPTER ONE

Second in Size

Customers enjoyed themselves at the Bell Tavern in Philip Street, Birmingham. There was always the chance of a good sing-song, and the regulars particularly appreciated those evenings when they could join in the chorus of the latest ballad composed, and sung by their uninhibited host, John Freeth.

How the rafters rang! for

> Birmingham must (whose fame shall sing),
> Second in size to London be;
> Every month fresh houses spring.
> Every year new streets we see.

And the speed of change as observed and admired by those eighteenth century roisterers continued unabated until halted by the bombs of the second world war. The blitz devastation and the lack of building materials, checked the insatiable developers but enabled far-sighted planners to make rebuilding preparations for the future.

Now, a generation later, Birmingham is a city of vast new industrial estates, new houses, new office blocks, new stores, new shopping precincts—all linked to a network of new, fast motorways—roads cut between and below or rising three tiers high, all contributing to a radically altered urban scene.

Even well established residents have to buy an up-to-date street map in order to find their way around.

Favourite shops and old-established business premises have been demolished. The backyard workshops of the city's craftsmen have had to make way for flatted factories—highrise buildings containing workrooms to rent. Many of the one-man businesses had insufficient capital to survive the move and pay the increased rents and extra travelling expenses. Larger enterprises have re-appeared in districts as far out as Solihull.

For centuries after the Domesday survey, Birmingham remained a community of small traders, clustering along the banks of the River Rea at Deritend, with St Martin's Church, and the market rising up the hill towards the market cross.

It was not until the beginning of the eighteenth century, when the Mines Royal and Battery Company ceased to have a monopoly of brass and copper, that the rapid development began. This attracted the many

15

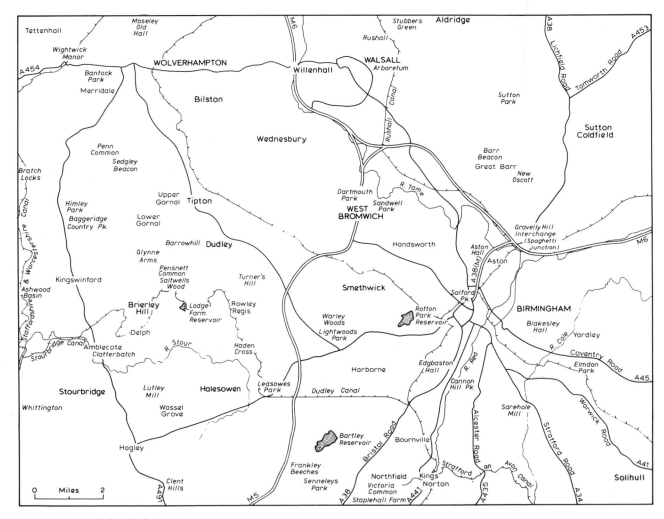

Birmingham and the Black Country

smiths, already settled in the community around St Martin's Church, to turn their skills to non-ferrous metals. In those days, the metals came into Birmingham in the form of thin sheets and the first items of 'Brum Brass' were 'Battery' wares, so-called because they were made by hammering these sheets.

The town had no guilds or companies, so a man was free to set up his own business and rise or fall by his own efforts. This attracted many craftsmen from the neighbouring counties.

Another factor was the religious freedom which attracted the persecuted. The Quakers arrived from Wales, among them, Sampson Lloyd, who was born while his parents were in a Welshpool prison. His son Sampson, together with John Taylor, a button maker, gave the town its first bank. The Lloyds' friends, John Cadbury and his father soon followed them to Birmingham and, fortunately for the south-west side of the town, succeeding generations of Cadburys, realising the importance of trees and parkland, preserved many acres of land, reaching far beyond the Lickey Hills.

Buttons and buckles are but small items in themselves, but along with coins, medals and 'toys', they were largely responsible for the lack of open spaces in the centre of Birmingham.

The Colmore estate, which covered extensive areas on the higher ground above St Martin's Church, was sanctioned for development, by a private Act in 1746. Then, with the break-up of the Holte estates at Aston at the beginning of the nineteenth century, the speculative builders were able to spread out to the east and west and northwards to meet Matthew Boulton's 'Manufactory', already established on the warren at Soho Heath.

Typical of the workshop-cum-houses of the period, was a property advertised in the town's newspaper, *Aris's Gazette*, in 1774. After a description of the house, it listed a "good warehouse to the front, two counting houses, a stable with three stalls, a yard, a large garden, and a brewhouse." Soon, however, the gardens had to go to make way for the small houses required for the ever increasing number of employees.

Business boomed. The old pack-horse roads were superseded by the canals, the narrow boats bringing supplies of coal and iron and other raw materials from the nearby Black Country. Emptied, the boats were immediately re-loaded with manufactured goods for delivery along the main system of canals to the ports of London, Liverpool, Bristol and Hull. As these ports became increasingly accessible and with the tremendous expansion in trade, space for recreation for the town's crowded workers became more and more limited.

Small wonder their sports were bull and bear-baiting

in the streets and terraces. Even the space available for bull-baiting must have been a confined one, as an infuriated bull outside the King's Arms in Harborne tossed a man through the bedroom window of the house opposite. Whether he was badly hurt or found an attractive occupant is not related, but he did not reappear for two days.

The provision of open spaces in the centre of the town had to wait for Joseph Chamberlain and a few other enlightened Victorians. They formed the Open Spaces Association, to raise money to buy land for recreation and to urge the corporation to do the same. This led to the first public park, on land rented from the Hon. Charles Adderley in the crowded district of Saltley. In 1878, the Birmingham Closed Burial Ground Act enabled the Corporation to convert eighteen graveyards in the town into public gardens.

Working as a voluntary ambulance driver during the last war, I was familiar with many of the city's slums, where street after street of back to back houses had no gardens and no trees. Today, it is a pleasure to walk through some of these re-planned districts: to walk from the Bristol Road, up Lee Bank, over the hill of wide lawns and newly planted trees, past the paddling pool and playground, to St Thomas's Church. The main body of this church was destroyed, but the columned façade and elegant clock tower withstood the blast. These have been carefully restored and the remainder of the site is now a garden of rest.

Many of the former inhabitants have been re-housed at Garretts Green, a council estate near Yardley. A new St Thomas's Church, designed by S. T. Walker, has been built in Garretts Green Lane. This St Thomas's is one of the best of Birmingham's modern churches; simple and unpretentious, in grey stone and light wood and lit by ample windows. The interior is dominated by the painting of St Thomas, a mural designed and painted by Matvyn Wright, which covers the entire wall above the altar.

Returning to the city, the most central oasis is the old burial ground surrounding the cathedral. Some 60,000 of Birmingham's citizens were buried here before the ground was closed. A few tomb stones remain, and some head stones lie flat in the lawns, where the young sprawl under the trees in their summer lunch hours.

On one side of the cathedral entrance is the imposing bronze statue of Bishop Charles Gore, the first Bishop of Birmingham, 1905–11. On the opposite side, almost hidden in the grass, is the churchyard's smallest stone, to the memory of—

Nanette Stocker, May 4, 1819, smallest woman ever in this kingdom.

*Lee Crescent. A
hidden beauty revealed.*

She was an African midget, 33 inches tall, which is the exact length of her stone.

As part of the new city plan, a space has been cleared at either end of Colmore Row, but neither is as popular as the central cathedral garden. To sit in the pedestrian part of Colmore Circus, with double-decker buses rushing around behind the high wall, is like sitting in a concrete pit, despite the mosaic mural and the potted plants. The grassed slope which has replaced buildings in Victoria Square was soon reduced to a mud patch by the trampling feet of demonstrators. It is now crossed by a neat asphalt path and the re-laid lawns are railed off, their future undecided.

St Phillip's Cathedral is built on land purchased by the Church Commissioners about 1711 and at that time was known as "Mr Phillip's barley close". The builder was one William Shakespeare and the architect was Thomas Archer, whose family lived at Umberslade Hall, at Hockley Heath.

At the suggestion of Sir Richard Gough of Edgbaston Hall, King George I gave a much needed £600 towards the completion of the tower of St Phillip's and, as a gesture of thanks to Sir Richard, the boar's head crest of the Goughs adorns the weather vane, instead of the traditional cock.

When the tower was completed, a peal of bells was cast by local craftsmen at Joseph Smith's foundry, which was opposite the still flourishing 'Swan' in Harborne Road, a district known as Good Knaves End.

A painting by Birmingham's David Cox depicts the fashionable townspeople entering St Phillip's in the early nineteenth century. Another artist who earned world renown, Edward Burne-Jones, was christened there in 1833. In later life, he presented monochrome cartoons to the church of his youth and these were translated into the cathedral's beautiful stained-glass windows. In the City Art Gallery, there are examples of the work of Sir Edward Burne-Jones, William Morris, Rossetti and their large group of friends who became known as the Pre-Raphaelite Painters.

After the war, when the bomb damage had been repaired, the Friends of the Cathedral presented a new altar cross and candlesticks, designed by John Donald. The cross, in gold, silver and crystal, is a particularly fine example of modern design, completely different from the work of Birmingham's king of silversmiths, Matthew Boulton, but in the same first class tradition.

It was said that St Paul's Church by New Hall Hill, was not built to honour God but rather to honour the industrial pioneers who worshipped there. It stands in Birmingham's only surviving eighteenth century square; a square surrounded by houses with their workshops

The Cathedral Church of St Phillip, consecrated in 1715.

behind them, built to accommodate the rising manufacturers, who were working with a great variety of raw materials.

What well-known names many of those early industrialists became! The Chance family from Newhall Street, whose glass lenses are in lighthouses around the world; the Rabones from Broad Street, makers of accurate rules; Ralph Heaton, a button maker who is buried at St Paul's; also Benjamin Cooke, who brought prosperity to the city by inventing the iron bedstead. Thousands of these were shipped to termite-infested countries to give many an empire-builder more peaceful nights.

Three of Birmingham's distinguished doctors worshipped at St Paul's—Dr Ash, who with several other parishioners was responsible for instigating the building of the General Hospital; Dr Hall Edwards, a pioneer in the use of X-rays; and Dr Pearson, a distinguished surgeon and nephew of Mr Aris, founder of Birmingham's first newspaper, *Aris's Gazette*.

To the joy of local historians, copies of this paper, dating from the first issue in 1741, are available in the Reference Library.

Matthew Boulton and his partner, James Watt, an infrequent worshipper but holder of the freehold of pew no. 100, brought their families to St Paul's. With them came many of the craftsmen employed at Matthew's nearby factory, who themselves became industrialists. Edward Thomason, one of his silversmiths, later Sir Edward, built his own large manufactory in Church Street. Francis Eginton, Matthew's artist and one-time partner, started working in painted and stained glass at his own premises in 1784. These were situated at Prospect Hill House on Soho Hill and from here, commissioned work for many buildings was sent out. Some of his earliest work is in St George's Chapel, Windsor.

Eginton's brother John was a celebrated engraver, whose work can be seen in Aston Hall, and his son William became 'Glass Painter in Ordinary' to Princess Charlotte.

The only well known writer who worshipped at St Paul's was the American, Washington Irving, the brother-in-law of Henry Van Wart, a merchant who lived at the corner of Newhall Street and Frederick Street. As an alderman, Van Wart devoted much of his time and money to the benefit of the town.

Irving, whose parents were emigrants from Great Britain, was a frequent visitor to his sister's house. There, he wrote his *Sketch Book*, with the immortal story of Rip Van Winkle and a description of an English Christmas—

Christmas is still a period of delightful excitement in England . . . even the sound of the Waits, rude as may be their minstrelsy breaks upon the mid-watches of a winter night with the effect of perfect harmony.

He was a keen, humorous observer of the English and the *Sketch Book* was followed by *Bracebridge Hall*, a story of country life, in which the Hall is believed to be Aston Hall, then the home of James Watt's son, another James.

St Paul's, designed by architect Roger Eykins, was built in 1779, on land given by Charles Colmore. The Colmores came from France and a William Colmore acquired property in Birmingham in the middle of the sixteenth century.

Their house, New Hall, was approached by a tree-lined avenue from what is now Colmore Row and this avenue later became Newhall Street. Since the last war, this street has completely lost its character. The nine-teenth-century families who lived in the large stone houses moved to the country and the houses were occupied by solicitors and doctors, a select nursing home and fashionable men's clubs, where brown bowlers were not unknown. Many of these houses in their turn are now no more and the porticoed façade of Elkington's, the silver-smiths, has made way for the Science Museum. The street no longer has its sweeping vista; it is cut in half by the walls of a new tunnelled road and the Assay Office, which Matthew Boulton worked so hard to achieve, is Newhall Street's only remaining period building.

St Paul's is not remarkable but is typical of its period,

as Eykins was influenced by James Gibbs, the architect of St Martin's-in-the-Field, London.

Francis Eginton was asked to supply the stained-glass window, *The conversion of St Paul*, copied from a painting by Benjamin West, then President of the Royal Academy.

Why Matthew Boulton, the great silversmith who belonged to the church, did not supply the chalice and flagons, history does not relate; they were made by a woman, Hester Bateman, the queen of silversmiths.

Hester, illiterate and poor, married John Bateman at Fleet Street prison for the price of a gin. She acquired her training from her husband, acting as his indispensable assistant when she was not having his babies. In 1760 John died of consumption and Hester was left with six children and few assets other than the tools of his trade, bequeathed to her by John. Nothing daunted, she registered her silver mark the following year and became one of England's finest silversmiths. Her designs are simple, with clean-cut lines and her silver has great elegance, with fine bead-edging and masterly saw-piercing.

As prosperity increased in the workshops around St Paul's Square, the wealthy manufacturers gradually moved out of the industrial centre to the suburbs. 'The Jewellers' Church' became shabby and blackened by smoke. It might have been demolished like St Mary's, St

23

St Paul's.

Bartholemew's and Christchurch, the other eighteenth-century city churches, if it had not been an ideal centre for the churches' industrial relations work.

The excellent acoustics at St Paul's were immediately appreciated by the first vicar, William Young and his curate Rann Kennedy, both keen musicians. When the organ was re-built in 1965, concerts were held once again. How Rann Kennedy and his wife Julia, friends of the young Mozart, would have revelled in the music which so often fills the church.

In Kennedy's time as vicar, a great change came to the parish of St Paul's. A hundred thousand trade unionists gathered on Newhall Hill to press their demands and the capitulation of the government came with the Reform Bill of 1832, designed to end the sweated labour in the factories and workshops.

St Paul's Square is a conservation area and it is hoped that what is left of the Georgian façades will be preserved. The most imposing one is that belonging to John Betts's metal refinery on the corner of Charlotte Street, which was originally three houses. The firm was started by Alexander Betts in 1760. He is said to have built up his business from the precious metal which he swept up from the floors of the neighbouring jewellers' workshops. Betts and Sons Ltd, is one of the oldest firms in Birmingham which is still run by ancestors of the origin-

John Betts.

al founder.

No. 35 bears another well known Birmingham name, George Mewis. He moved his family to the Square from Spring Hill, and for his Ropery built a single-storey factory in Caroline Street, adjoining No. 35. This still retains its iron window-frames and an original rain-

25

water head. George Mewis was a warden at St Paul's and a keen supporter of the church's work in the parish.

On the other corner of Caroline Street is St Paul's Club, which was originally two houses. Henry Hutchinson, a partner in the firm of Rickman and Hutchinson, who built the Town Hall, lived there and Rann Kennedy died there.

Conservation could not save Easy Hill; too many changes had taken place on John Baskerville's estate.

A man of many interests, with a great talent for calligraphy, Baskerville made his fortune from his japanning business, which was managed by his wife Sarah. At the age of 50, he was in a position to devote himself to the printing of fine books. He was a distinguished typefounder and produced type far superior in elegance and distinctness to any previously used. He set up a printing house at Easy Hill and a windmill, where he made his paper. In 1751, he produced his first book. This was a Virgil, followed the following year, when he was made printer to the University of Cambridge, by his now famous edition of Milton.

He was an erratic, restless character in life, and even in death he was not allowed to rest in peace, for he had insisted that his windmill should be his mausoleum; sixteen years after his death, his house was burned down in the Priestley Riots in 1791 and his windmill destroyed.

This was followed by the final break-up of the estate. The Crescent and Easy Row had already been made and their charming Georgian houses have in their turn been demolished. Easy Row has had to make way for a wide road and a new Central Library, which will house a complete collection of Baskerville's books.

James Brindley's canal at the back of the estate, was opened in 1769. In 1820, Thomas Gibson demolished the base of the old windmill in order to build wharves on the canal side. Discovering Baskerville's coffin was an embarrassment to him, until he persuaded his friend Job Marston to keep it in store. Baskerville had been an atheist and his body was unacceptable in Christian burial grounds, so the coffin remained with the Marston family for some years. Eventually, by devious means, they managed to get it into the Christchurch catacombs.

Christchurch was erected "for the lower classes", but they were able to worship there for less than a century, as the church was pulled down to make way for more profitable buildings.

John Baskerville's coffin was on the move again—to the cemetery in Warstone Lane. The cemetery chapel has since been demolished but so far the vaults beneath have not been disturbed. The complete history of Baskerville's coffin has yet to be written.

The new civic centre was planned for Easy Hill many

years ago and after the first war, the Hall of Memory was built, with its garden and colonnaded terrace. Behind, stood the first block of new Council Offices, Baskerville House. Then came the second world war and it was 1969 before any further change was effected.

Streets and factories behind the Civic Centre were then demolished, further land cleared and landscaped and high rise flats built beside the old Crescent Canal Basin. Fortunately, everything of historic interest appertaining to the canal has been carefully preserved.

At Cambrian Wharf, Farmers Bridge, where the canal used to be joined by the Newhall branch, there is a narrow boat marina.

Great care was taken over the preservation of the cottages, which are now sought-after residences—a far cry from the days when they were the handiest theatre 'digs' for the poorer members of the companies performing at the Prince of Wales Theatre. One of the bow-fronted cottages is used by British Waterways as an information office and a shop for narrow boat enthusiasts. On sale are scoops, cans, scuttles and stools, all painted with the traditional patterns. But the brown pottery teapots on sale are many sizes smaller than those used by the bargee families who tied up at the Crescent on Friday nights.

The ridged brick slope in Kingston Row, used for a hundred years by the barge horses, leads down to The

Gas Street Basin. A convenient tie-up on a small branch canal connecting the Birmingham and the Birmingham-Fazeley with the Worcester-Birmingham Canal.

Long Boat pub. To be true to Midland canal tradition, the pub should be called 'The Narrow Boat' as Long Boats were those used north of the Midlands. The name Long Boat originated in friendly derision, for in fact they were 20 feet shorter than the 70-foot-long Midland boats.

27

In front of the flats, a memorial walk in honour of James Brindley, follows the canal. Brindley was a Derbyshire boy and the pioneer of the country's canal systems. Brindley Walk is on the site of the original Birmingham Canal, built by him in 1769. It was this, which laid the foundation of the town's canal navigation and greatly contributed to Birmingham's prosperity.

The week-enders on the boats moored in the marina are not the bargees we used to paint in our art student days, but they are no less colourful—certainly as busy. Appetising smells drift up from the galleys, while the owners mop the decks and polish brass fittings to keep their gaily painted craft shipshape and 'Cut' fashion.

Although Baskerville is remembered chiefly for his books, he was indirectly responsible for the flourishing trade in japanned or lacquered goods and for Birmingham's papier mâché trade. At his factory in Moor Street, where his money was made, his research on hard lacquers was invaluable to both trades—one of his assistants was a young man named Henry Clay.

'Dick Whittington' was Birmingham's affectionate name for Henry Clay, a poor boy who through his hard work, flair for business and upright character, rose to be High Sheriff of Warwickshire in 1790 and 'Japanner in Ordinary' to his Majesty, King George III.

For centuries, the East had made small articles by glueing pieces of paper together and pressing them into moulds. This craft, developed in France by the Frères Martin, became known as *papier mâché*. It fascinated the young Henry Clay, when he first saw a sample in the form of a box, in John Baskerville's office.

Henry improved on Baskerville's lacquer and invented one which was heat-resisting. He made papier mâché articles as a hobby in his spare time and discovered that his new lacquer made them so strong and hard, it was obvious papier mâché could be used to make large trays —even furniture.

Before long the go-ahead Henry Clay had a factory of his own at 19 Newhall Street and by 1757 he had won a prize for producing a clear lacquer equal to that made by the Frères Martin.

With his new hard papier mâché, he began to make large articles: chairs, tables, ships' cabins and panels for coaches. He employed skilled artists to decorate his work and many of Clay's products were beautifully inlaid with mother-of-pearl, as thin as one hundredth of an inch. He made coach panels for John Baskerville and for Queen Charlotte, wife of George III. Henry Clay's papier mâché work has been collected ever since George III made it popular. The Blakesley Hall museum at Yardley is fortunate in having many excellent pieces.

Leaving 'The Long Boat' for a nostalgic walk back to

Brindley Walk. This replaces a clutter of canal warehouses.

Broad Street along King Edward's Road, the route passes a cast iron urinal. Numbers of these were erected in Birmingham in the last century and quite a choice of designs for the plate casting and gallery edging was used. If none of these urinals can be preserved on its original site, it is hoped that at least one will find its way into a museum.

With the canal basin at the end of the street, it used to be difficult to keep the nearby Prince of Wales Theatre free from rats. Like the autograph hunters, they were always ready to dodge the busy stage-doorkeeper and sneak into the theatre.

I remember a great disturbance one night. A lady who had put her hat and fur tippet under the seat, picked up a rat instead when she reached for her finery. She was revived with sal volatile by a theatre attendant, who happened to be one of the local rat catchers. According to him, the rat's fur was far superior to that of the tippet.

In Broad Street, the new Repertory Theatre was completed in 1971 to replace the old one in Station Street, where as students, we were so spoilt by Sir Barry Jackson. We were every bit as 'way-out' as modern students, with our short skirts, long strings of beads and foot-long cigarette holders. Perhaps our hair was more hygienic, as Eton crops were in fashion.

In spite of our outrageous appearance and stage-struck behaviour, Sir Barry encouraged us to meet his important guests.

"Furnish a pleasant dressing room", he said, "for Dame Ethel Smythe, who is coming to conduct her own operas for us."

Expecting a dulcet, romantic lady, we raided the property room for elaborate gilded stage furniture upholstered in satin. We were dismayed by the mannish figure, with severe trilby hat, collar and tie, who strode into the room and threw up her expressive hands in horror.

"I never use upholstered chairs—full of fleas!" she announced.

Bernard Shaw did not suffer the young gladly. When he became more than usually irritated by us at rehearsals of his *Back to Methuselah*, which he produced himself, he would retaliate by watching us with evil glee, while we ate his stale vegetarian sandwiches. Too polite to refuse, we dreaded to see the fluff-covered morsels emerge from the large pockets of his Norfolk jacket. Barry Jackson suggested we should have pressed them between the pages of one of Shaw's plays, for the benefit of posterity.

One consolation was his compatriot W. B. Yeats, who, during the long rehearsal waits, would sit on the steep stalls stairs with us and tell us fey tales of Ireland.

Sir Barry, who presented so many plays and players to his home town, in the steep, cramped little theatre in Station Street, would have been delighted with the spacious new building, designed by Mr Graham Winteringham, who also designed the smaller nearby Crescent Theatre.

The fountain garden between the new Repertory Theatre and the Hall of Memory is not quite the "Seven acres of rich pasture land, part laid out in Shady Walks, Fish Pond and Grotto" advertised after John Baskerville's death. An electrically operated fountain, floodlit at night, replaces his fishpond and a covered colonnade the shady walks. Although the garden occupies only one acre rather than seven, it is welcome in the city centre and is overcrowded on fine days.

Unfortunately, few of Birmingham's really early buildings have survived the ever increasing need for business premises. The oldest building is the Crown Inn, Deritend. A timbered manor house, built at the end of the fourteenth century, it has been used for centuries as an inn. Now owned by Ansell's Brewery and including two shops, it is kept in good repair.

The other half-timbered buildings which led up to the Bull Ring have gone. Even the tall spire of St Martin's Church is dwarfed by the Rotunda and a conglomeration of new buildings.

Near Deritend is Banbury Street, an interesting cul-de-sac near the imposing façade of Curzon Street Station. On one corner is the 'Eagle and Tun', with its

Crown Inn, Deritend (circa 1400). A domestic, timber-framed building.

Victorian interior, on the other, another decorative cast-iron urinal. Facing up the street, is the Birmingham Proof House, with its elaborate coat-of-arms in strong relief, a familiar landmark to the train passengers entering New Street Station from the east.

31

During the reign of William III, the Birmingham smiths were quick to change from the manufacture of knives and swords and try their hands at gun-making. When Sir Richard Newdigate, a Member of Parliament for Warwickshire, heard the King say that he was obliged to procure his guns from Holland, he assured him that the smiths of his constituency could supply them. And supply them they did, so much so that by the time of the American War of Independence, Birmingham was a flourishing centre of the gun trade.

The gunsmiths used to proof their own guns. In many cases this was far from satisfactory. Consequently in 1813, the Proof House was built in Banbury Street. From then on, all guns had to be proved there and the inhabitants of Deritend were deafened by a new noise, which they cheerfully called "Birmingham Thunder". It occurred when fifty guns were fired simultaneously, by an antique machine then in use in the Firing House.

I first knew the Proof House after the last war. I was looking after five separate theatrical companies playing *Annie Get Your Gun*, each supplied with twenty ·22 rifles, and I was honoured to be asked to sign the Proof House visitors' book. The first signature was that of Prince Albert, followed later by "Wellington, F.M."

On a recent visit to the Proof House, it was a sign of the times to find the export of Birmingham shot guns had declined and Japanese guns were being proofed in Banbury Street. These sell for £100, as against the £900 British model. The Japanese shotguns were also beautifully engraved with traditional designs.

Another old building recently restored, is Stratford House, built by Abraham Rotton in 1601. Fronting on to Stratford Place, at Camp Hill, it was not very old when the Rotton family must have witnessed the fight which took place on Camp Hill on Easter Monday 1643, during the Civil War. The townspeople had been advised to allow Prince Rupert and his troops to pass through the town on their way to Lichfield but a small company of infantry stopped them at Camp Hill. The result was the burning and looting of many houses on the march into the town by way of Deritend and the destruction of Porter's Blade Mill, which was supplying swords to the Parliament supporters.

Although Prince Rupert made his headquarters at the Ship Inn at Camp Hill, Stratford House remained undamaged.

Another building of two-fold interest, is the Museum of Science and Industry in Newhall Street, because it is housed in premises used by George Elkington and his brother, electroplaters; it was designed for them by their business partner, Josiah Mason, a pen-maker. The latter began life as a street hawker in Kidderminster and came to Birmingham to try to make a living. He was so successful that he was able to endow the Mason Orphanage and the Josiah Mason College, since incorporated into the University of Birmingham. Even in the 1880s, these endowments cost him £550,000.

Distinguished visitors came to Elkington's from all over the world to see their showroom in Newhall Street. The Elkingtons gathered fine craftsmen around them in order to produce copies of the works of the great silversmiths, such as Cellini and Caradosso. Their showroom became a veritable museum of fine arts.

A hundred years later, it has become amongst other things a museum of 'Steam'. Considering that this was the first of its kind in the world and that it was only started after the second world war, it has acquired a remarkably representative collection of period machinery. Wherever possible these machines are workable.

One of the latest acquisitions, a full sized railway engine, has necessitated the destruction of the porticoed façade of Elkington's and a high roof, glass-fronted building has replaced it.

The engine, the *City of Birmingham*, can thus be seen from the street in all its shining glory. Not so glorious is its movement—a mere ten feet, operated not by steam but by remote electrical control.

The exhibits range from replicas of the small workshops of Birmingham's first button makers, to aeroplanes; from pen-nibs to motorcars and from clocks to steam organs. Every year, the museum authorities organise a Steam Rally and this has led to similar events being held all over the country.

The rally takes place on a Sunday in May and the steam engines come puffing into Newhall Street from far and near, all polished and gleaming. Friends of mine, great steam enthusiasts, own a Burrell Showman's Locomotive, age 55. The names of Bostock and Wombwell, noted showmen in their day, are carefully preserved around the rim of the canopy.

Crowds fill Newhall Street and the obliging owners take on loads of boys for rides and hand out potatoes baked in their jackets under the boiler fires. These steam enthusiasts have helped to save a beam pumping engine. Too large for the Science Museum, which is already proving to be too small, the engine is installed on the traffic island near its original home in Dartmouth Street. Having travelled to pumping stations as far apart as Otterbourne and the Isle of Dogs, to see beam engines at work, I am strongly in favour of the Dartmouth Street venture.

Period machines are not only the landmarks of industrial history but also, when isolated, provide interesting industrial sculptural pieces.

Stratford House (1601). A beautifully preserved building in Stratford Place, Camp Hill.

CHAPTER TWO

Trees and Spaghetti

An aerial photograph of the residential suburb of Edgbaston resembles one of a well established forest—there are more trees to the acre than in many rural districts. The trees in a large part of Edgbaston are carefully tended by the forestry department of the Calthorpe Estate, which also holds the freeholds of many of the Georgian houses.

Although building in other parts of Birmingham expanded rapidly around 1760, Sir Henry Gough and later his successors, the Gough Calthorpes, refused to allow the building of workshops or warehouses alongside the newly cut canal and as a result, Edgbaston developed into a quiet residential suburb.

Owing to the lack of domestic servants and gardeners, some of the larger houses with extensive grounds have been demolished and replaced by smaller houses and high rise flats, but wherever possible, the well-established trees have been retained and new ones planted.

Edgbaston Hall is used as a golf clubhouse and much of the park is taken up by the golf links, but the lake, Chad Brook and the woods, have been left undisturbed. On the brook, below Edgbaston Pool, are the ruins of Over Mill, which in Tudor times was owned by miller Kynge, who lived on the other side of the Bristol Road at Pebble Mill, on the River Rea.

There have been several previous houses on the site of the present Edgbaston Hall and many owners, from the medieval de Edgbastons to the Gough Calthorpes. Dr Withering, a friend of Matthew Boulton and a member of the Lunar Society, lived there for a time.

The Lunar Society, so called because it met when the moon was full, consisted of a group of Matthew Boulton's friends, who met at one-another's houses for discussions which ranged over many subjects. Dr William Withering is remembered for his work on British plants and for his research on digitalis.

The last private owner of Edgbaston Hall was the city's first Lord Mayor, Sir James Smith.

The extensive playing fields of the boys' and the girls' schools of the King Edward's Foundation, and other land, formerly used by the Edgbaston Tennis Club and now taken over by the University, enclose many acres of

Edgbaston. The Beadle's Cottage in Ampton Road.

open space before Edgbaston meets the built-up suburb of Selly Oak. On the opposite side of Edgbaston Park Road is another large area occupied by residential blocks of the University, with a newly landscaped pool and pleasant grounds which slope down from the Judges' House in Church Road.

It was not long before the swans and a number of Canada Geese discovered the pool and they are now as much a part of the scene as the University students.

Some of the oldest pools in Edgbaston are in the extensive gardens of No. 6 Sir Harry's Road. Historians believe there was a Priory in Edgbaston, but so far, no record has been found of the exact site. Because of an area surrounded by a moat, the pools fed by a good spring, an ancient right of way which leads from the garden to Priory Road and the presence of three yew trees which are one thousand years old, it is considered possible that the site of the Priory was on the land surrounded by the moat. The garden is one of the few in Edgbaston to possess excellent water-cress beds.

This quiet retreat, now surrounded by private gardens and by the grounds of the Priory Tennis Club, is visited by many birds including swans and moorhens which enjoy the peace of the pools.

Because the land surrounding Edgbaston Hall is used only for golf, it also makes a natural bird sanctuary and is

Number 6, Sir Harry's Road. The moat and pools suggest a possible site for Edgbaston's Priory.

home to foxes, hedgehogs and squirrels. My house is near the golf club and only one mile from the swirling traffic of the Bull Ring Circus, but the garden has many visitors. Apart from the common small birds, magpies chatter at the ring doves which live in a large monkey-puzzle tree. Occasionally a greater spotted woodpecker

37

comes into one of the almond trees. In the autumn, grey squirrels rush around, busily burying the fruits of the Spanish chestnut, to return in the winter, wondering where in the earth they hid them. A hungry fox frequently jumps up the bird table and makes off with the tits' net of suet.

Nearby, are the Botanical Gardens, which cover 16 acres and here records are kept of visits by kingfishers. The gardens were planned and laid out by J.C. Loudon and opened in 1832. There is a small entrance fee—for keen gardeners, this is money well spent. Tropical shrubs and exotic orchids are grown in the hot houses and the gardens are of considerable horticultural interest at all seasons. The gardeners are always willing to discuss their latest acquisitions and give helpful advice: it is Birmingham's Kew.

The sloping grounds have lawns, sheltered flower beds which catch the sun and a well-equipped playground for the very young. Aviaries of rare birds are spaced around the gardens, adding great interest to the walks, where one may meet peacocks roaming free around the gardens.

Edgbastonians are often accused of having a snobbish, affected accent, which is admirably mimicked by the Garden's mynah birds. On entering the bird house, one is apt to be greeted by "Hay-low, how nace to see you," followed by a lively wolf whistle and "Wal rayally".

On Edgbaston Reservoir, a flock of gulls has settled, which will welcome anyone with a bag of crusts, taking them expertly on the wing. The Reservoir was made from Roach Pool at Rotton Park, which in Tudor times was reported to contain, "Lytell fysshe or non". The pool was enlarged to supply the Birmingham Canal, which joins it by making a horseshoe loop around Rotton Park Street. The reservoir is now used for sailing and has a thriving club with a large clubhouse.

A footpath encircles the lake—willows grace one end and at the other is a long industrial view across Spring Hill to Hockley.

On the southern side of Edgbaston Hall and Park, there is a long sequence of public parks. Calthorpe Park is nearest to the City centre, followed by Cannon Hill Park, the Moor Green Recreation Grounds, which lead up to Highbury Park and then to Kings Heath Park.

The 80 acres of Cannon Hill Park, opposite the Edgbaston County Cricket ground, were given to the town by Louisa Ryland, grand-daughter of John Ryland, a wealthy manufacturer who was living in John Baskerville's house on Easy Hill, at the time of the riots.

Cannon Hill Park has boating and fishing lakes, an area for games and a Japanese Garden for quiet contemplation. The River Rea flows beside one boundary and along its bank is the well-patronised Arts Centre for young people, with its studios, cinema, squash courts, music rooms and small open-air theatre. This centre grows gradually larger as funds permit.

The pools are frequented by flocks of Canada geese. Near the boathouse a pair of Chinese geese is usually to be found. They are aggressive ankle-nippers and push their way into the keeper's office if the door is unlatched. When they have eaten all the scraps, he has to offer them a lighted cigarette before he can get them to waddle off to the water squawking furiously.

On one of the main walks through the park is the re-constructed fifteenth-century Golden Lion Inn, rescued from a re-building project in Deritend. Part of the ground floor is open at the back, making a wind-free shelter from which to look across the sloping lawns to the boating pool.

Another enjoyable feature of this park is the beauty of the flower beds. Starting in early spring with aconites and snowdrops, working up to the magnificent display for the Spring Festival, when the blaze of colour is enhanced by the open-air art exhibition. The flower beds continue to delight until late autumn and all too soon are followed by the Christmas fairy lights. Near one entrance to the park, there is an exact working model of the Elan Valley reservoirs in the Welsh hills, from which Birmingham draws its water. It is in a pleasantly land-scaped corner, with miniature hills and shrubs and a ground cover of seasonal heathers.

Highbury Park, once the home of Joseph Chamberlain and his famous orchid houses, stands on much higher ground than Cannon Hill Park, has more open parkland and is much less sheltered and therefore fresher.

The small lake does not attract the flocks of geese which fly around Edgbaston from pool to pool, announcing their travels with incessant honking. Highbury's trees are frequented by numerous magpies, forever chattering at the squirrels. Fieldfares are common visitors and, more rarely, pairs of jays.

From Highbury to King's Heath Park is only a short distance along Dad's Lane. The large house in the centre of this park is used by the Horticultural Training School, run by the Birmingham Parks Department. The park is used extensively in the training of students and future staff. The rock gardens, vegetable gardens, shrubs, flower borders, the water gardens around the lake, the fruit trees and various specimen trees, are used for teaching purposes. Turf maintenance is demonstrated on the actual turf of the areas used for various sports.

Members of the Tree Lovers League, who are regular visitors to the city parks, are offered every opportunity for study.

Sarehole Mill, not far from King's Heath Park is now more rare than rural, as it stands beside a busy bus route between the suburbs of Hall Green and Moseley. My mother was friendly with the Andrew family, who had worked the mill for many years and it was our great joy as children, to be allowed to visit there—to sail our home made raft on the mill pool, paddle in the River Cole and on special occasions, watch the great iron wheels at work.

At that time I was too young to have read about Matthew Boulton but it was exciting in later years, to discover that he had actually worked in the mill we knew so well. He leased Sarehole Mill for rolling sheet metal before he built his Soho factory in 1761. There has probably been a mill on the site since the Middle Ages but the present building, Birmingham's only surviving water mill, dates from the eighteenth century. Over the years, its water power was used for many purposes other than grinding corn and in the 1850s, a steam engine was installed to supplement the water power.

Milling ceased in 1919, and in 1946 the mill was bequeathed to the City of Birmingham but due to lack of funds, it was not until 1969 that it was opened—as a branch museum. It has been most carefully restored and the three-storey interior with its machinery, mill wheels and mill stones makes a fascinating exhibit. The mill pool

Sarehole Mill, on the River Cole. The last of Birmingham's water-mills, now preserved as a museum.

is shaded by some fine old willows and the River Cole flows by the side of a small park. The kingfishers no longer fish its waters but the local youngsters hopefully fish for tadpoles and tiddlers, much as we did.

The small villages which surrounded eighteenth-century Birmingham gradually developed into suburbs

40

for the wealthy, before the pressure for artisans' houses forced them further and further into the country.

Because of the control exercised by the Calthorpe Estate, Edgbaston has been able to retain some of its period character, but Harborne did not fare so well.

In the days when Harborne Hall was built, the local haulier was Abraham Westwood, proud owner of 27 donkeys and 3 mules, which he stabled by his cottage in Turks Lane, now Queen's Park Road.

The building bricks for the Hall came by canal in the narrow boats and were unloaded near the entrance of the Lapal Tunnel and transported the three miles up the hill by Mr Westwood's pack train. In later times, the growing demand for bricks was met by brickmakers who established themselves in the fields to the north of Harborne, in a district known as California.

Little now remains to connect Harborne with village life, although one still hears the elderly shoppers in the supermarkets refer to the High Street as 'The Village'. What is left of old Harborne, clusters round the church, some distance from the High Street.

The parkland which lay between Metchley Lane and Harborne Park Road has been built over and so have most of the Roman camp sites at Metchley. Only a small section of them can still be seen in the grounds of the Queen Elizabeth Hospital. When the latest hospital car park was sited the local archaeological society was given the use of the land for the summer months and much useful information was added to the plan of the camps.

Both the railway and the canal were cut through this Roman site and the remains lie partly on University land and partly under the Queen Elizabeth Hospital buildings. Many interesting items from the inner small camp were found when the foundations for the laundry block were excavated.

I was exceptionally lucky on the occasion of my one visit to the 'dig', when some of the original Roman timbers were uncovered. This was on the Metchley site and the timbers in the surrounding sandstone were well preserved. They had clearly supported the remains of one of the camp walls. I could appreciate the thrill and excitement at such a find, and I had to admire the philosophical way in which the archaeologists leading the 'dig', were content to have been able to confirm their theories and were quite resigned to the fact that the hospital car-park was more important than an exposed layout of a Roman camp.

I went from here to some pleasant gardens on the other side of Harborne Park Road from Metchley. These are on the site of a house called The Grove, at one time the home of the banker and reformer, Thomas Attwood. He may have walked in these same gardens in 1819, when a group of working men called to persuade him to go and speak for them at their meeting on Newhall Hill. They were reputed to have been in such a hurry, they could not wait for his horses to be harnessed but themselves pulled his carriage the four miles into the town. In my schooldays, I knew nothing of Attwood's political career —to us, he was just 'Old Attwood', whose statue at the top of Stephenson Place was our rendezvous. We came off our various trains at New Street Station and waited for a gossip with our boy friends by 'Old Attwood' before we poured into our respective buildings, at King Edward's School, then in New Street,

It was like losing an old friend when his statue was moved to the comparative obscurity of Calthorpe Park. By then, I had learned of the political career of Birmingham's first M.P.—of his long fight which resulted in the passing of the Reform Bill and of his currency reforms which saved the nation from bankruptcy in 1825.

Attwood's house, later the home of the Kendrick family, was demolished only a few years ago and the gardens and parkland were opened as a much needed public park in the wide expanse of Harborne's housing estates.

Walking from The Grove along Old Church Road, on one side there is Bishop's Croft, home of the Bishop of Birmingham and on the other, Harborne Hall, now a convent. Both stand in ample grounds and in the seclusion of Old Church Road, the traffic and bus routes of the neighbouring roads could be miles away.

In front of Bishop's Croft are the local sports and cricket grounds and one of Harborne's few remaining footpaths passes between them: tree-lined, it is respectfully named 'the Avenue'. Tickle Belly Lane and Lie Close Way, have long since disappeared, though War Lane still recalls the days of the Civil War.

An old man, who remembered the days when there were farms at each end of the High Street, was feeding the squirrels in the churchyard. One of them took food from his hand, rushed up a nearby gravestone and perched like a fur hat, on the head of a marble angel, nibbling furiously. One nibbling squirrel soon attracts another and they came towards the old man, skating across highly polished marble tombs like cartoon chipmunks.

The land drops steeply from the front of the church to give a long view across to the large reservoir at Bartley Green. Beyond, lie Frankley Beeches, a group of trees on the top of a small hill, which with its walks, is now preserved by the National Trust.

On the bend where Old Church Road becomes Vicarage Road, there is one of those quiet corners so hard to find in Birmingham. Here is a group of buildings com-

Harborne. A quiet corner by the Bell Inn.

prising the Bell Inn, a row of cottages with the church behind them and opposite, an elegant Georgian house. The whole group, together with the land of the Hall and of Bishop's Croft, the playing fields and The Grove, are all part of a conservancy plan. Long may they remain so!

Conservancy plans were laid for Bournville nearly a hundred years ago, when George and Richard Cadbury moved their cocoa and chocolate factory from Bridge Street, off Broad Street, to their newly built premises on the banks of the Worcester canal at Bournville in 1879.

Because of his work with the Adult School founded by Joseph Sturge, George Cadbury was more than familiar with slum housing conditions and was determined to provide better conditions for his own workpeople. He began by building a few semi-detached houses close to the works and from this, conceived his plan for a model village—each house to have its own garden and leaving plenty of land for recreation.

In 1900, he established the Bournville Village Trust, to ensure his ideas would be given permanent form. As a result of his vision, although Bournville has trebled in size, it still retains its original character in spite of having been absorbed into Greater Birmingham.

With great foresight, many trees of various kinds were planted at Bournville some sixty years ago and these are now well grown. Many of the roads which cut through the estate bear names such as Linden, Laburnum, Maple and Mulberry, in contrast with the roads on the Calthorpe, the Colmore and the Gooch estates, which were named after members of the families.

The centre of Bournville village is The Green, which is shaded by trees and in spring, is carpeted with flowers. Surrounding it are various schools, including the Ruskin School of Art, the Meeting House, a church and row of shops. The Rest House in the centre of the Green, modelled on the Yarn Market at Dunster in Somerset, was given to the village by George Cadbury's employees, to commemorate his silver wedding in 1913.

What George Cadbury envisaged in the 1890s, is now "a green and pleasant land". Beside the Bournville works are two pools, fed by Griffin's Brook and there are linked Parkways following the course of the brook up to Northfield.

Crossing only the occasional road, the walks cross Bournville Park, pass through Valley Parkway and on to Manor Farm and Dame Elizabeth Cadbury's estate, with its beautiful lake.

Several of the University Hostels have been built in the grounds of the Manor House estate.

Where possible en route, farms, houses, barns and pools have been preserved. The children's pool in Valley

Parkway, constructed in 1932 for the relief of unemployment, is especially suited for model boat racing, as it is shallow and has a concrete bottom. On a Sunday afternoon, small boys have to take a back seat while their fathers crouch over the intricate electronics of remote controlled miniature speedboats.

"Oh come on Dad! get it going!" they grumble, until at last the boat cuts through the water at great speed, with a deafening noise, often to stop alas, with a splutter, in the centre of the pool. The boys jump in, in their wellingtons, but eventually it is Dad who makes his precarious way out to the boat, the audience eagerly waiting for him to slip and get a ducking.

The waterfowl which make their home on the pool during the week, are conspicuously absent on Sundays, flying off to neighbouring pools as the first speedboat starts up.

Other walks cross the Rowheath recreation grounds, one to the Cotteridge, another, through Valley Parkway Recreation Grounds, crosses Hole Lane and St Laurence Road and then continues right up to Victoria Common and Northfield.

The trees and bluebells in (the Civil War) Camp Wood, have been carefully preserved, although some of the land behind 'The Old Houses' has had to be used to provide a car-park to relieve congestion around the Green.

'The Old Houses', as they are known locally, are Selly Manor House and Minworth Greaves House. George Cadbury purchased the derelict Selly Manor House, which stood about a mile away at Selly Oak and had it carefully dismantled, restored and re-erected near his Village Green. Similarly, Minworth Greaves came from Kingsbury Road, near Minworth.

They are fine examples of thirteenth- and fourteenth-century building. Many famous people are reputed to have stayed at the Manor House from Selly Oak, among them Richmond (later Henry VII), Oliver Cromwell, and Catesby, one of the catholics engaged in the Gunpowder Plot.

On their new site, the houses have been suitably furnished and Minworth Greaves houses an interesting collection of weapons.

The Bournville Estate now stretches out across the tree-centred Bristol Road to Shenley Fields and Weoley Castle. On either side of the Bristol Road are the Selly Oak colleges, each in its own grounds and with a number of furnished houses and flats for visiting missionaries.

Woodbrooke, once the home of George Cadbury, is one of the largest and is near the Library and the George Cadbury Hall, a central meeting place for students from

45

all the Selly Oak colleges.

The stretch of double carriageway from Selly Oak to Northfield, which cuts through the Bournville Estate, was created long before the last war. The trams rattled through the centre reservation to the Lickey Hills, where the people of Birmingham could enjoy fresh air and uninterrupted views. The trams have disappeared but the central reservation is lined with trees and this is one of the more pleasant approaches into Birmingham.

The Lickey Hills were moulded by glacial action in the ice age. Legend has it that the Malverns and the Lickeys are surplus ammunition left over after a battle between two giants, who threw rocks at each other—good overarm bowling which covered twenty miles.

The city boundary only encloses Rednal Hill but the Lickeys have been one of Birmingham's natural parks since the beginning of the century. I enjoy them at all seasons of the year. In winter, with the snow weighing down the branches of the pines and firs, Bilberry Hill might be in Switzerland. In spring, when the bluebells cover the ground with a blue haze and the magnificent beeches are in bud—it must be England.

On hot summer days, the air is fresh on the open wind-swept heights of Beacon Hill, 1,000 feet above sea level. Using the directional map up there, you can look across Birmingham to Barr Beacon or down, to Lydiate Ash, which inspired Mrs Henry Wood's novel *The Shadow of Ashlydat*.

At Red Hill is the Roman Catholic retreat where Cardinal Newman is buried. For nearly forty years, he read his brilliant and controversial sermons at the Birmingham Oratory. His poem, 'The Dream of Gerontius', inspired Edward Elgar, then Professor of Music in Birmingham, to write one of his best compositions—but the music heard on Beacon Hill is the song of the skylarks.

Many footpaths radiate from the Lickey Hills, some by way of Cofton Hacket and the National Trust land to Bittell Reservoir, which is kept as a bird sanctuary —others by way of Cofton Park, returning to Birmingham across the fields, towards West Heath.

On the west side of the Bristol Road, in the valley of Stonehouse Brook, lie the excavations of the principal ancient monument in Birmingham. In the centre of a modern housing estate, is the site of Weoley Castle, a fortified manor surrounded by a wide moat. Apart from its archaeological interest, this is a well kept site, with lawns on which to walk and seats under the trees, from which to sit and contrast the ancient with the modern.

In the small museum, drawings show the three building periods which followed one another and list the various owners. At the Domesday survey, the land was taken from the Saxon landlords and granted to the

Norman, William Fitzanculf.

It passed by marriage to the de Somerys of Dudley and then to the de Botetorts. In 1536, the manor was bought by Richard Jerveys, Sheriff of London. It remained in the Jerveys family until the early nineteenth century, although it was described as a ruin soon after the Civil War.

There was no George Cadbury to provide park lands on the Northern side of the town. Most of the Holte estates at Aston and Duddeston were sold before the Birmingham Corporation had realised the need for an open space there. They purchased the last remaining acres of grassland surrounding Aston Hall and in due course, these were opened as a public park by Queen Victoria in 1858.

By the time the park was opened, the districts of Aston, Witton and Saltley, near to the park, were reputed to have more people to the acre than any in Birmingham. Many residents of these areas have been housed further out of the city and now it is the old residential area of Handsworth, to the west of the park, which is overcrowded.

From the new interweaving, three tier road complex, officially known as The Gravelly Hill Interchange but already aptly nicknamed 'Spaghetti Junction', the Aston Express-way, on its tall concrete columns, interrupts the view from Aston Hall across to Duddeston. With the high Nechells cooling towers, the Saltley gasometers overshadowed by towering blocks of flats and offices, it is a very different view from the open country Sir Thomas Holte saw in 1613, when he decided to move from Duddeston and build his magnificent new home on the hill above the church.

Very different too, are the guests who now enjoy his gardens. Quiet Sikhs in brightly coloured turbans sit in contemplation on the park seats, while East Pakistanis sit in family circles, cross legged on the grass. Young West Indians play energetic games in the park playing fields. In 1970, there were more black babies born in Handsworth than white, but no matter what race, creed or colour, all get fresh air and exercise in the remaining acres of the Holtes' deer park.

Aston Hall is considered to be "an architectural jewel in the finest Jacobean style". Its chimneystacks and gables make a rare pattern against the sky. It houses one of the city's finest domestic museums, with furnishings carefully chosen to enhance the various rooms and give an overall picture of a seventeenth century hall.

The floors and the furniture gleam with polish and the great kitchen looks ready and waiting for an army of cooks and scullions to start work with the period cooking equipment.

47

Aston Hall. A seventeenth-century architectural gem, which houses a domestic museum of the seventeenth and eighteenth centuries.

Among the many treasures to be seen in the Hall are two splendid examples of English japanning, the thriving Midland industry of the early eighteenth century: one a black lacquer chest, the other a lacquer cabinet, each on a stand.

In the servants' hall, over the fireplace, is a local iron casting depicting the elephant crest of the James Watt family. James, son of the famous James Watt, leased Aston Hall for thirty years and died there in 1848.

Also in the servants' hall is a box mangle. These were made by the thousand in Birmingham in the early nineteenth century. The large stones placed in the rolling box made turning very hard work—far removed from the press button spin driers of today.

Even with its tall spire, Aston Church has been dominated for centuries by the hall on the hill above it. Now, the high new Express-Way offers almost a bird's eye view and the Hall and the park have not been seen so well since before the sale of the Holte Estate.

Aston's present church of St Peter and St Paul was built in the 1880s but there are records of a Saxon community, settled around the banks of the Tame, with their resident priest. The first name on the list of vicars is Ralphe de Crophill in 1200. Inside the church, there are two examples of Francis Eginton's stained glass. One is a memorial window, which unfortunately is behind the organ, re-built in 1967. The other, is a stained glass panel inserted in the window over the north door—a gruesome armorial of a bloody hand and some crossed bones —not the happiest of heraldic designs. In this Holte shield, the red hand is the Baronet's badge of Sir Lister Holte and the crossed bones are the arms of his wife, Sarah Newton, granted to Sir Isaac Newton, President of the Royal Society, who was knighted in 1705.

The church contains many monuments and memorials to local families. The oldest tomb, dated 1360, is thought to be of Ralph Arden, husband of Isabel Anselm de Bromwich. He was an ancestor of Thomas Arden of Aston Cantlow, grandfather of William Shakespeare's mother, Mary Arden. The effigy is believed to have been brought to Aston from Maxstoke Priory.

The monument of William Holte and his wife is in white sandstone and has the squirrel family crest. The Holte squirrel is well known throughout the Midlands, as the trademark of Ansell's Brewery at Aston Cross, who acquired it from the old Holte Brewery. The only brass left in the church and preserved in the Baptistry, is to Thomas Holte of Duddeston, grandfather of the Thomas Holte who built the Hall.

In the 1920s, I lived in a wing of one of Aston's large houses. It was built on the top of a small hill, and a beech wood, full of bluebells in the spring, dropped steeply

49

down to the Tame Valley canal. Alongside the canal flowed the River Tame and beyond, was the Aston Reservoir.

At the foot of the beech wood was a cave, cut in the sandstone, and before the reservoir was made, there was reputed to have been a secret passage leading from the cave to Aston Hall.

The house was demolished before the last war and, with the building of 'Spaghetti Junction', the hill was lowered, the new road cut through the wood and the cave and passage have finally disappeared.

Much of Birmingham, including this cave, was photographed by Sir Benjamin Stone, one-time Member of Parliament for Aston. An excellent photographer, he was the first amateur to receive a Royal Command from Queen Victoria. He was also given the important assignment of photographing the Lying-in-State of the Queen but unfortunately, the telegram telling him of this never reached him.

He photographed many of the famous people of his day, Guglielmo Marconi, the inventor of wireless telegraphy, and Louis Bleriot, the first person to cross the Channel by aeroplane, in 1909, were both photographed by him outside the Houses of Parliament.

He was an enthusiastic traveller, photographing the people and places he saw and often exploring unknown territory. The main collection of his photographs is now in the Birmingham Reference Library, but many, including the one of the Aston cave, are in the possession of the families of his friends.

The five acres of the Aston reservoir have since been converted into an open air athletics stadium. The canal is lost to view beneath a labyrinth of concrete columns, the course of the River Tame has been diverted to flow round the Witton side of the smaller reservoir but the whole adds up to the extremely pleasant Salford Park.

A group of highrise flats, reminiscently named The Holte Estate, with individual blocks named after Boulton, Watt, Murdock and Priestley, tower above the park at one end, with 'Spaghetti Junction' at the other. There are new pictures to paint, looking across the lake into the maze of giant columns reflected in the water. The complex, as seen from the park, is an elegant feat of engineering—by Sir Owen Williams and Partners.

Now that the massive engineering project is complete and only the roar of traffic remains, moorhens and coots have made themselves at home on the lake, in spite of the excessive decibels. New trees have been planted along the side of the river path and the lake is to be re-stocked with fish. Before long, the 'Sons of Rest', sitting in front of their clubhouse, should be able to watch the anglers who fish so hopefully in park pools.

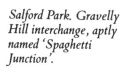

Salford Park. Gravelly Hill interchange, aptly named 'Spaghetti Junction'.

On the way to Witton Lakes, I came across another exciting subject for a picture—the view down Moor Lane. The new road runs above the old Moor Lane and as you pass under it on the way to the lakes, there is an almost endless perspective view of hundreds of columns, shadowed by the road above and striped with diagonal shafts of light.

Witton, like Aston, was one of the ancient manors on the banks of the River Tame and has developed rapidly in this century. George Kynoch had already built his powder factory and magazine, when the General Electric Company acquired the 240-acre site opposite, and Witton became a centre for electrical engineering. The first broadcast by the BBC locally, was made from the GEC factory in 1922 with the call sign 2WR.

The River Tame, near Kynoch's, flows alongside Brookvale Road for some distance, and it was good to see that some of the firms had tidied up their river banks and planted trees. It was even better to find the walks around Witton Lakes open to the public.

Before the large Elan Valley reservoirs in Wales were completed in 1904, Birmingham's water supply came from eight deep wells and from the Rivers Bourne and Blythe, Plant Brook and Perry Stream. The Upper and Middle Reservoirs at Witton were used for storing surface water. These lakes and the fields surrounding them are connected by a narrow strip of grassland to Brookvale Park, on the east side of Marsh Hill. On the west side, they are joined by a large area of school playing fields and Perry Common Recreation Grounds, which together make quite a stretch of open country for the surrounding houses.

The new tower blocks of flats are separated from the lakes by sloping lawns but are tall enough to be reflected in the water. In this reflection I noticed a pair of black and white tufted ducks, rare birds among the more common Midland waterfowl.

On the rising ground to the west, stands the Catholic College of St Mary, at New Oscott, with Pugin's Gothic towers silhouetted against the sky.

Boating is available on Witton Lakes during the summer but, as yet, the lakes are not stocked with fish. Trees have been planted along the west side and the walks opposite are sheltered by banks of gorse, their brilliant flowers turning to orange in the rays of the setting sun.

L.M.S. Goods Office, New Canal Street, formerly the terminus of the London-Birmingham Railway. Designed by Philip Hardwick in 1839.

CHAPTER THREE

Villages and Craftsmen

My grandmother was born at Ley Hill Farm, Northfield and, for several generations, her family had farmed land behind the Bell Inn. Unlike the north-east side of the town, agricultural work continued in Northfield until the present century, when Street Farm in Church Road was the last of the farms to be parcelled out for building sites. The railway came through Northfield in 1838, the Austin Motor Works was begun at Rednal in 1905 and, with the Corporation Tram Service reaching out to Rednal and Rubery in 1923, Northfield rapidly developed into a residential suburb. But farm names remain to remind us of the past—Beech Farm Croft is behind a small group of nailers' cottages, Ley Hill Farm Road is behind the Bell, Bank Top is still marked on the map as a farm. The house has been demolished though the farm buildings are rented to a pony club, which enjoys the rides in the fields on either side of the River Rea.

The Rea rises nearby on Windmill Hill and its clear waters flow through the fields of Bank Top shaded by trees until it passes Lifford Reservoir, after which it soon reaches an area where it becomes polluted by industry.

A river walk has been planned for the future—to start in Daffodil Park at Longbridge, pass through the playing fields at King's Norton, past Lifford Reservoir, through Pebble Mill Fields, Cannon Hill Park and Calthorpe Park, until it meets the town at Gooch Street. If this can be achieved, it would make a delightful walk into the city.

The fields on the side of the Rea beyond the farm buildings, rise to meet the gardens of the houses on Staple Lodge Road. The whole area is marked on the map as Staplehall Farm Recreation Ground—as yet undeveloped. The pony club enthusiasts and the local children who fish and paddle in the Rea, are petitioning for the land to remain as fields—they enjoy their recreation in less formal surroundings.

On the top of Church Hill, clustered around a hazardous bend in the road, is all that is left of old Northfield —the Church of St Laurence, with the Rectory on one side and a group of old buildings opposite.

Among these, is The Great Stone Inn, named after a large stone which stands in the adjoining village pound. These small yards or pounds, were to be found in most

Northfield. The Great Stone Inn adjoining the village pound.

villages and were used for housing straying cattle.

Before the last war, I experienced the usefulness of a cattle pound. Our house was at the end of a cul-de-sac and had a small paddock. One evening, a group of terrified ponies raced up the hill and into the front drive. We were able to close the gate behind them and shepherd them into the paddock before the police car arrived, together with the distressed owner of the ponies, a circus proprietor. He was so relieved to have his ponies safely housed for the night that he loaned one of the ponies to the children for the remainder of the winter. To their great delight, he told them the commands to use to get the pony to count, to dance and to give a low bow. They tried all winter to get their own pony to perform but they discovered that you can't teach old dogs new tricks.

The Northfield cattle pound is preserved as a small garden and in the centre is the great boulder, believed to have been carried from the Arenig district of North Wales by glacial action. The pound is about 500 years old and the well-worn sandstone wall, with its iron grilles, certainly looks its age.

Cattle pounds also housed the unemployed in the eighteenth century. If they applied for parish relief, they were compelled to stand in the pound for so many hours each day in order to qualify. History does not relate what happened if the pound was full of cattle.

There has been an inn on this corner since Tudor times but the present one was built on the old site in the eighteenth century. The nailers' cottages beyond the inn are old, but undistinguished except for a pigeon loft built into one of the chimney walls. The whole corner is part of a conservation area but until something can be done about the traffic on the blind corner, it is difficult to appreciate it.

The church was built during the thirteenth and fourteenth centuries and in spite of three periods of restoration, still retains some of the original structure, including a fourteenth century timbered porch in a remarkably good state of preservation. It was easy to visualise the Northfield of my grandmother's day, as I stood in the rectory garden under the shade of a tulip tree. Ring doves were cooing in the tall trees surrounding the church. On the rectory lawn—

'. . . like busy curates
Hands under coat tails clasped, are
Dapper wagtails bobbing, black and white'

as Barbara Ellis, in her poem, 'A bus ride in the country', so aptly described them.

Behind the Bell Inn and Bell Holloway, Merritt's Brook flows through the Ley Hill Recreation Ground

Northfield. The last of the nailers' cottages.

and the road leads down the hill to Bartley Reservoir and Senneleys Park.

Except for the playing fields, Senneleys has been preserved as a natural park and looking down on it from the seats by Bartley Reservoir, it is a good stretch of open country in a built up area. In addition to the trees which follow the winding course of a brook, it is well-wooded

and many of the paths make welcome short cuts to Genners Lane and the walks round the reservoir.

Quite near to Northfield, is King's Norton. Although a mass of busy roads and housing estates, King's Norton has yet managed to retain the charm of a village, where The Green is much as it has been for centuries. Although most of the buildings around it have changed, the group has the atmosphere of a village, where people come for their daily shopping and gossip with their friends. The village aspect is met as soon as the traffic island is left behind and one enters the short approach to The Green.

At the top of the slope stands the church, with its elegant tapering spire, a landmark for miles around. To the left, is the half-timbered 'Saracen's Head' and to the right, under the trees behind the church, the small grammar school.

It was here that young John Baskerville developed his love for calligraphy and taught writing, after doing duty as a footman at the Rectory.

A hundred years later, after the canal was cut, King's Norton became such a busy manufacturing centre that it claimed the postal address of Birmingham should be 'near King's Norton'. Many manufacturers took advantage of the cheap land and the ease of transport and built premises around King's Norton. Among these, Nettlefold and Chamberlain made screws, Ellis and Son,

57

King's Norton. One of the oldest village greens within the city boundary.

German Silver, Baldwin's made paper, Deakin's gunbarrels and bayonets, while Heaton's minted coins. Pennies minted at King's Norton between 1874 and 1882, with an H under the date, are now collectors' pieces.

William Lucas Sargent, the educational reformer, was born at King's Norton in 1809 and fought for better education during the industrial boom.

Times have changed again. The battle has died down and houses and a large park occupy the land above The Green. Owing to extensive alterations, little of the original church remains, though there is a list of incumbents going back to 1310. There is an alabaster tomb supporting the effigies of Sir Richard Greves of Moseley and his wife Anne. Sir Richard was High Sheriff of Worcester in 1609 and was a considerable landowner in south Birmingham, though the family was eventually reduced to penury. Moseley Hall became the home of John Taylor, a manufacturer of fine snuff boxes and a partner of Charles Lloyd in Birmingham's first bank. His snuff box lids were decorated with delicate swirls in the enamel, which baffled his competitors for years, until Taylor finally revealed they had been made with his own thumb print, in the privacy of his office.

The small half-timbered building in the churchyard was the free Grammar School, and is thought to have been built on the site of a school founded in 1344. By 1875, the building was too small for the growing population and a new school was built on the Pershore Road. The old premises, now restored, are used by the church for social functions.

The 'Saracen's Head' also belongs to the church, having been presented by the brewers in 1929. This building is well cared for and now houses many church activities, although the bar serves coffee only. The part of the building flanking the churchyard was built in the fifteenth century, with later additions facing on to The Green.

> Sets the sun o'er Norton crest,
> Stay they all at the Queen's behest.

It was not Queen Elizabeth who slept there but Queen Henrietta Maria, wife of Charles I, on her way to meet the King at Edge Hill. The 'Saracen's Head' is claimed to have been one of the oldest licensed premises in the country.

On the lower side of Pershore Road South, along Wharf Road, there is a good view of the church from the canal towpath, looking up across the playing fields. A number of gaily-painted narrow boats tie up here and it is only a short distance along the canal towpath to the guillotine lock, which is under the bridge that carries Lifford Lane over the canal.

59

This type of lock was not built for the usual purpose of lifting or lowering the boats, but was in effect a double door, to prevent the loss of the jealously guarded water from the Worcester to the Stratford Canal. Before nationalisation, the two canals were owned by rival companies but communicated with one another at the same level. The guillotines now remain open but their iron supporting columns and the winches are still in good condition and one hopes will be preserved.

The River Rea also flows under Lifford Lane, through the grounds of Lifford Hall. Part of the curtain wall of the old hall and a round tower, are all that remain of the home of James Hewitt, who became Viscount Lifford of Lifford in Donegal, in the reign of James I.

Lifford Reservoir lies behind the grounds of Lifford Hall and, together with the tree-lined walk along the River Rea, gives pleasure to walkers and fishermen and is home for many water birds.

The more one explores Birmingham, the more the same familiar names recur. Lifford Hall is now used as a works canteen by the firm of Joseph Sturge and Co. Joseph Sturge, a Quaker, was one of the town's first aldermen in 1838. His statue at Five Ways, Edgbaston, has survived the upheaval there in the last few years, caused notably by the construction of a traffic circus and underpass. The inscription below his statue reads—

Lifford. Unique guillotine lock, which controlled the water supply between the Worcester-Birmingham Canal and the Stratford on Avon Canal.

He laboured to bring freedom to the Negro slave, the vote to the British workman and the promise of peace to a war-worn world.

During the last war, when his "promise of peace" seemed almost impossible, I lived in one of a row of small Georgian houses opposite the statue, which, along

60

with the Grammar School, were demolished to make way for the new road. Intrigued by the name Five Ways, as there were six roads which radiated from the clock tower in the centre, I found an old picture of the toll-gate. This was removed in 1841 and the field path which formerly led from Edgbaston Hall to the Turnpike cottage, was made into Calthorpe Road, but the old name of Five Ways remained.

The road from Lifford to the ancient manor of Yardley passes through many crowded suburbs and although Yardley has a long history, it presents a dull face to the seventies, with few open spaces.

There is a succession of recreation grounds along the banks of the River Cole between Hay Mills and Stechford, but these have an unkempt look. There are various others scattered round the district but the only semblance of a public park is the small garden behind the old school house.

Yardley, like King's Norton and Handsworth, had a flourishing community of master weavers in the early eighteenth century and the presence of so many weavers working in the outlying villages no doubt spurred Lewis Paul and John Wyatt to invent the first spinning and carding machines.

It was at John Wyatt's funeral that the eccentric John Baskerville ran true to form by attending in a gold lace coat instead of the required sombre black.

As was the case in all the Midland villages, there were many cottage industries in Yardley at the beginning of the eighteenth century, mainly engaged in the production of small metal items—industries which had been growing steadily since 1600.

By the mid-nineteenth century, it had become a fashionable suburb for the business men, who moved out to Yardley from the congested districts, which spread along the Coventry Road through Bordesley, Small Heath and Hay Mills. When the tram service was extended from Small Heath to the Swan Hotel in Yardley in 1890 and penny fares were introduced, streets of small houses were cut through the remaining agricultural land. The business men moved further out and Yardley developed into a middle class residential area. Since the War, many of the meaner properties have been demolished to make way for new council house estates. Now, the old village is closed in on the Coventry side by the Kitts Green and Garretts Green estates and by Wells Green and Sheldon, on either side of the Coventry Road.

In the centre of all this maze of roads, crescents and avenues, is the parish church of St Edburgha, dedicated to the Saxon princess. Some of the thirteenth- and fourteenth-century building still remains, but like so many old churches, it has suffered from many alterations.

61

One of the interesting items in the church is a cracked tombstone taken from the floor of the Este Chapel when it was re-tiled in the particularly ugly designs so popular with the Victorians. The incised stone appears to have held a brass. On the wall, despite a fracture across the centre, it is possible to discern the outline of two figures. They are Thomas Este Governor of Kenilworth Castle, and his wife, Marian de la Hay, the last of the Hay family, whom he married in 1493 and who lived at Hay Hall.

This old hall is on land belonging to a factory and is now used for offices and reception. Built by Robert de la Hay about 1300, part of the original building still survives and has been well restored.

Another item of interest within the church is an unusual brass which depicts a wife with a husband kneeling on either side. The wife is Dame Wheeler, who died in 1598. She was related to the Catesbys of Gunpowder Plot fame, one of whom is buried in the churchyard.

The handsome marble monument commemorates the Reverend Henry Greswolde, Rector of Solihull, who died in 1700. The Greswolde family has many Birmingham connections. Coming originally from Greet, north of Yardley, they also lived for many years at the old Shaftmoor Hall at Hall Green before moving to Malvern Hall at Solihull. The chancel of St Edburgha was repaired by a Henry Greswolde of Malvern Hall in 1797.

The Manor of Yardley is mentioned in a charter of AD 972 (preserved in the British Museum), confirming the previous gift of the manor to the Abbey at Pershore. Thus, Yardley was able to celebrate its one thousandth birthday in 1972.

The Manor of Yardley was later begrudgingly given to Catherine of Aragon by Henry VIII, after he had married Anne Boleyn. Poor Catherine had a hard time raising enough money to support even her meagre household and it was not long before she sold the manor to the Duke of Northumberland. Her ownership is recorded in stone over the north door by a Tudor rose and a pomegranate, the emblem of the Spanish Aragon family.

A less distinguished owner of the manor, was John Taylor, of Taylor and Lloyd's Bank. Wishing to be called Squire, he bought the title of Lord of the Manor of Yardley in 1759, for £9,000 and lived for a time at Sheldon Hall.

The exterior stone at the base of the fourteenth-century tower of the church is well grooved—maybe from the practice of sharpening arrows, as arrows sharpened on a church wall were believed to shoot more accurately. Or they could have been caused by well-wishers scraping the soft sandstone to sprinkle a little

Yardley. A manor which was one thousand years old in 1972.

over newly weds, a gesture believed to ensure fertility.

Beyond the churchyard is the half-timbered School-house, built in the latter half of the fifteenth century, though the interior has been completely modernised. With the group of cottages opposite and the sharp bend in the road, this is a very similar scene to those at Harborne and Northfield, though not so attractive, owing to the poor Victorian houses nearby.

Walking in the small formal garden which lies beyond the Schoolhouse, I saw a rare white-headed blackbird. Piebald blackbirds with white streaks on their wings are not uncommon. This bird followed me around the garden, from bush to bush, until I entered the open fields of the recreation ground.

Blakesley Hall at Yardley is a sixteenth-century timber-framed house, built by a wealthy merchant, one Richard Smallbroke. The family name is recalled in Smallbrook Street, Birmingham, which ran from the Bull Ring to the Horsefair. Until the bombing of the second world war it was a narrow street of thriving small businesses, carrying some of the most comprehensive ironmongery stocks in the country. I remember asking at one of the ironmongers for a length of pierced brass strip, needed to make a gallery for Prince Albert's shaving stand in the production of *Victoria Regina*.

"Give us some idea of the style you want: plain or fancy, like," said the assistant. "We have hundreds of different ones in stock."

I described as best I could, the elaborate design I required.

"I get you—RC rather than C of E."

The once busy little street is now a double carriageway with too many double yellow lines and many of the new shops, like those in the new shopping precincts at Five Ways, are still unoccupied. The car parks needed by their customers are either too far away or too expensive.

Blakesley Hall also suffered during the air-raids but unlike Smallbrook Street, has been carefully restored, to become one of the city's most interesting museums, dealing with the archaeology, the history and the industrial growth of Birmingham, beginning with an excellent model of the town and its environs, as it was in 1731.

This model clearly shows Deritend Bridge spanning the River Rea. One old legend tells how Alice Clopton, betrothed to Sir Harry Wade, was stolen by a lovesick yeoman on her wedding morning.

Sir Harry in chase. To the River Rea,
Where Deritend slumbers, they sped that day.

While the rival lovers fought, poor Alice fell into the Rea and was drowned.

Sir Harry plunged swiftly down the spate
And grasped his love. Too late! Too late!

In 1625, Deritend Bridge was in need of repair but an argument arose between the authorities and the taxpayers as to who should pay. The matter was unresolved at the start of the Civil War and by 1651 the bridge had collapsed "through the neglect of such as ought to repair it." In 1652, the ratepayers won the argument and the bridge was re-built, but the authorities were so mean, that it was years before the stonemasons were paid for their work. In order to save wear and tear on their precious bridge, chains were placed across it, —the authorities having decided that as the Rea was so shallow and there was a good ford, the bridge would only be opened for carts and carriages in times of flood.

Confined in a brick culvert, the Rea still flows under the road at Deritend and there is no longer any need for the floodgates, which gave their name to a nearby street.

After seeing the model at Blakesley and the excellent collection of views of old Birmingham, there are the displays of the many examples of the work of the town's early craftsmen. Particularly the papier mâché articles from Henry Clay's factory. There are also some made by his successor, Ebenezer Sheldon, whose descendants continued to manufacture papier mâché until the first world war.

One of the trays at Blakesley thought to have been decorated by Edward Bird, bears Clay's mark—'Clay's

Blakesley Hall. Early seventeenth-century timber-framed manor house, restored and now a museum.

Patent', with a crown superimposed, on the back.

Little is known about John Thorpe, an heraldic artist working in Birmingham at the beginning of the nineteenth century. He supplied painted truncheons to the Birmingham Commissioners. Blakesley Museum has some of these decorated truncheons but the best examples

65

of his heraldic work I have seen are in the boardroom of the Proof House in Banbury Street. On the wall there is a royal coat-of-arms signed John Thorpe 1835 and on the ceiling, the arms of the Proof House, dated 1836.

The garden at Blakesley Hall has been designed and planted to show the style of garden common to a house of that period. Lawns, yew hedges, fruit trees and a herb garden, all combine to make it a most suitable setting for the beautiful old house.

After enjoying the work of Birmingham's nineteenth century craftsmen at Blakesley, it was interesting to find a modern one, at work in his garden studio, just round the corner from the museum.

Claude Price designs and makes stained glass windows, but stained glass with a difference—it emphasises light, as well as colour. The designs in his windows have a subtle three-dimensional quality. He obtains this by fusing pieces of glass, one on top of another, in his electric kiln. Put simply, he makes glass sandwiches, three or even five layers thick. He demonstrated his method, with a beautiful head of Christ. The crown of thorns, which he wished to remain sharp in outline, was in the middle, No. 3 sheet; the features and hair line, sheets 2 and 4, were more rounded; and the contours of the face and hair were even softer in outline, having been in the hottest layers, sheets 1 and 5.

On the carefully selected pieces of coloured glass, the design is drawn, cut and etched—possibly the colour is strengthened and, after the sandwich has been assembled, the whole is placed with great care in the kiln. The great heat which is applied fuses the individual sheets together, softens the outer sheets most and leaves the outline of the centre sheet quite sharp.

Claude Price evolved this method as an improvement on the Victorian windows, many of which, he considered, were over-drawn, stained and etched and therefore gloomy. As he explained, no amount of cleaning can lighten this type of window.

A master craftsman and a brilliant designer, he fits his beautiful sections of fused glass into their leaded channels and prefers to erect the finished windows himself, no matter how large. The fitting of the windows into grooves cut in the stonework is exacting work.

A painter works with a palette of colours. Claude Price's palette consisted of racks of hand-made coloured glass, carefully graded from dark to light, from deep purple to the palest pink, and from dark green to pale yellow.

The large windows of his studio-shed were covered with small sections of his latest work, with the light shining through them. Like any artist with a painting, he studies and adjusts them until they meet his high standard of perfection.

After absorbing so much information, I needed a walk in the country. Elmdon Park, near the Coventry Road, just beyond the city boundary, is the nearest to Yardley. Turning off the road to Coventry at Damson Lane, the lane to this park passes between a sports ground and a car testing ground, both covering several acres.

The car park, which also serves the small parish church of Elmdon, is surrounded by magnificent beech trees. Beyond, the parkland slopes down towards the small stream in the valley below, which feeds a lake. There are a few paths with seats under the trees but the main area of land on the slopes of the hill has been left as a natural park. Walk where you will, under the old oaks and Spanish chestnuts which are scattered throughout the park and hear the laughing call of the green woodpeckers and the raucous squawks of the jays.

Like Yardley and Northfield, Handsworth was once a village. It lay on the heathland between Aston and Perry Barr and began to develop after Matthew Boulton built his Manufactory on Soho Warren in 1762.

Land was acquired on Handsworth Heath by many wealthy manufacturers who wished to live further out in the country. Before long, a smart suburb developed, with large houses standing in their own grounds, complete with stabling for horses and coach houses for elegant carriages.

To this desirable district came James Watt, to live at Heathfield Hall, and William Murdock at Sycamore House. Many of their friends lived nearby, and by the middle of the nineteenth century it was necessary to enlarge the small parish church of St Mary. But so rapid was the growth of Handsworth that by the end of the century the corporation was having difficulty in finding a large enough area of land for a public park.

Most of the grand houses have now been demolished. The few which remain stand as shabby relics of a bygone age, their paint and plaster peeling, used as business premises, night clubs or as crowded lodging houses.

Soho House, the home of Matthew Boulton, has so far survived, but it has been deprived of its grounds and long driveway and is at present being used as a police hostel. Gone are the days when the crowned heads of Europe came visiting in search of the beautifully designed articles made at the 'Soho Manufactory': when the carriage of the victorious Admiral Nelson was pulled up the drive by the cheering villagers from Hockley. The ghostly carriage with the sound of horses' hooves, heard in November by the police cadets who sleep in the bedroom over the porch, always appears to turn in the drive and depart hurriedly.

67

Handsworth. The original sixteenth-century 'Town Hall', which has served as a work-house, a lock-up and a parish office.

Unlike Nelson, I entered the house by the kitchen door, as the present approach road is at the rear of the house. Only a minute piece of garden now separates the original handsome portico from the backs of dozens of small houses built around it.

The house is warmed by the latest central heating, but so it was in Boulton's day. When he built the house, he incorporated air ducts within the walls and boasted that his house was the first to have efficient central heating since Roman times.

The walls are thick and the damp and the cold are kept out by a lining of slates under the plaster façade. Two hundred years ago, he had elegant metal window frames (and they are still as good as new) in the room where the famous Lunar Society met. Among the members of this society were Boulton's friend and partner, James Watt, inventor of the steam engine; Dr Erasmus Darwin, botanist and grandfather of Charles Darwin; Dr Joseph Priestley, the discoverer of oxygen; Josiah Wedgwood, the potter; Sir Joseph Banks, President of the Royal Society; Sir William Herschel, the astronomer and James Keir, the engineer. They gathered at Boulton's hospitable table to talk, with great good humour and ready wit and to discuss the latest scientific discoveries.

Handsworth Park, which expanded gradually from land first purchased in 1888, has been famous for many

Soho House, 1764–89. Designed by Samuel Wyatt for Matthew Boulton.

years for its annual flower show, which runs a close second to Chelsea. There is ample space for it on the high ground which lies between the railway cutting and Hinstock Road. On this same high ground is a well established heather garden, which hides the foundations of the old Manor House. Some historians say the moated manor house of the de Parles family was on the site now occupied by the lake, but before the present lake could be made, it was the old rectory on the site which had to be demolished.

Weeping willows now trail their branches in the lake, making a contrasting foreground to the sandstone church and the tall beech trees on the rising ground behind it.

It seems sad that the church, containing as it does, memorials to so many of the city's great men, has to be kept locked against vandals. It is even sadder when one thinks of the wealthy congregation which worshipped there in the last century, to hear the vicar say that they do not have the funds to pay for a printed church history.

In the nineteenth century, the parish church of St Mary had to be enlarged, to accommodate the rapidly increasing population. Even after the re-building, it still remains rather small and insignificant, dwarfed by the tall trees in the extensive churchyard.

Within the church are some of the memorials to the great industrialists. Matthew Boulton's memorial is small and discreet, a marble bust above a wall tablet. The memorial to Sir James Watt is a life size statue by Chantrey, standing in its own chapel. The difference in the memorials corresponds strangely to the difference in their characters.

Francis Eginton, a partner in so many of Boulton's enterprises, lies buried in the churchyard, but with ne'er a headstone to commemorate him.

The two really old tombs in the church are rather hidden away. The one which lies under the organ pipes, belongs to the Wyrley family. The de Wyrleys of Wyrley were Crown tenants of Handsworth in Queen Elizabeth I's reign and subsequent de Wyrleys were Lords Lieutenant of Staffordshire in the reigns of some of the Stuarts and the Hanoverians. Like many of the local families, they were interconnected by marriage. The Wyrleys had connections with Bishop Vesey of Sutton Coldfield, with the Lanes, who were supporters of Charles II and with the Wyrley-Birch family, whose name was perpetuated in one of the earliest of Birmingham's allotments.

The other tomb, dated about the mid-fifteenth century, is thought to relate to the Stamford family. William Stamford, a Catholic judge in the reign of Queen Mary, owned the nearby Perry Hall and a later William Stamford, eldest son of Sir Robert Stamford, added an old mansion to his Perry Hall estate. This was called New Inn. In the twelfth century, it was quite common to call a family mansion an 'Inn'—usually preceded by the family name, as in 'Clifford's Inn', which was originally the site of the de Clifford's home. Similarly, Lincoln's

Inn, was the site of a town house of the Earls of Lincoln. The New Inns public house, well known in Handsworth, is reputed to have been built opposite the site of the old Stamford mansion.

Also buried in St Mary's churchyard, is the forger William Booth, who came to Great Barr with his family in about 1800 and settled in a house which had originally been part of a monastery. There, he posed as a farmer but, in the upper storeys, behind the massive walls, he set up presses for making on a large scale, both base coins and forged bank notes. His illicit business thrived, until feeling secure and well hidden, he became incautious and began to send his base metal to be rolled in Birmingham. This eventually led to his capture and he was sentenced to be hung at Stafford on 15th August 1812. Booth's hanging must have been bewitched, for at the first attempt the rope broke and he was knocked unconscious by the fall and, at the second and third attempts, the mechanism failed. When the sentence had eventually been carried out, his coffin was caught in a flood in the River Tame on its way to St Mary's. Locally, he was known not as 'Booth the forger' but as 'Booth three times dead.'

King's Norton. The old Grammar School endowed by Edward VI.

CHAPTER FOUR

Satan Stood on Brierley Hill

There is nothing throughout the length and breadth of England to compare with the Black Country. It is unique. Much of its appearance is due to a man-made landscape created during the last two centuries, in a ruthless exploitation of its mineral riches. It is a separate and distinct area and not, as often supposed, an extension of Birmingham.

The Black Country of today, part of the industrial West Midlands, is made up of five county boroughs: Wolverhampton and Walsall in the north, and Dudley, West Bromwich and Warley covering the central part, with the two smaller municipal boroughs of Stourbridge and Halesowen in the south.

It is not a large area—approximately ten miles from the western boundary of Dudley's Himley Park, to the eastern edge, where Walsall meets Aldridge and the roads leading north to Cannock Chase. From north to south it is barely fifteen miles from Wolverhampton's Moseley, made famous by Charles II, to the most southerly part where the Stourbridge borough has expanded beyond the old natural boundary of the River Stour, to meet the Clent Hills.

The land within the West Midlands' boundaries is one of abrupt contrasts of hills and flat plains. The ridge of broken hills includes the Rowley Hills, where the many tributaries of the Tame and the Trent have their source and Turners Hill, almost eaten away by centuries of quarrying. Next comes Dudley Castle Hill, a military stronghold since Saxon times, with the adjoining limestone ridge of the Wren's Nest and finally the heights of Sedgley Beacon.

It was once a land of dense forests and heaths, hunted over by kings, nobles and clerics. Small towns developed at Dudley, Wolverhampton and Walsall after the granting of market charters and Halesowen grew beside the wealthy Abbey of Hales.

Beneath the forests and the heaths lay the cause of their destruction—rich deposits of ironstone, limestones, coal and fireclay. These were within workable distance of the surface and offered readily accessible raw materials to the industrious people living in small communities near the rivers.

By the fourteenth century, coal and iron were being

Warley. Decorative cast-iron in Light-woods Park.

mined in the Wednesbury district and smiths soon began to establish their forges in the neighbourhood. Coal mining extended along all the accessible outcrops of Thick Coal and trains of packhorses served the local industries and the ever growing needs of the smiths at Birmingham.

The River Stour, which rises in the Clent Hills and flows round the chain-making districts of Cradley and Lye, past Stourbridge town and Amblecote, was an important source of power before the era of steam. No other river of its size in England fed so many water mills and supplied so much power for small industries.

In the nineteenth century, the industrial growth of the Black Country was meteoric. With the advent of steam-driven pumps for use in coal mining, fuel no longer posed a problem and with the cutting of the first canal, in 1769, to be followed by a network of canals connecting the Black Country to the principal ports, the transport of raw materials and manufactured goods became economic. From then onwards, the extraction of the earth's riches became a miniature gold rush. The name 'Black Country' was given to the one-time rolling heathlands; black by day but red by night, for the fiery glow from the great blast furnaces, sent spurts of fire leaping high into the sky all the year round.

Many times, on the trams at night, I used to rattle out towards Oldbury and Dudley with fellow students and climb the spoil heaps. With a torch fixed to our sketchbooks, we tried to record the inferno below.

When Satan stood on Brierley Hill
And round about him gazed—
He said "I never will again
At Hell's flames be amazed".

We students also sketched with meticulous care, the people in the village pubs. The women, in their flat black caps and shawls, gathered around and criticised our work, in a dialect which, although we were so near to Birmingham, could be understood only by the speakers and their friends.

The flat black caps are no more and the appearance of both the land and the people has changed. Schools have standardised the dialects. The younger generation can be understood. Photography has also changed our art—no longer the careful drawing! We look for sweeping abstracts and find them in plenty in the West Midlands, in the great quarries cut deep into Turner's Hill, or at the scarlet graveyard of the Midland Red buses, or the swirling masses of sombre colours, before the filling in of the open-cast mining restores the land for future parks and open spaces. One time, it looks as if Macbeth's witches had stirred up a black and sinister Lake District, while on the next visit, the good fairies, disguised as yellow bulldozers, are busy straightening it all out again.

The greedy Victorians, sometimes admittedly through lack of capital, mined in an un-planned and wasteful way. Consequently millions of tons of coal are inaccessible because of flooded mines and uncharted workings.

The rape of the land has now almost ceased. Limestone quarrying ended in the 1920s. Deep coal mining is, in the main, confined to the Cannock area. Many of the clay-pits, brickworks and iron foundries have closed down. But the burrowing underground has left a legacy of serious subsidence problems, though to the joy of the conservationists, there are also 'hollow lands', which will not support buildings.

Due to modern smoke control, Dickens' description in *The Old Curiosity Shop* of the Black Country's belching chimneys, whose "plague of smoke obscured the light and made foul the melancholy air," no longer applies.

The authorities who at present control the West Midlands, are faced with the gigantic task of re-planning the area and ensuring that the air is neither melancholy nor foul. Many of the railways are closed, pleasure craft use the discarded canals and goods are transported on the wide new roads. High Rise flats and new housing estates are gradually ousting the nailers' cottages and workshops and many of the scattered villages are now joined together, in great stretches of industrial and urban development; though not all. There is plenty of country to be found within the West Midlands boundaries—and, for an artist, dramatic and exciting country.

Subsidence cracks many roads and buildings but it also creates opaque pools, often azure in colour, due to the clay beneath the water. Others are a deep rust colour or dark and sinister. The local boys call them 'Swags' and fish in them for tadpoles, water beetles and tiddlers, which seem to thrive in their murky depths, no matter what the colour. Reeds grow round the edges of these pools, making homes for water-loving birds, and grass and stunted shrubs gradually appear on the spoil heaps. Not green grass—no matter what the time of the year, the grass is like stubble, in shades of yellow ochre and raw sienna, with an occasional patch of jet black, where the coarse grass has not yet succeeded in overwhelming a rash of cinders.

Open country within the West Midlands comes in small doses, well worth searching for, as its character is unique. Except for the south east corner where it meets Birmingham, the people living within the area can find many beauty spots preserved for public use.

To the south west, lie the Clent Hills, Kinver Edge and Enville Common. In the midst of the agricultural

75

land on the western border are the beautiful parklands surrounding Himley Hall, with walks across Penn Common.

To the north lies Cannock Chase, with its miles of woodland walks and drives, less than 10 miles from the crowded suburbs of Walsall and Wolverhampton.

Barr Beacon rises over 800 feet above sea level on the eastern boundary, commanding magnificent views, and finally, before returning full circle to northern Birmingham, there are the 2,400 acres of Sutton Park.

All these open spaces mean that people living in the industrial centres, such as Tipton, Bilston, Darlaston or Oldbury, have real country easily accessible.

The authority nearest to the centre of Birmingham is the new County Borough of Warley. Opposite the King's Head on the Hagley Road, Warley meets the Birmingham district of Harborne, and close by, is Lightwoods Park. This is a small stretch of the parkland which once surrounded Lightwoods House, built by Madame (not The Mrs) Grundy, in 1791. It is not a distinguished building. Nikolaus Pevsner describes it as "restless and looking early Georgian". For some years it has been threatened with demolition but it has now been reprieved and will shortly be used as a stained glass studio by John Hardman of Newhall Street, Birmingham. This is an old established Birmingham firm, which

Warley Woods. Park land which surrounded one of the grange farms of Hales Abbey.

originally made church metal work until persuaded by the architect Pugin to tackle the stained glass he required for Oscott College.

The pool at Lightwoods has had to make way for road widening but it is a pleasant walk through the park to Warley Woods, which cover over 100 acres. This land was saved from becoming a maze of small streets, by the Birmingham Corporation, which purchased it in 1907 for use as a public park.

The rolling parkland with its birch and beech woods, is closely surrounded by small houses, but the area is so large, they are soon out of sight and mind and one can peacefully listen to the song of the birds.

The ancient Manor of Warley, like so much of the Black Country, belonged to the Barons of Dudley before some of the land was bestowed on Hales Abbey in 1328. The monks had one of their many granges or monastic farms there, to which in 1490, they added a small chapel dedicated to St Michael. This could not rightly be termed an abbey—the misnomer was given by the owner of a Victorian house on the site, Sir Hugh Gilzean Reid, who was the first M.P. for Aston Manor (and who was knighted in 1893). Prior to that, the freehold of Warley Hall was held by the Galton family, Birmingham bankers and gunsmiths.

The Galtons entertained many visitors at Warley, including the ghost of the grey lady, who was so often seen walking in the park. When the Punch artist, Harry Furness, was staying with the Galtons, he not only saw but also drew and published his version of the apparition.

Though it has been one of my favourite walking places since childhood, I have never caught a glimpse of her.

Perhaps the chatter of the squirrels and the magpies has frightened her away.

After leaving Warley Woods, drive along the Hagley Road towards Halesowen and when halfway down Mucklow Hill turn left, into The Leasowes Park.

The Leasowes has always been a stretch of beautiful countryside and although William Shenstone would no doubt have preferred to be remembered for his poetry, he is appreciated locally for the tree planting and landscaping which he accomplished at The Leasowes. He was born in 1714 at the Leasowes farm house on the large grazing farm, which at that time occupied most of the estate.

Following an academic life at Oxford and the death of his uncle, William had to take over the management of his Leasowes estate. He saw at once its natural potential as a landscape garden. The undulating land, sheltered by hills and watered by two streams emptying into pools, together with the distant views of Halesowen Church, framed by the Clent Hills, made it an ideal site.

He certainly achieved a beautiful garden, spurred on by the friendly rivalry with his friends, the Lyttletons at Hagley Hall. In its heyday, The Leasowes must have resembled the present gardens at Stourhead in Dorset. John Wesley, who was a much travelled man, was certainly impressed by its beauty. While staying at Hagley

77

Leasowes Park.
Landscaped by the
eighteenth-century
poet, William Shen-
stone.

Hall in 1782, he wrote of The Leasowes, ". . . I have seen nothing in all England to compare with it . . .such walks, such shades, such lawns, such artless cascades, such waving woods with waters intermixed, as exceeds all imagination."

After Shenstone's death, The Leasowes had various owners. They felled his carefully sited trees and demolished his romantic ruins and few cared for his beautiful gardens. All the same walkers of today are left with acres of open country, now carefully conserved as natural parkland, with the occasional stone bridge and cascading stream to remind them of William Shenstone.

The canal was cut through The Leasowes grounds in 1797—across the lake, necessitating a high embankment, thus spoiling the uninterrupted view from the house to the church. The once busy canal is in its turn deserted but the walk along the towpath would have delighted William Shenstone. From the high embankment, there is a view straight down to his lake, along his streams, over the trees which line each dingle, to the house on the hill. The present house was built shortly after Shenstone's death and is used as a golf clubhouse.

If the entrance to The Leasowes Park is well disguised, the access to Hales Abbey is positively discouraging; rightly so perhaps, as the ruins are now part of a busy farm. The ruins are listed as an ancient monument and genuinely interested visitors are allowed to walk around.

The best view of the site is from the top of the hill on the Bromsgrove to Dudley Road. From there, it is possible to see the farmland site originally chosen by the White Canons and also the ruins of their abbey. They came from Premonstratum in Picardy in 1215 and were described as "Homely and retired lovers of country, and enterprising farmers." Judging by the activities at Manor Farm today, it is still run by enterprising farmers.

As it stands at the moment, it is an artist's dream; at every turn, there is something to draw. The garden wall of the Victorian farmhouse is part of the original abbey's *frater* or dining hall, with two rows of windows towering above a small garden gate. Sections of finely carved fan vaulting rise high above the hay ricks and the canons' infirmary, which remains almost intact, is used as a barn. The farmyard is the old cloister garth and all around, built in with the brick walls of the farm buildings, are the warm red and yellow stones of the abbey.

After the Dissolution in 1538, the abbey was owned by the Dudley family and was later sold to the Lyttletons, who used much of the stone for the building of Hagley Hall.

The ruined sections of the abbey were obviously suited to be the nucleus of farm buildings and were utilised accordingly. No matter that heavy stone buttresses sup-

Hales Abbey ruins at Manor Farm, near Halesowen.

house anything from old sinks to expensive cars. Cattle, not canons, look inquisitively through the lancet windows.

The hospitality of the White Canons was renowned and profitable, as they accommodated many travellers and pilgrims. They had their own attractions, the shrine to St Barbara, and also a shrine to St Kenelm at their chapel on the lower slopes of the Clent Hills, near Romsley.

Owing to modern building, it is no longer possible to see the small church of St Kenelm's from the abbey ruins, but after leaving Manor Farm, continue along Manor Way towards Hagley; to the left of the roundabout where the Bromsgrove to Dudley road crosses Manor Way, is Halesowen Grange and its park, which was one of the monastic farms belonging to the abbey. After the dissolution, much of the property belonging to the abbey was made over to Henry's notorious Duke of Northumberland, John Dudley and The Grange became the seat of the co-heirs of the barony of Dudley, the Lea-Smiths. Now it is a clubhouse, sports centre and a welcome open space for the employees of the great Somers Works on Mucklow Hill.

Further along Manor Way, is a narrow lane on the left, signposted Clent, which passes St Kenelm's Church on its way up to the top of the hills.

port a slender brick wall or that the row of rick staddle stones which stand beside the track leading into the farm-yard carry incongruous caps. Those which have lost their mushroom tops are crowned with pieces of trefoil stone, carved seven centuries ago. Corrugated lean-to shelters, which are hitched on to the towering transept walls,

80

The legends tell of Kenelm as being a boy of eight and King of Mercia in AD 819, who was murdered by the courtiers of a jealous sister and buried under a thorn bush on the site of the present church. The story goes on to tell of a white dove, which flew out of the thorn bush, on the long journey to Rome, bearing this message—

In Clent, in Cowbach lieth under a thorn,
His head off shorn, Kenelm King-born.

The Pope sent to England to locate the royal martyr, who was eventually re-buried at Winchcombe Abbey, beside his father, King Kenulph. After that, curious things happened at the scene of the murder. Cows refused to leave the field and gave a double supply of milk. A spring of water spouted from the place from which the body had been removed and the fame of its healing properties made it a place of pilgrimage. Following this, a shrine was built in honour of King Kenelm.

In the present small church, there are traces of Saxon stones and of thirteenth century building. There are also three windows of interest—one to the memory of child war victims, appropriate to the boy king; one designed by Burne-Jones, and one given by Mr Gladstone, the nineteenth century Prime Minister, who worshipped at St Kenelm's, when staying at Hagley Hall.

In the Middle Ages, the village of Kenelmstone sur-rounded the church but with the growth of the new village of Romsley, which was nearer to the road to Dudley and as a consequence of the decline in pilgrim traffic, the village became deserted. There is no sign of it today, nor of the busy fair which was one time held on St Kenelm's Day, 17th July.

But St Kenelm's, the parish church of Romsley, still has many visitors. It is once more a pleasant resting place —not for pilgrims but for walkers on their way to the top of the Clent Hills.

The Clent Hills, which have not suffered from the various enclosure acts, have for many years been a place of recreation for the people in the south of the Black Country. There are 355 acres of the hills, including the farm and woodlands of the Clatterbach Valley, which are now safely in the hands of the National Trust, thanks to several benefactors and to the foresight of twenty local authorities.

The walkers who rest at St Kenelm's or refresh themselves in Clent village, have some wonderful country to explore as they climb the hills. To the west are wide views of the Wrekin, the Clee Hills, and the Malvern Hills; looking back, they can contrast these with the view of the crowded suburbs they have left behind.

Whether you approach Halesowen from the Clent

Hills, Bromsgrove or Hagley, you will see it spread out before you in a hollow, with a sweep of hills surrounding it on all but the Dudley side. After Henry II gave the manor of Halas, or Hales, to David ap Owen, it gradually became known as Hales Owen—Halesowen.

The church of St John stands on a high ridge of sandstone in the centre of the town, where a Saxon church once stood. The tall spire can be seen for miles around but getting to the church is another matter. Wide new roads encircle the town and the nailers' cottages have had to give way to large traffic islands. Unless you are determined to see what Halesowen has to offer, you will find yourself being hooted on to the next town, for the direction signs to the town centre are discouragingly small. Once you have turned into one of the narrow roads leading to the church and arrived at the car park in front of it, there is a chance to look around.

Immediately below the car park are some of the restored Tudor cottages, known as Whitefriars. On the sites of those which had gone beyond repair before Councils had become preservation conscious, small gardens have been landscaped.

The church has a fine Norman font and west door, which have survived the inevitable restorations. Among the memorials to local families, notably the Lyttletons of Hagley Hall, there is one to the novelist Francis Brett Young, a son of the local doctor. He took his own medical degree before joining the R.A.M.C. in the first World War. Many of his novels, particularly *My Brother Jonathan* and *Portrait of Clare*, contain vivid descriptions of the Black Country he knew so well. He mentions the rhythmic beat of the great steam hammer at Somers' Works, beating night and day like a gigantic pulse. Somers are still in business alongside the canal, at the foot of Mucklow Hill.

Halesowen also claims William Caslon as one of its citizens, for, although born at nearby Cradley, he was baptised at St John's in 1692. After starting life as an engraver, Caslon set up his own business in London for letter-founding. By 1734, he had issued his first specimen sheet and he is regarded as England's first type founder. A type is named after him, as another is named after that great admirer of his work—John Baskerville.

Another of the town's famous citizens was Thomas Attwood the reformer, who was born at Halesowen and began his education at the Free School. His father was an iron founder, who owned large estates around Halesowen, including The Leasowes. In Attwood's time there were considerable brick works at Halesowen and it is most probable that the bricks used to build his house at Harborne came from his own home town.

Halesowen. Restored cottages in Church Lane.

J. J. Shaw, the amateur seismologist, who died in 1948, recorded many earthquakes while living in Halesowen. One of his early seismographs, produced by an apparatus made from an empty treacle tin, wheat straw and an alarm clock, recorded the Messina earthquake in 1908.

One of the beauties of St John's is the large churchyard and the adjoining cemetery, which is a veritable arboretum. The magnificent beech and copper beech trees compete with limes, pines and sycamores for pride of place—an area obviously appreciated, judging by the seats provided and occupied. The walks under the trees are shady short cuts from the modern shopping centre to the other side of the town. In the corner of the churchyard are the remains of the market cross, said to have been a symbol of honest trading, erected in the Cornbow – 1540 when the market house was built.

At that time, the busy weekly markets were held on Sundays. Because Halesowen was the ancient centre of the social, political and religious life of the district, with people coming from the outlying villages to worship there, it was obviously advantageous to hold the market on Sundays.

The cross was blown down in a gale, at the beginning of the present century and was subsequently rescued from the council's scrapyard by a member of the Garratt family. Old Job Garratt was a great figure in nineteenth-century Halesowen. His father left Hawne Colliery to him and he became a shrewd business man. When he died in 1909, he left the equivalent of £½m. Like many wealthy manufacturers, he liked to pose as a country gentleman, and lived at Wassell Grove, near Clent, where he regularly feasted his workpeople.

He had a private theatre at Wassell Grove and his son, Shenstone (named after the local poet) produced plays for his family and unfortunate friends.

Hawne Colliery did not survive the General Strike in 1926, as a result of which it became uneconomic to pump out the flooded workings.

Looking for what was left of old Job's colliery, I came across a typical corner of present-day Black Country. The lane dips steeply from Haden Hill down to the River Stour, which flows along one side of the old colliery site and the old trade of gun-barrel-making is continued at the works in the dip. On either side of the river is a new housing estate, with Job's spoil heaps rising sheer, like ragged cliffs, before them.

After the colliery was closed, the shafts were filled in, as safety demanded, but the covenant to make the land fit for tillage and cultivation was not observed. Then, as now, it was deemed too expensive. But in forty five years nature has worked wonders on the spoil heaps. Birds carried the seeds of hawthorn, willow, elder and silver birch to the site, the trees have now grown and given the birds a natural sanctuary. Among the more common birds at Hawne are the chiff-chaff and the willow warbler.

Turning the corner into Hawne Lane, there is an unexpected stretch of agricultural land dropping down again to the Stour and Corngreaves Hall. This old house stands in rising woodland, a grey Gothic mansion, now converted into flats. It was at one time the home of James Attwood, brother of the famous Thomas. Their father, Matthias Attwood, who lived at Hawne House, rose from humble nail maker to iron master and became the first proprietor of the Corngreaves Iron Works. His grandson, John Attwood, sold the flourishing Corngreaves business to the New British Iron Company. Unfortunately, he did not receive his payment and so began a long and most memorable lawsuit.

The countryside towards Hayley Green is developing into a well planned housing estate, looking out across Hagley Park to the Clent Hills and old Job's Wassell Grove.

Haden Hill rises high above Hawne Colliery on the north side of the Stour and on the right of the road is a district called Haden Cross. This is where one of the Hales Abbey boundary crosses stood, on Hayseech Common, which was enclosed in 1799.

I climbed to the top of Station Road to see if there was anything left of the Common, but on the top of the hill is a new housing estate. It was high and windy up there, with wonderful views across to the Clent Hills but all that is left of the common is a stretch of waste land enclosed by buildings.

The more you explore the Black Country, the more you find the unexpected. A small front garden of one of the new houses in Station Road, is completely covered by a round blue brick ventilation shaft of the old Dudley Canal, which runs underground from the tube works by Coombeswood Colliery to the far side of Station Road.

At one time, all the Stewart and Lloyd boats came through the tunnel, laden with tubes and pipes. For the time being, a new lease of life has been given to the narrow boats on the canal at Bilston, as they are used to bring the pipes which are being laid under the towpath for supplying natural gas to the West Midlands.

A dedicated craftsman must have made the dome of iron rods which covers the brickwork of the shaft. It has four sectional irons, terminating in an elegant finial. I stopped to make a drawing of it but I doubt if the lady of the house appreciated this work of art and I should imagine she strongly objected to the bluebrick wall which blocks the daylight from her sitting room and the dank smells which waft into her bedroom.

Coombeswood and Cherry Orchard are the old names of the lands in the estate of the Haden family. Their manor house still stands on the top of Haden Hill, surrounded by a considerable area of the beautiful park, landscaped in 1876 by George Alfred Haden-Best to rival The Leasowes. Not so beautiful is the Victorian house he built on to the back of the old one. All there was to admire here was a fountain rising from three beautiful cast-iron swans, which stands outside one of the french windows.

At the moment, both houses stand empty but there is considerable local enthusiasm to preserve and re-open Haden Hill House and the money is steadily being raised. As the park on the hillside, with its lakes and magnificent trees, is a public park, the house is ideally situated for use as a domestic museum. It is a brick building of the early seventeenth century, with stepped gables and canted bay windows—an uncommon house with its pointed arches above the windows. It has an air of romance about it, perched up there on the hill, with views of the sprawling Black Country below.

The much earlier Norman house of Ricardo Haden, would have been fortified and also the house which followed, but the present house was built in a peaceful land, for country gentlefolk. Eliza Haden, the last of the

Haden Hill House (circa early seventeenth century). The last house built for the Haden family, who owned the land for 600 years.

Hadens to own the estate in a direct succession of 600 years, died there in 1876.

The River Stour, from just below Haden Hill, forms the Halesowen boundary and flows along the northern boundary of the Borough of Stourbridge until it is crossed by the railway at Clatterbach. It is possible to

86

follow the course of the river for much of the way on foot and for anyone who is interested in industrial history, to see how this busy little river, which has supplied so much power through the centuries, is now serving modern industry.

At Clatterbach, railway historians can see the original wooden bases, on which Brunel's Viaduct was built, to carry the O.W.W. (Oxford, Worcester and Wolverhampton) Railway.

The site of an ancient glass works was discovered at the time of the excavation for the viaduct. Nowadays, it is usually only possible to trace the whereabouts of these historical sites by searching old maps.

A small stream, Pudding Brook, flows into the Stour by Hawne Colliery from the Lutley Valley. This for centuries powered Lutley Mill. There has been a mill on this site from Elizabethan times, possibly earlier, and the present mill, with the charming house beside it, is to be preserved. It is a four-storey brick mill, not yet restored, but it can be seen to advantage from the small bridge over Pudding Brook, at the end of Lutley Lane.

To enjoy the Black Country, be selective and avoid where possible, the areas which are a maze of twisting roads, factories and houses. With this in mind, I left the Stour valley for the heights of the Rowley Hills. Rowley Regis, as the name implies, was King's Rowley, part of Pensnett Forest, which remained one of the royal hunting grounds until the time of the Tudors.

Quarrying is the main industry on the south-eastern slopes of Turner's Hill and is so deep and extensive that it is a distinctive feature of the district. Where the igneous rock thins out, seams of coal were mined and the old village of Rowley has had to be demolished owing to subsidence. Rowley dolerite, which was used in the building of many of the old cottages, ceased to be used as a building stone almost two centuries ago, when bricks became cheaper. Stone can be seen in the walls which still enclose some of the fields on the windswept hill top.

The buildings of the new Rowley are spreading up the more stable slopes of the hill to the church on the summit. Built in 1913, this is the fourth church to be built on the site since 1199—so far, it has escaped the surrounding subsidence, though the old vicarage which stood near the church, was in imminent danger of collapse before the vicar could be persuaded to leave it.

From the windows of the new vicarage, on the one side was a vista of desolation and on the other, rising up towards the vicarage and the new pub, a completely new housing estate.

The vicar told me of a pot of Roman silver coins, which was found under one of the stone walls in 1794.

This pot contained nearly 1,200 coins of 40 different varieties, some with portraits of the Roman Emperors Galba and Otho.

He talked of Rowley's cobbler poet, James Woodhouse, a friend of William Shenstone and a one time land steward for Lord Lyttleton at Hagley. As country lovers are apt to do, we deplored the lack of country at Rowley but he sent me on my way with the consoling thought that it was still possible to buy eggs from a farm by the Portway.

Portways were the ancient market roads, little better than trackways, which sensibly followed along well drained ridgeways. The name occurs several times in the Oldbury district, as a portway ran from Rowley, through Oldbury and West Bromwich to Wednesbury.

Passing Tippity Green, a typical Black Country name which derives via Ibbity Green from Isabel's Green, I found that Isabella de Botetort, sister of John de Somery at Dudley Castle and wife of Thomas de Botetort, had lived nearby and owned land round Rowley in the reign of Edward II. It was Isabella who gave some of her Warley lands to the canons at Hales Abbey.

From the top of Turner's Hill the views are magnificent. The hill is nearly 800 feet above sea level, like Sedgley Beacon and Barr Beacon, whose fires gave news flashes long before the days of radio. On a clear day, one

Turner's Hill, rising 876 feet. A line of quarries on the southern and eastern slopes expose the brown and blue igneous rock.

can see the line of hills to the south west, from the Clees to the Clents.

Looking down into the great quarries from what remains of Turner's Hill, there is a swirl of colours—the strong blues, browns and greys of the exposed igneous rock. This hard and durable rock was quarried to pave the streets of Birmingham and the Black Country in the frantic rush of nineteenth-century building. It is still being quarried for road metal and even at the present more rapid speed, the supplies of Rowley Rag, as it is known locally, should last another 50 years. I wondered, as I sat on one of the stone walls and listened to the larks high above me, whether the hole down below, when stripped of its rock in the twenty-first century, would still provide a home for them or whether it would be developed into a new overspill 'Turner's Town'.

Unlike Turner's Hill, there is no gentle approach to Castle Hill at Dudley. The wooded sides rise steeply above the maze of the traffic in the streets below and dwarf the surrounding buildings. Dudo, the Saxon, chose a fine site for his castle, which commanded a view of the Midland plain embracing nine counties. The site, with a succession of castles, remained a military stronghold until after the Civil War and the lords who owned it, owned many of the Midland manors.

From William Fitzanculf at the time of the Conquest, the lands passed through the centuries to the Paganels, the de Somerys and the de Suttons, to the Tudor John Dudley, Earl of Warwick and notorious as the Duke of Northumberland, who tried unsuccessfully to put his daughter-in-law, Lady Jane Grey, on the throne of England.

At the castle he employed Sir William Sharington to design the domestic buildings on a magnificent scale.

Except for the Norman earthworks, the thirteenth-century keep, built by John de Somery and the residential rooms added in the seventeenth century, the general structure is largely as John Dudley left it, prior to his execution on Tower Hill.

In the reign of Charles I, the extravagant Lord Edward Dudley, father of the illegitimate iron-master Dud Dudley, nearly ruined the estates before he managed to retrieve the family fortunes by marrying his granddaughter to a wealthy London jeweller, Humble Ward. The latter was created Baron Ward of Birmingham by Charles I and the eleventh Baron Ward was created Viscount Ednam and Earl of Dudley in 1860.

Towards the end of the eighteenth century, the Dudley family moved away from the rapidly developing town to more modern accommodation at Himley Hall. This lies just west of the new boundaries and with its many acres of wooded parkland and its beautiful lakes, is now owned jointly by the corporations of Dudley and Wolverhampton and is a public park.

After the Dudleys vacated the castle, it was used to meet the demand for premises by the manufacturers of metal smallwares and was rented out as workshops. The forges set up in these unsuitable premises were the cause

Dudley. Market place fountain, presented by the Earl of Dudley and Ward in 1867. The president of the Temperance Society expressed thanks on behalf of the water drinkers.

of a disastrous fire in 1750. This happened on the day of St James Fair, 24th July, when the town was crowded with people, who, watching the blaze, saw the molten lead from the roof pour down the wooded hillside, leaving a blazing trail behind it. It was three days before the fire burnt itself out.

The eighth Baron Ward restored the castle ruins in the 1790s and laid out the grounds as a much needed place of recreation for the townspeople.

Over the centuries, Castle Hill, like most of the Black Country, became pockmarked with surface mine workings. The hill is precipitous and the walk up to the top of the 180 feet to the castle ruins formerly spiralled round the hill, avoiding the deep indentations left by the workings.

In the 1930s, the Council decided Castle Hill would be an ideal site for an open-air zoo. The designers, Lubetkin and Tecton, who were called in, used the pockmarks on the hill to great advantage, converting them into paddocks in which the larger animals could roam freely and yet be clearly seen by the visitors. The sea-lion pool has a particularly natural appearance and is one of the largest in the country. A chair-lift is provided so that the Castle ruins with their wonderful view of the adjoining counties can easily be reached and the walks down through the woods enjoyed without effort.

I had the occasion to be grateful to the zoo authorities and particularly to the keeper of the alligators. In an American play, *The Happiest Millionaire*, a crazy crank keeps a number of alligators in his home and inevitably, a full grown specimen had to appear and walk on to the stage. In Britain, unlike America, dangerous animals are not allowed on the stage, so a walking alligator had to be made. Many evenings were spent in the alligator house at Dudley Zoo, while the patient keeper persuaded his charges to 'move along' until we had perfected a mechanism which was an exact replica of their leg movements.

The play was destined to continue its association with Dudley, for Viscount Ednam was a constant visitor backstage and married the leading lady, Maureen Swanson. He succeeded to the title of Earl of Dudley in 1970.

In addition to the many attractions of Castle Hill, the town has a stretch of parkland behind the hill. This was originally the land belonging to the Priory of St James, founded in the twelfth century by Gervase Paganel. After the Dissolution, the Priory was closed in 1540 and became a desolate place, until like the castle, it was occupied around 1770 by a small manufacturers, including a tanner and a thread spinner. Fire-irons are known to have been manufactured in the building and there are traces of a large kiln, used sometime during its industrial occupation.

The ruins of the Priory are surrounded by tall beech trees and, where possible, the open park land has been left undisturbed. There are a few flower beds in front of the Victorian Priory Hall and a well designed stone shelter with seats facing towards Castle Hill. This peaceful place is only a stone's throw from Dudley's busy freight-line terminal, which like the canals of the eighteenth century, connects Dudley with all the main ports.

Dudley. The ruins of the Cluniac Priory of St James, founded by Gervase Paganel, Lord of Dudley about AD 1160.

Behind Priory Park, towards Tipton, is the site for the Black Country open air museum, which is at the junction of Tipton Road and the Birmingham–Wolverhampton Road. Considerable money and labour will be required before this industrial museum is finished, but at any stage, it is interesting to visit. When completed, it is hoped the museum will illustrate the history of the region and show aspects of Black Country life.

It is intended to erect the head-gear and the winding engine of a coal pit, also a nineteenth century forge and it is hoped to have canal boats, a slipway and boatyard, and to exhibit some of the old Black Country trams and trolley buses. Cast-iron canal bridges are already on the site awaiting erection. Already on display in full sight of the main Birmingham–Wolverhampton Road—a small gauge railway engine named the *Winston Churchill*.

I was welcomed to a Sunday morning 'dig-in', perhaps more suitably described as a 'dig-out', as the main work on hand was dredging the canal. The horse-shoe loop of water on the site, is known as Lord Ward's Arm. When the Arm and the approach to Dudley Tunnel (opened in 1792), at the north end of the site, are cleared, and the tunnel, with its associated limestone caverns re-opened, a further exciting interest will be available for museum visitors.

The caverns were popular with boatloads of trippers during the Dudley Castle fêtes in the 1850s. Many of the boats belonged to Monk, of Tipton, who ran a special passenger-carrying packet called the *Euphrates*. This was captained by John Jevon, who fancied himself as a skipper, though he wore an incongruous uniform of jockey-cap, and scarlet sleeveless jacket adorned with rows of brass buttons. The trippers saw the great caverns lit by thousands of candles and had all the excitement of being 'legged' through the tunnels.

'Legging' was the only method of propulsion through many of the canal tunnels, as they were too narrow to allow for towpaths. One or two men lay on their backs on barge-boards and propelled the boat along by pushing against the roof of the low tunnel with their feet. The visitors were shown the limestone workings under Wren's Nest and the large cavern under Castle Hill. It is hoped in time, when safety permits, to organise similar trips.

Beside the entrance to the tunnel are old lime kilns, which are to be restored and included in the museum. David Cox, responsible for providing many records of the nineteenth-century Midlands scene, painted a water-colour of these kilns.

Cox was a Birmingham boy. He was too delicate to assist his blacksmith father in making bayonets for the Napoleonic War and was sent to learn how to decorate buckles and snuff boxes. Fascinated by the art his work entailed, he became a scenic artist to the tragedian Macready. After his marriage, he became a professional artist, teacher and a prolific painter of the English scene. He finally settled in Harborne and he was buried at Harborne Church.

Visitors to the 'dig-in' were greeted by a student who was allotting various jobs to those keen enough to help. When I saw the crowds of young enthusiasts, the men stripped to the waist in true Black Country fashion and all hard at work, I was thankful to be a mere subscriber.

Great yellow excavators were delving into the green water and bringing up the slimy remains of old boats, depositing them on dry land, there to be broken up by eager helpers, ready for the bull-dozers to take to the bonfire sites. Any small treasures were carefully cleaned of slime and preserved. Towpaths and walks were being levelled, scrub and willow-herb cleared and new lawns laid out.

The extensive site adjoins land belonging to the Upper Tame Drainage Authority, and there was a surprising number of small waterfowl nesting among the reeds and bullrushes. The two areas combine to make an interesting open space in an industrial district, with Dudley Castle Hill rising up behind it and the Wren's Nest

93

nature reserve beyond.

Wren's Nest, with Mons Hill, is one of the Black Country's almost unique features. It is internationally known as a classic geological exposure of Upper Silurian rocks.

Millions of years ago, the Dudley area was beneath the sea and today, fossilised remains of sea lilies and corals, shells and trilobites, can be found in the limestone.

While the limestone quarries were being worked, the sale of fossils became a profitable sideline for the quarry-men, who soon became wise to their saleability. More than 300 different species were available and sold to collectors and to museums.

The nature reserve, established in 1956, now covers 74 acres. The area is so vast and there is so much to see, that it is best to go first to the Dudley Museum to view the permanent model of the whole reserve and to buy the guide book. Then, the quarry, the clay pit and the canal basins beyond the nature reserve, which have all been scheduled as Sites of Scientific Interest by the Nature Conservancy, will not be missed.

Looking for the old caverns at the end of the ravine, I asked the way from some boys who were kicking a foot-ball against the wall of The Caves pub on Wren's Nest Hill. I was advised, if going alone, to watch out for the 'cave men,' with which well worn advice and amid their peals of laughter, I climbed up the hill path along the top of one side of the ravine.

The caverns at the head of the ravine, including the famous Lions' Den cavern, were railed off, as they are now considered unsafe, owing to mining subsidences.

The high, spiked metal fence was no deterrent to the local boys, they were giving one another a leg-up and wrecking their jeans on the spikes, before slithering down towards the gaping black holes. The ravine would be a striking feature anywhere but it is especially so at Dudley, as it is completely surrounded by the contrasting industrial landscape.

Dudley townspeople are also blessed with ten other more conventional parks and four large expanses of water, including Lodge Farm Reservoir at Netherton.

The spoil heaps which almost lean against St Andrew's Church, are a lustrous blue grey and the view of the reservoir from high on Church Hill, magnificent when the sun shines on the 14 acres of water, is especially so when a regatta is in full swing. Small sailing boats scurry along, their red and blue sails billowing in the breeze.

Due east of the reservoir and beyond Rowley Regis, are the giant columns which carry the M5 Motorway across Titford Pool. Here, the willows and alders at the edge of the pool are protected from marauding boys by the Titford feeder arm of the canal. Thus an unexpected nature reserve has been created by the new motorway and as the surrounding land is unsuitable for building, the pool has been designated as a bird sanctuary.

The birds have certainly taken advantage of this and seem to sing louder than before, perhaps to make themselves heard above the roar of the traffic. In addition to the waterfowl, which seem to know immediately a pool is 'to let', the chaffinches, wrens, robins and warblers were busy nesting.

St Kenelm's Church. A shrine to a Saxon boy king.

CHAPTER FIVE

Lords and Commons

Pensnett Chase, which lay to the east of Kingswinford, between the Gornals and Lye, was once the hunting ground of kings. Later, except for the commons, it was owned by the Earls of Dudley, who became Lords of the Manor and the commons were grazed by the cattle of the common people. Villagers were allowed to collect dead wood for fuel and to burn limited quantities of peat. Despite severe punishments, they also poached the lord's preserves for deer and rabbits.

During the industrial revolution, the Chase was turned over like a giant's Christmas pudding and the owners became richer than ever from their mining royalties. The commons were enclosed and the Pensnett commoners were pressed into mining around the rapidly growing villages of Wordsley, Brettel and Bromley.

By 1849, the once beautiful, berry-laden slopes of Brierley Hill, to the south of the Chase, were covered with dirt and dinginess. A contemporary observer described it as "scene of industry and wealth, where, within the memory of man, little else was to be found but open common."

Now the greedy turmoil has ended and the burrowed lands are quiet again, a scheme has been proposed to conserve some of the land to the west of Lodge Farm, around Barrow Hill and the Pensnett Pools.

The Earls of Dudley, who were responsible for churning up much of the land, almost destroyed their own church in their enthusiasm. Pensnett Church, known as the Cathedral of the Black Country, was built for the Earl's miners and their families. William, Baron Ward, provided the land and the money and the church was consecrated in 1849. Like many another Victorian industrialist, he gave with one hand what his industrial greed took back with the other. Further and further he tunnelled his mines under Barrow Hill, until the fabric of the miners' church cracked and its foundations sank. Not until the third restoration in 1958 did the church seem safe and sound—by which time the mines had closed and the miners departed.

Inside the church, the three-lancet window in the north transept depicts many of the Black Country craftsmen and their products. The over-ambitious design includes a miner's candle, a steam train, a typewriter, the

Kingswinford. First among the royal manors of Staffordshire to be recorded in the Domesday Book.

badges of Wolverhampton Wanderers and West Bromwich Albion football clubs and the arms of Keele University and Lichfield Cathedral.

From Pensnett Church, a good walk leads to the summit of Barrow Hill, down through Barrow Hill Copse, around the valley, past a small swag, until finally, under the tall beech trees, it returns to the church.

Beyond the churchyard, with the exception of the road frontage, it is hoped to develop the remainder of the land into a natural park, though even in the present condition it provides good walks and pony treks.

The landscaping of the area surrounding the three Pensnett pools will pose a more difficult problem, because the tips are still being used by the Round Oak Steel Works. The pools which are natural ones, not swags, are the last relics of the old Chase. Fishing and boating are already established on two of them and the swans seemed at home, in spite of a fringe of rotting oil drums at the water's edge.

The disused arm of the Stourbridge Canal, which enters the site from Pensnett Road, is already graced by lawns along its banks near the road, but nearer to Grove Pool, there are a number of industrial ruins. The local children will be sad if these have to go, as they obviously serve as a fine adventure playground. It is a welcome site for a park, fringed as it is by small houses, whose even

smaller gardens are taken up with cycle sheds, dog kennels and pigeon lofts.

Still in search of the Chase, which, until the enclosure act of 1784, covered the land round Kingswinford, as far west as Kinver Forest, I circled round Pensnett to Saltwells Wood. This is one of the oldest standing timber coppices in the Black Country, dating from medieval times. The quickest way to it from the pools was along Level Street, which cuts through Round Oak, an iron and steel works founded in 1857 and later modernised to produce several grades of steel from its five open-hearth furnaces. Level Street crosses the Stourbridge Canal and two level crossings, before it reaches Pedmore Road, which is all that divides the large area covered by the steel works, from the open fields.

In the fields on either side of the lane leading to the woods, ponies were grazing—the skewbald and piebald ponies so common in the Black Country and so popular with the local pony clubs. The woods run north to south on either side of a valley and in the seclusion of the woods is Saltwells House, which is used as a children's home.

It is hard to imagine the Tipsiford Bridge end of the woods as a Spa, but in a directory of 1836 it is advertised as "Beautifully situated in a woody district, amid pleasing walks on the banks of a large pool, is Cradley Spa, where warm and cold baths have been erected. The water has sulphate of soda and magnesia . . . A mile to the north in a plantation of firs, is a spring of salt water called Lady Well, frequented in summer . . . ".

The bath house was used until the 1914 war, when the saline stream became polluted by the Earl of Dudley's mine workings and the war put an end to the merrymaking of the Wakes.

The Spa and the woods were a popular venue on the first Sunday in May, the day of the Saltwells Wake, when the merrymakers took a great deal more than the waters.

Saltwells Clayfield, which lies between the woods and Lodge Farm Reservoir, was Doulton's clay pit, which supplied the Springfield Pottery at Rowley Regis. Bands of fireclay lay beneath the coal seams between Stourbridge and the Gornals. Resistant to high temperatures, these clays have been used for the last two centuries for crucibles by the glass industry and for the manufacture of firebricks and sanitary ware. The Saltwells clayfield was worked out some years ago. It now remains as a steep wooded dell below the clubhouse of the boating enthusiasts of Lodge Farm Reservoir.

It is a pity to leave the Dudley area without visiting The Crooked House, or Glynne Arms. It is a rare example of the effect of subsidence on a building. Now safely

The Glynne Arms, or Crooked House where mining subsidence is good for business.

shored up, the upper storey windows, at an angle of almost 45 degrees, will still open, and on the ground floor bottles appear to roll upwards on the steeply sloping bar tables. This house is at the end of the narrow wooded lane which winds around Himley Wood, passing under the old Askew railway bridge, which is almost

99

as crooked as the Glynne Arms.

Subsidence, often caused by the acute angle of the underlying coal, has played extraordinary tricks on some of the buildings. The seam ran roughly from Cannock to Halesowen. After the coal was mined and the workings collapsed, the land dropped both vertically and laterally, like an underground landslide. Thus, many buildings which were some distance from the coal seam were affected. Few were as lucky as the Brade Iron Works which, over the years, sank vertically some eleven feet but remained undamaged.

Glass making, like iron working, is one of the Black Country industries which has been fed for centuries by the wealth of raw materials underground. It was around Stourbridge and the River Stour, that the French refugee families, the Henzeys and the Tyzacks settled in 1557. They brought with them their glass-making skills and made good use of the local fireclay for their crucibles. Their skills were passed on to their workers and in time, small glass houses sprang up like mushrooms in the surrounding districts. By 1700, glass making was a thriving industry.

Like most Black Country industries, it has had its fair share of ups and downs. Many of the small firms have either given up or have been absorbed into the five large firms now in business.

Most of the beautiful lead crystal table glass, so popular today, is made at Brierley Hill and an excellent Glass Museum is housed at the Brierley Hill Library.

After a tour of the nearby glass works, where visitors are welcome, followed by a look at the cut glass in the showrooms, which is positively dazzling, the peace of the museum is most welcome. Like all Black Country museums, it is carefully arranged to present the history and the development of the local industry. It has amassed a rare collection of glass dating from Roman times. Items not on show may be seen on request, as may the pattern books of many firms now extinct.

One of the most famous of these firms was Richardsons of Wordsley, just north of Stourbridge—now the Stourbridge Glass Company. Richardsons had their heyday in the nineteenth century and were awarded a number of medals for their glassware at the Great Exhibition of 1851. They employed many skilled artists to decorate their glass—the two Frenchmen, Alphonse Lecheverel and Jules Barbe, are names well known to collectors, for their cameos and gilding, as well as that of George Woodall, who was a local man. Examples of their work are in the museum, including a particularly fine loving cup gilded by Jules Barbe. There are also many amusing pieces of glass trivia—spun glass ships, birds and fountains and the flowered paper-weights, fly-catchers and oil lamps so dear to the Victorians.

One room at the library is equipped with lathes, where apprentices from the local glass works, come to practise their cutting and to study the extensive library of books and illustrations.

The museum is at the foot of the hill, no longer covered with the briers which gave it its name. It is worth the climb through the narrow streets to the summit of this hill, for a rewarding view of the famous nine locks (not surprisingly, only eight), of the Delph section of the Stourbridge Canal. The name Delph refers to the shallow coalmine workings, which were the chief occupation of the district in the eighteenth century. Glassware was carried by narrow boats and many of the old side-ponds were used as wharves for loading.

An old bottle cone, not far from the canal, part of the works of Stuart Crystal, is to be preserved as an industrial monument.

One of the streets by the canal is named 'The Home Made' and home brewed beer is still available in the pub of that name, which has its old name—'The Blessings of Your Heart'—inscribed over the door.

The glass school at Stourbridge, part of the Fine Arts College, is one of the best equipped in the world and students from other countries are accepted.

A student may use the facilities of any of the various departments teaching ceramics, metalwork, photography, fibreglass moulding etc, in the making of one object. In this way, a chess set made by one student was part ceramic, part glass and was stored in a moulded fibreglass case. Photographs were being printed on glass and the image sand-blasted into the glass. Another student, making a glass and metal table lamp, was able to complete the article herself. There was a surprisingly large percentage of girl students.

The work produced at this college is outstanding. The students are lucky to have the internationally famous glass sculptor, Harry Seager, as one of their tutors. In his own studio this shy, modest man produces large, exciting glass constructions supported by metal which forms an integral part of the design. His constructions often weigh nearly a ton of carefully placed glass. Built up of narrow strips, they take their colour, their lights and their shadows from their surroundings. From every angle, as you walk round them, they offer a different and wholly satisfying view.

His work has been well known in Europe and the United States for some years and is at last on view in England in the grounds of Syon House, near Kew. He is one of the sons of Esther Seager a remarkable mother, a J.P. for many years and a one-time Mayor of Smethwick. I knew her during the 1939-45 war, when she was

Wordsley. The Stuart Crystal bottle cone, preserved beside the Stourbridge Canal.

a skilled surgical corsetière, working hard to give her sons the art training she wished them to have. Unconsciously an artist and sculptor herself, she was most receptive to my requests for actress's corsets and would create anything, from the steel cage worn by Elizabeth I to the waist-stranglers of the Victorians. No construction problem daunted the mother of Harry Seager.

Stourbridge is on the extreme south west of the West Midlands boundary and there is open agricultural land, watered by the River Stour and the Smestow Brook, between Stourbridge and Kidderminster.

Travelling northwards from the Stewpony Inn, the beautiful stretch of country along the western boundary can be enjoyed from the towpaths of the Staffs and Worcestershire Canal.

For canal enthusiasts, it is an interesting trip from the junction with the Stourbridge Canal at Stourton all the way to Aldersley, which is well inside the Wolverhampton boundary.

The Staffordshire and Worcestershire Canal was part of James Brindley's 'Grand Cross' scheme for connecting the rivers Trent, Mersey, Thames and Severn. He surveyed this in 1758 and lived to see its opening in May of 1772, before his death in the following September.

From the beginning, it has been a popular canal for pleasure cruising and judging by the converted narrow boats and motor cruisers moored in the Ashwood Basin, it is even more popular today.

Ashwood Basin is also a site of historic industrial interest, for it was here the Earls of Dudley developed the natural basin as a loading dock for the coal and other goods from their estates.

Following this, the Pensnett Railway reached Ashwood in 1829 and branched along either side of the waterway. This was the first steam haulage to be used in the West Midlands. The celebrated engine *Agenoria*, now in the railway museum at York and coveted by the Black Country Museum, travelled the Pensnett line. It was built by Foster, Rastrick and Co. of Stourbridge, in 1829. It was almost identical with the *Stourbridge Lion*, built by the same firm in 1828. This was sent to America, where it was that continent's first locomotive to run on rails. Engine and tender weighed 11 tons, the wheels were of cast iron with tyres of wrought iron.

Some of the original sandstone sleepers can be seen in the track which remains, others were used in the construction of a wall near the entrance to the basin.

A wide road bridge, with eleven sandstone and brick arches spans the basin and provides a good vantage point from which to see the gaily-coloured boats below and the wooded country beyond. Historians regret the loss of

103

The locomotive Agenoria. *Built for the Shutt End Colliery railway of Kingswinford, which it opened on 2nd June 1829.*

the last traces of the sidings, limekilns and weighbridges, which disappeared when the site was converted into a marina. Only the original boat dock survives.

Further along the road, in the hollow by the Greens-

forge Lock, is the Navigation Inn, built in 1744 to serve the iron workers at Greensforge. The inn no doubt also served the canal builders, for the second date on the building, 1767, is thought to have been cut by one of the masons working on the Greensforge lock. Thanks to the large car park provided, the service at the small Navigation Inn is still in popular demand.

Just up the hill from the 'Navigation', the road to Swindon cuts through the ramparts of a Roman encampment and at Swindon is the site of one of the old water-powered forges on the side of Smestow Brook. The present steel works was developed from the Baldwins Slitting Mill during the second world war. Due to its isolation, it was an ideal site, remote from the main bombing targets. It made a useful contribution to the war effort and is still a busy outlier to the industrial West Midlands, which perhaps accounts for the three pubs in the small village of Swindon.

North of Swindon, the canal passes through Giggety and Wombourn to the locks at The Bratch. This is a favourite place for artists, particularly for the view looking up to the cottage high above the three locks and the small octagonal toll house, perched perilously on the edge of the wall. From the higher ground beyond the cottage, one looks down on the extraordinary architecture of the red brick pumping station. These buildings

Wombourn. The Bratch Locks, an example of James Brindley's outstanding engineering skill.

in the Midlands are usually described as 'Waterworks Gothic' but the one at The Bratch, with its four minaret-cum-turrets, appears to be apeing a Scottish ancestral hall or a castle on the Rhine.

When they were built, The Bratch locks were an outstanding engineering work. The flight of these locks is not a true staircase, since each lock is separated by a short pond and the water is diverted by side paddles into side ponds. From an artist's point of view, these ponds make the site even more attractive, as they are crossed by the Trysull road and are fringed with reeds.

Regretfully, I left the canal at 'The Mermaid' at Wightwick, where, together with the Smestow Brook and the Bridgnorth road, it passes through a gap in the warm red sandstone. On the hill above 'The Mermaid', is Wightwick Manor, which was given to the National Trust by Sir Geoffrey Mander.

The house, built around the 1890s, is an early example of what is popularly known as 'Stockbroker's Tudor'. S. Theodore Mander bought the old Wightwick estate and employed as the architect for his country seat, Edward Ould, an expert in half-timbering. If the exterior is an impure copy of past glories, the interior is very different. It is largely influenced by William Morris and his contemporaries, who were utterly sincere in their attempts to produce a great variety of domestic furnishings of good design and workmanship.

William Morris was an intellectual giant, better known to the majority as a poet, writer and as a socialist but to the art world as a designer. His designing career ranged through architecture, fabric and wall-paper printing, carpet weaving, glass and furniture making to typography. His aim was to produce articles of sound construction and good hand-workmanship instead of the usual cheap and shoddy products of the time.

The Mander family have collected examples of Morris's designs and also the work of many of his contemporaries, whom he had enthused with his own determination to raise the standard of design.

Many of the walls at Wightwick are decorated with Morris fabrics, which after nearly a century, are still in excellent condition. There are examples of his use of natural forms and colours, his favourite acanthus leaf and his floral and bird patterns, influenced by Persian ornament. There are tiles by Morris and also by the more famous tile maker, William de Morgan and some beautiful examples of painted glass by C.E. Kempe, whose work is to be found in many English churches.

Towards the end of his life, Morris devoted most of his time to typography and the printing of fine books; his last and most valued one is the Kelmscott Chaucer. Several Kelmscott books are on display at Wightwick, including a facsimile of the Chaucer.

Most interesting also is the attempt being made to start the Wightwick Press. A fellow artist, Kevin Reilly, has his studios in the outbuildings of the original Wightwick Manor, home of the Wightwick family for generations. He is repairing and binding old books and setting up a press to print books of high quality, hand printed, on hand made paper and bound in tooled leather. His outlook is modern but his craftsmanship is knowledgeable and thorough, in the best Morris tradition. Morris believed in mastering the working details and the practical handling of each craft for which he designed.

The pictures in the house are mostly by the Pre-Raphaelites, the group of literary artists started by Hunt, Millais and Rossetti and later joined by Burne-Jones and Morris. They were denounced by Dickens and defended by Ruskin. Their major works can be seen in English provincial galleries but only at Wightwick have I seen such a comprehensive collection of their more personal drawings and sketches, which also includes a rare line and wash landscape by Ruskin.

The gardens at Wightwick are beautiful, being a subtle mixture of formal and landscape, with their woods, pools and yew hedges. Morris and his contemporaries are remembered in a charming way in the gardens —by shrubs and plants from Morris's garden at Kelmscott Manor, other plants from the gardens of Tennyson, Kempe, Burne-Jones and Ruskin and also some from the garden of The Pines, Putney, the home of Theodore Watts Dunton and Algernon Swinburn whose life together was immortalised in Max Beerbohm's brilliant story—"No. 2, The Pines".

Himley Park is only a short distance from Wightwick and here are beautiful walks round the lake and through Baggeridge Wood.

The snowdrops were out in great drifts beside the pools by the stable blocks. The waterfalls were sparkling in the February sunshine and all around were the signs of an early spring. There were no longer any indications beneath the tall beech trees of Dud Dudley's iron works, once powered by the dammed up stream—or any traces of his struggle to introduce to the wood-starved Midlands his method of iron-smelting with coal.

Dud, born in 1599, was the natural son of Edward, Earl of Dudley, the fourth of eleven children by the same mother and a great favourite with his father. As a boy, he delighted in his father's iron works near Dudley, a great centre of iron manufacture, for within a ten mile radius of Dudley Castle, there were, in Dud's estimate, 20,000 smiths, making nails, chains, tools, horse-shoes, keys and locks—their industry shortly to be halted for lack of wood.

When Dud came down from Oxford, he took charge of his father's furnace and forges on the Pensnett Chase and, hampered by the rapidly approaching fuel famine, gave his mind to using pit coal as a substitute. Although he was successful, he was beset by jealous competitors and by the conservationists of those times, who thought iron works should be prohibited—"They so devour the woods."

In spite of all the opposition but backed by his father, he set up a second furnace at Cradley, powered by a dammed-up pool fed by the Mousesweet Brook. This had been in successful operation for only one year, when it was swept away by 'The Great May-Day Flood', which swept through the countryside and sent the people of Stourbridge to the safety of their upper rooms.

His fellow iron-masters delighted in his misfortune and when Dud had re-built his Cradley works, they fastened law-suits on him and succeeded in ousting him from Cradley. Nothing daunted, he set up a pit-coal furnace on his father's land at Himley and another near Sedgley, but both were destroyed by mobs of rioters, instigated by the charcoal iron-masters.

Eventually, overwhelmed by debts, he was imprisoned in London and the honour of successfully smelting iron using coal went to Abraham Darby in 1709.

At the beginning of the present century, shafts were

Himley Hall in Himley Park. Built by the Earls of Dudley, now used as a teachers' training centre.

being sunk just west of Baggeridge Wood, for the Earl of Dudley's new colliery. When the mines were nationalised, the Coal Board took over the management of the Baggeridge mine and when the Earl moved further south, Himley Hall became one of the Board's Midland headquarters.

The coal seams are worked out and hundreds of thousands of pounds are being spent to make a country park from the industrial wastelands.

The 66 acres of land purchased by the Seisdon and Staffordshire authorities, lie between the Dudley boundary at Gospel End and Baggeridge Wood. They run south west, across the Earl's parklands to include his four pools and link up with the Great Pool within the present Himley Park, which is already open to the public.

The site was only acquired in 1970 and there is much to be done before it will be officially opened. There is the old vexed question of the great pit mound, so large that it would probably be too expensive to move and may have to be developed into a natural hill.

The colliery buildings have been demolished and thousands of trees have already been planted. When the deposits of coal dust and clay have been dredged from the pools, what wonderful walks and nature trails there will be along the banks. The pools will be a unique feature of the park, as they form an almost continuous stretch of water along the valley, from White Wood Pool, nearest to the old colliery workings, followed by The Spring Pool, Island Pool and Rock Pool.

The Earl's Pensnett Railway, which was one of the oldest in the country, already existed to serve his blast furnaces, his steel works at Round Oak and his barges at the Ashwood Basin. The railway was extended through Himley Park to connect with the new colliery at Baggeridge. Railway enthusiasts deplore its demolition by the Coal Board. What a unique feature—to have a period railway running through a country park! Would its return be impossible? Only time will tell.

The slopes which lead up to Sedgley Beacon from Himley Park are gentle and have been used for housing estates. Admittedly, they were good sites for houses but the ancient Beacon Hill now rises like a green knob, from a sea of roofs. Luckily they have reached the limit of their encroachment and when the reservoir is completed and roofed over with turf and when the temporary water tanks have been removed, Beacon Hill will once again become a fresh and windy place for walking.

In 1810, the Sedgley scholars had three recommended walks, Himley, Penn Common and Beacon Hill and, in spite of all that has happened in the intervening years, these three walks are still to be recommended.

Penn Common adjoins Himley Park at Gospel End and from the top of Beacon Hill, you can look down on this beautiful stretch of country. The rights of way crisscross the Common from Upper Penn, right through Baggeridge Wood, to the pools round Himley Hall, through Himley Wood to the Glynne Arms and Daffydingle Pool.

Sedgley Beacon was believed to have been used by the Druids and known to the Romans, as coins have been found at Turlshill and there is still a lane at Lower Gornal called Roman Way.

Little of Old Sedgley is to be seen, except for the Courthouse Inn by the church. The crypt is the oldest part of the church and although the restored church has little of interest, the church records have survived since 1550 and offer many blunt statements. Some of the baptismal records refer to children born in fornication and one "begat in fornication by a soldier as she saw". Many of the deaths have been faithfully recorded—"Old Mary Payton of Over Gornal, barbarously murthered by grandson, young Richard". In addition to the records of further murders by thieves, highwaymen and needy relatives, there is a pathetic record of centuries of deaths from industrial accidents.

Many of the old trades are recorded in the Parish Register. In the 1730s, before industry swept through the Black Country, there were peruke and coffee-mill makers, signs of a more leisured way of life. Sedgley was a great centre for dassel makers. Dassels was the local name for the extremely strong paniers used for transporting coal on pack animals. These animals, donkeys, ponies and horses, criss-crossed the Black Country from mine to mill and many of the remaining rights of way were originally created by these heavily-laden beasts.

To the south of Sedgley Beacon lie the Gornals, fast developing into pleasant housing estates on the western edge of the Dudley, Worcestershire border. One of my earliest memories is the 'Gornal Girl'. She called in spring and autumn with my mother's supply of salt and scouring sand, which were carried on her gaily painted cart, pulled by a donkey. The salt was in long rectangular blocks, which were stored in the larder and chipped and crushed as required. The scouring powder came in long cotton bags.

It was years afterwards that I learned of the 'Travellers'. They were Gornal families, who, rather like gypsies, toured the Midlands in the summer months, with the metal items they had made during the winter. Gornal's pure white sand, which was crushed from the rock by a stone wheel pulled round by a donkey, was packed into long cotton bags by the Gornal girls, as their contribution to the summer sales. No salt was available near Gornal but the Travellers found salt was in demand, so they bought this from the salt works at Stoke Prior and had it delivered by rail to various towns on their route.

Years later, knowing I was always looking for period

stage furniture, a Gornal man rang me up to go over there and buy his mother's four-poster bed. The address was one of a row of empty nailers' cottages but I found the son awaiting me in his 'local' and unknown to us both, he was an old acquaintance who had delivered tons of Gornal rockery stone to the house in Edgbaston. The cottage was a typical nailer's cottage—two up and two down, with the stairs hidden by a door in the kitchen wall. The four-poster was anything but typical—it filled the room. It was just possible to open the door and walk along one side of the bed. The foot was tight against the fireplace and the window could only be opened or cleaned by kneeling on the bed.

To sleep in a four-poster had been his mother's dream, so her six sons had made it for her—magnificently carved by brother Sam and lovingly draped by his sisters. His mother had died in it some weeks previously.

I was implored to buy the bed at my own price, as the authorities were waiting to demolish the cottages and the family couldn't bear to see their mother's bed crumble with the bricks. I had to get an amused demolition man to remove the bedroom wall, before Mum's bed could be lowered down with infinite care to the waiting lorry.

The Gornals and Sedgley are in the most northerly corner of the Borough of Dudley joining the Borough of Wolverhampton. Although Wolverhampton has few rural attractions other than its public parks, it is an old town. It suffered from the plague and also from a great fire in 1590, which swept through the town and destroyed its wooden buildings. The small half-timbered shop in Victoria Street is one of the few which escaped destruction.

A thriving town, for arts Vulcanian famed
And from its foundress, good Wulfruna named.

Lady Wulfruna, widow of Anthelm, Duke of Northumberland, built and endowed a church in 994 and the town which grew around it became known as Wulfrun's-hampton—Wolverhampton.

Wolverhampton is a town which in each century has moved with the times and few of its buildings have survived these advances; except for the Saxon Cross and the fine old church which stands beside it on the hill—a site hallowed by Christian worship since the time of Wulfruna, nearly a thousand years ago.

The oldest parts of the present St Peter's Church are the four arches which support the tower, dated 1205, which were later incorporated into the main structure, begun in 1425.

At the beginning of the fifteenth century, Wolverhampton was becoming a thriving centre of the wool trade and the present church was the gift of the rich wool merchants, whose coats of arms are blazoned in the windows of the clerestory.

The best known were the Levesons—the family now known as the Leveson-Gowers, Dukes of Sutherland. James and Nicholas Leveson became so wealthy from their wool stapling, they were able to purchase much of the surrounding land as it became available after the Dissolution. When James Leveson died in 1545, he left bequests to 58 parishes in the Midlands, ranging from Wellington across to Cannock.

Other reminders of the Dissolution are to be found in the church, which contains the priests' stalls brought from Lilleshall Abbey and the reading desk from Hales.

In the Lady Chapel is the bronze statue of Sir Richard Leveson by Hubert le Sueur, whose statue of Charles I stands in Whitehall, London. Sir Richard led a small English fleet in a successful attack against the Spanish Armada in 1588.

All round the church are traces of the town's history. The monuments of the Lane family recall the Civil War and the dramatic escape of the future Charles II from the Midlands, after the battle of Worcester in 1651. This was only made possible by the help of Colonel John Lane of Bentley Hall.

It is inspiring to see the beautifully carved pulpit and to realise that the people of Wolverhampton have listened to sermons preached from that pulpit for over 500 years. The preacher was protected from evil by the stone lion, perched like a giant newel post at the foot of the balustrade. Generations of Wolverhampton citizens have been christened at the medieval font, with its carving of St Anthony and his pig.

The inner south porch is a memorial to one of the town's more recent benefactors, Sir Charles Tertius Mander, Mayor and Freeman of the Borough, who died in 1929.

The chancel, restored in 1968 and panelled with modern woodwork at its best, is set off by the sparkling gold leaf on the fine roof, which is continued in the small roof above the clerestory of the nave. The gold leaf, together with the new organ and the light fittings, are the gifts of modern business men and give St Peter's the atmosphere of a well cared for and much loved home.

Even older than Wulfruna's church is the stone pillar in the churchyard. From its ornate carving, it is possibly of the period of Ethelwulf, in the eighth century. It has suffered severely from atmospheric corrosion and I thought it a pity that there was no plaque giving its history, nor any covered photostats of the drawings, made in 1877 and now lodged in the Victoria and Albert Museum in London, which show the detail of the carvings.

Also suffering from the corrosion of the atmosphere, particularly during the last century, is the stone work of the simple church of St John. This church, built in 1755, is reminiscent of St Paul's in Birmingham, in that it was built for "a large and prosperous trading place".

St John's stands in its own square, which adjoins the busy new ring road but the churchyard, which was made into the Hayward Memorial Garden in 1969, provides a quiet and pleasant refuge. Robert Noyes, the celebrated Staffordshire water-colourist, who died in 1843, is buried in the churchyard. He had had a long association with St John's. Behind the church there are a few Georgian façades left in George Street, once the homes of well-to-do manufacturers, now used as business premises. This was the church attended by Wolverhampton's japanners and William Ryton, a celebrated japanner, of Old Hall Works, was a churchwarden in 1819.

My interest in the art of japanning led me to Bantock Park.

Among the many benefactions Alderman Bantock made to Wolverhampton, were Merridale House and grounds, which he left to the town in his will. The grounds make a welcome park, offering sports facilities to a crowded suburb. The house is used as a library and museum and contains among other items, a collection of japanned or Pontypool ware.

At the beginning of the eighteenth century, many Welsh people working in Wales came to the Midlands, like the Lloyds and the Cadburys, to avoid religious persecution. Among them were some who practised the art of japanning. They came from the district around Pontypool and settled in Wolverhampton. Half a century before their arrival, Andrew Zaranton had established a tin plate manufactory in the Forest of Dean, and the availability of tinplate was one of the attractions of the Midlands. Previously the plate had had to be imported from Bavaria.

In Wolverhampton at that time, there was a moated Tudor manor house, built by one of the wealthy Levesons in the reign of Henry VIII. The Levesons became Leveson-Gowers by marriage and the Manor House was their ancestral home for many years. Then it passed to the Turtons and one of the Turtons leased the property to William and Obediah Ryton, who lived in part of the house and used the remainder for their business of japanning.

Bantock House not only has the Pontypool Ware, but also a number of the pattern books of various firms. There is always one of these on display in a case and the designs show the meticulous care with which they were drawn and painted by skilled artists before being transferred.

The Rytons employed many artists, including Edward Bird, who, born in Old Lichfield Street in 1772, later worked for Henry Clay and eventually became a member of the Royal Academy.

Another famous man in the art world, who began work at Old Hall, was George Wallis. He became Keeper of Art at the Victoria and Albert Museum. As Deputy Commissioner, he was responsible for much of the great exhibition in Hyde Park in 1851, at which, not surprisingly, was displayed the beautifully decorated and inlaid japanned and papier mâché ware of the Midlands.

The two trades were closely allied, as they used similar styles of decoration and the same hard varnishes. Unfortunately for collectors, the Victorians turned from the beautifully decorated Pontypool Ware, to the cheap brass and copper goods which were flooding the markets. After a desperate struggle for survival, the Old Hall was demolished in 1883.

The Rytons and a later partner, William Walton, were not the only japanners in Wolverhampton. By 1834, there were fourteen known factories and one of these was owned by the Manders in John Street, established by Benjamin Mander in 1773. Next door, in Victoria Street, were the chemical works of his brother John, and soon Benjamin's son Charles, was experimenting with varnish in his father's garden shed. He set up his own varnish works in John Street in 1803, which grew out of the requirements of his father's japan trade.

Almost two hundred years after Benjamin Mander founded the business, the Manders are still in John Street and I found it romantic to look out of the Board Room window on the ninth floor of the new Mander House, which towers above the Mander Shopping Centre and look down on the old John Street, where it all began. Below also was the site of the garden shed, where young Charles began work—the same Charles whose beautiful pastel portrait hangs at Wightwick Manor. Under the new Mander shopping centre, with its two-storey shopping precinct, and roof car park is the site of John's chemical works.

The Mander factory moved to a larger site at Heathtown in 1932, which eventually made the John Street land available for the development of the Mander Centre. This now dominates the town, as the wool staplers' church on Wulfruna's Hill dominated it centuries ago.

While the japanners were busy in Wolverhampton, the enamellers were no less busy in nearby Bilston.

Enamelling on copper is an ancient craft, practised by the Greeks 3,000 years ago and it became a thriving commercial craft in Bilston about 1750. Many of the beautiful boxes, candlesticks and scent bottles, which though attributed to the more famous Battersea enamellers, were made in Bilston. George Wallis tried to rectify this mistake with a special exhibition of enamels at the South Kensington Museum in 1874.

Gerald Mander (1885–1951), well known as an antiquary, also knew that the Bilston work was of the highest quality. With his friends, Bernard Rackham (successor to George Wallis), and Egan Mew, all three set about forming magnificent collections. It was Gerald Mander who was instrumental in acquiring Egan Mew's collection for the Wolverhampton Art Gallery.

The best known of the eighteenth century Bilston enamellers was Benjamin Bickley, who, like many of his contemporaries, was put out of business by the pressure of the Black Country heavy industries offering better wages, possibly owing to the Napoleonic War.

After two hundred years, Bilston enamels are popular collectors' items, particularly with Americans and the craft of enamelling has returned to Bilston.

In a new works, on an industrial estate, the old craft has been revived with modern equipment. The enamels are still made using powdered glass and metallic oxides for colour and fusing these to the copper, by firing in a kiln. But no lead is allowed for modern enamels and an excellent ventilation system removes the foul vapours from the acids and chemicals, which formerly ruined the health of the old enamellers. The enamels are sprayed on to the copper by compressed air before firing and only the final decoration is done by hand.

But how far have we advanced? On my visit, owing to a power cut, the girls were crouching over their work of transfer application, lit only by the light of candles. The electrically operated ventilation system was off and the workroom resembled the dark, stifling shops of old, which caused so many of the workers to suffer from blindness.

The modern work is distinguishable from the old by the stream-lined smoothness of the enamel application, but the designs, in some cases hand painted, were extremely suitable. In the sale catalogue alas, for sale purposes, they are termed Battersea and Bilston enamels and George Wallis appears to have fought in vain.

The people of Bilston have been campaigning to keep their collection of enamels in their own art gallery —beautiful candlesticks, opera glasses and inkwells, which they are loath to see added to the main collection in Wolverhampton.

There is a permanent show of iron exhibits at the Bilston Art Gallery—a delight to industrial historians.

Bradley, the site of John Wilkinson's famous iron works, adjoins Bilston and its history is clearly displayed in the Gallery by models, photographs and by some of

Tettenhall. Here King Alfred's son Edward defeated the Danes.

the smaller products. These include some good examples of decorative fire-backs and fireplace surrounds. Bradley is now a new housing estate and only a small area of the old iron works site remains to be cleared.

The only reminders of John Wilkinson, 'Man of Iron', are the iron pulpit in the Hall Green Street chapel, which was cast at the Bradley works, Wilkinson Street, and a new public house called 'The Iron Master', which is decorated with pictures of the old works. If your taste is not for modern pubs, 'The Greyhound' in the High Street, Bilston's oldest, is fifteenth century and beautifully preserved, inside and out.

Fiery Holes recreation ground at Lower Bradley, now covers the historic site of Five Hole Furnaces, where steam was first used to power a blast furnace, an experiment which was to revolutionise iron working in the Black Country.

At the opposite end of the borough from Bilston, the old village of Tettenhall still retains its village green. It was once the scene of a battle between the Saxons and the Danes and has reminders of this, in the names of Danes Court and Danes Croft.

In the early nineteenth century, Telford brought his new road through Tettenhall, connecting Birmingham with Holyhead. When the road was completed, the rich industrialists built their large houses at Tettenhall, on the sandstone above the town. Now, much of Tettenhall is a conservation area and many of the large houses in their well wooded grounds, are used as schools, colleges and old peoples' homes. The conservation also includes the Rock House in Old Hill and two windmills.

Telford's road passes through the village green in a deep sandstone cutting, so it is possible to sit on the seats under the trees, undisturbed by the traffic. On one half of the green are mellow houses, a few of which have had their front parlours converted into small shops. On the other, is the large village pond, where the children sail their boats. This is surrounded by a small open park. Down the hill are the slopes of Tettenhall Wood and the ancient barrows, believed to be the burial place of the Danes and Saxons, killed when Alfred's son Edward defeated the invaders.

Tettenhall Church, built originally by the Saxon King Edgar and re-built by the Normans, was devastated by fire in 1950.

At the extreme north-east of the borough are the few remaining farmlands of Moseley Old Hall. This beautiful Elizabethan house became famous when Charles II was safely hidden in one of its priest-holes by Father Huddlestone.

After losing the battle of Worcester in September 1651, Charles made his escape and rode through Stourbridge, Himley and Wrottesley Woods to seek sanctuary at the White Ladies Priory. After hiding in the oak tree outside Boscobel House, he was lent a mill horse by the Penderel brothers and rode with them to be successfully hidden once again at Moseley Hall.

The Hall is now looked after by the National Trust and still contains the bed in which the king managed to spend a peaceful night after Cromwell's soldiers had searched the house and departed.

The Stourbridge Canal at Whittington, behind the sixteenth-century inn.

CHAPTER SIX

Tanners and Gypsies

With the rapid development of Birmingham after the 1750s, many of the craftsmen moved to outlying villages in search of cheaper premises. The tanners and the harness makers left the banks of the Rea for Walsall, where the malleable iron workers were producing the small fittings required for the harness.

The Walsall manufacturers were closely linked to horse transport and the old stage-coach lines, maintaining thousands of horses, were some of their best customers. One of the reasons why Walsall has remained a smaller town than Birmingham and Wolverhampton, was the refusal of the harness makers to allow the new railway companies to bring their main lines through Walsall.

In the end, it was no help to their business, for the coming of the motorcar saw the end of horse transport. The iron foundries looked to the agricultural industry for work and the harness makers had to rely on the cavalry and sporting horses for business.

Walsall is still a town world-famous for its saddles and harness and for those expensive tooled-leather goods one covets when gazing through the plate glass windows in Bond Street and Fifth Avenue. It is also a town where one of the oldest and largest markets of the Midlands is held.

Henry IV granted the town its first charter in 1399, which greatly encouraged the early traders, for it "Permitted the men of Walsall to be quit of all their goods, throughout England."

If you stand on the high limestone cliff of Church Hill on any working Saturday, you can see the whole patchwork of its brightly covered market stalls spread out below. They stand against the foot of Church Hill, cover the length and breadth of High Street, and spread out across the new shopping precincts until they are finally stopped by the main road.

To wander through the market and bargain with the barkers is a more vital experience than pushing a trolley through the regimented neatness of a supermarket. No '2p off' is marked up on the goods in Walsall Market. You pit your wits against the stall holders to get sixpence off, or more if you are lucky. The licked stub of a pencil on the back of a paper bag and a friendly "That what

Walsall Market. A trading charter was granted by Henry IV in 1399.

you make it, ducks?" makes a welcome change from the impersonal clicking of an electric till.

There may have been a church on the hill in Saxon times but the first record is of Serle de Sunning being King John's chaplain there in 1211. The present church of St Matthew was re-built in the 1820s by the architect Francis Goodwin and inside are many examples of his use of local cast iron. Particularly elegant are the slender iron columns of the arcades, the iron tracery of the windows and the perforated patterns of the floor grilles.

In the thirteenth century, the church and its tithes were acquired by the canons at Hales. The building which replaced it in the fifteenth century, was used by Cromwell's soldiers as a barracks and most of its woodwork was used by them for firewood. It is surprising that the handsome choir stalls, which came from Hales Abbey after the Dissolution, have managed to survive the destruction of soldiers and builders.

The stalls have a choice collection of misereres, sometimes called misericords or mercy seats (Latin *misericordia* = mercy). Aptly named, these were designed to give merciful support to the clerics and latterly, the choirboys, standing through long services—the misereres enable them to sit, while appearing to stand. Many of the misereres have the liveliest of medieval carvings, carved by craftsmen with a merry sense of humour. Do not miss

the old witch, riding on her cat while playing the fiddle. She and her fellows may well have bewitched the Cromwellian soldiers into leaving the stalls unburnt.

There is a memorial window to Walsall's Sister Dora, the Good Samaritan Sister, who, disappointed at being unable to join Florence Nightingale in the Crimea, put her nursing skill and unbounded energy to work amongst the poor people of Walsall.

Walsall was the home of the Siddons family. Mrs Siddons, whose portrait hangs in the National Gallery, was the talented daughter of actor-manager Charles Kemble. She married Mr Siddons, a young actor in her father's company who was born in Rushall Street—son of the publican at 'The London Apprentice'.

Equally famous in his heyday about 1796, was Askins, the ventriloquist at Sadlers Wells. His real name was Thomas Haskey, whose father rang the treble bell at St Martin's. After losing a leg in the American War, son Thomas returned to Walsall as a gardener's assistant, making holes for planting at great speed with his peg leg. He remained a favourite ventriloquist at Stanton's Theatre, Walsall and also at Himley Hall as the guest of the Earl of Dudley.

Walsall was also the home of Jerome K. Jerome, an author with a lively sense of humour, who was born in Bradford Street in 1859, son of a Nonconformist Welsh

121

mother and a father who was not only a mine owner but also a preacher.

Flooding ruined the Jerome mines and, in spite of the abject poverty of his childhood, Jerome K. educated himself. His *Three Men in a Boat* became a best-seller and I well remember a quote from it which a wag pasted up on the art school wall, after we had been lectured on the advantages of looking at our work.

> I like work; it fascinates me. I can sit and look at it for hours.

Some years later, I had to design a set for his play *The Passing of the Third Floor Back*.

In 1968, a leather exhibition was held at Walsall, sponsored by the London Council of the Museum of Leather-craft, and as a result of this, a permanent exhibition has been set up in the Walsall Art Gallery. Starting with prints, posters and photographs of Walsall's old leather industry, it continues with cases containing a great variety of period saddles, harness, helmets and gauntlet gloves. One of two smaller rooms is furnished with a surprising selection of domestic articles, from leather-covered furniture, leather jugs and bottles, to a beautifully tooled leather tablecloth. Particularly fine is one of the three-dimensional leather pictures of fruit and flowers, constructed like a Grinling Gibbons carving. Tucked away amongst the flowers is a tiny bird's nest, beautifully woven with shreds of leather and containing a clutch of minute leather eggs.

The other small room is a saddler's workshop, complete in every detail and the exhibition ends with a display of modern leather goods currently being made in Walsall and including an evening dress in shining silver leather.

Old Walsall has had to give way to present day demands for good roads and good houses and only two old buildings of interest remain. One is the County Court, built about 1773, at the corner of Lichfield Street. This stands at such a busy junction that it is only possible to get a good view of its pillared façade when looking down Ablewell. The other building is 'The White Hart' at Caldmore—pronounced 'Calmer'. It was here that Charles I's queen is thought to have stayed, in 1643, on her way to join the king at Edge Hill. At that time 'The White Hart' must have been a similar hostelry to 'The Saracen's Head', her resting place at King's Norton.

Walsall boasts few rural areas other than its public parks. Reedswood Park is an example of what can be done with reclaimed industrial waste land. Walking by the swimming pool and flower beds, it is hard to visualise the spoil heaps of the mines which covered these green acres not many years ago.

The Arboretum, rather a misnomer so far as rare trees are concerned, is a lake surrounded by well stocked shrubberies. Beyond, are extensive playing fields, which are crossed by the Rushall Canal, with a walk along the towpath to Daw End.

Rushall Castle was the scene of fierce fighting during the Civil War. What remains of the present structure was built by William Grobere to replace a previous fortified sandstone house. It passed to his son-in-law, John Harpur, who became Lord of Rushall and died in 1464. From the Harpurs, it passed by marriage to the Leighs and it was Sir Edward Leigh, a Parliamentarian, who strengthened Rushall Castle against the King. But not well enough, for its garrison was defeated and Rushall was captured by Prince Rupert in 1643. The castle was later held for the King by Colonel Lane of Bentley, whose son and daughter organised the famous escape of Charles II from Bentley Hall to Bristol, in 1651.

After the Civil War, like many similar strongholds, Rushall Castle was partly demolished. The ruins are now hidden in the trees behind Rushall Church but Harpur Road, which cuts through a new housing estate, bears an old name and leads to the castle keep, which still bears the coat of arms of the Harpurs.

The embattled castle walls are built of rough limestone, high, thick and strong, in great contrast to the modern bungalows, only a few yards away on the Harpur Road side. On the other side and behind the castle, there are extensive agricultural lands with woods, and field paths leading to Park Lime Pits Pool, Lady Pool and Daw End.

This area is likely to remain agricultural. It is known locally as 'hollow land', due to the considerable limestone mining beneath it. The original workings were extensive and led to a large subterranean lake in the Lindley Caverns. These, like the Dudley Caverns, were once popular with pleasure parties, for whom they were brilliantly lit, but they are now thought to be flooded. Perhaps the curlews which have returned to Park Pits pools, have chosen a good site where they may remain undisturbed.

Rushall Hall is built within and on to the castle walls. It is privately owned and the only entrance is still through the castle keep. Built into the castle walls are some incongruous bay windows, with a view across the terrace and the burial mound of the Civil War soldiers, to the recently restored church. Below and beyond, are the hollow lands and the once busy Daw End Branch Canal, making its way in a large loop to Walsall Wood.

Within this loop lie Stubbers Green and Dumble Derry, an expanse of once busy Black Country and beyond are the farmlands of Aldridge and the expensive houses of commuters, discreetly hidden in the woods of Little Aston.

It is the sudden contrast of areas which makes the West Midlands so fascinating. I continued the walk along the towpath, high above the disused colliery and the brick-works and looked down on the swags, with their occasional fishermen—the young ones were in school. The afternoon sun was casting long shadows and turning the yellow grass to orange, as I startled a flock of goldfinches feeding amongst the thistles.

The land around the largest pool, marked on the map as 'The Swag', has been landscaped as a small park. Stubbers Green Lane cuts off a corner of the swag water and the vibration caused by the occasional passing lorry, taking a short cut between its rush-laden sides, sends large ripples across the water—the swans riding these with their usual nonchalance. A small herd of cattle was grazing in the fields behind Shelfield House, near a tributary of Ford Brook and it was easy to forget the nearby main road from Rushall to Lichfield.

Although the Borough of Walsall has no rural areas, it is less than ten miles from the heart of Cannock Chase.

The 6,000 acres of Cannock Chase offer a unique stretch of open country to the people living in the northern part of the Black Country.

In 1286, this royal forest was bounded by four rivers, the Trent, the Penk, the Sow and the Tame and included parts of Walsall, Wolverhampton, Lichfield and West Bromwich. Edward I sold his rights over the land to the Bishop of Lichfield and thus, in 1290, it became a 'chase'—the hunting ground of a cleric or a feudal lord.

After the Dissolution, the Chase passed to William Paget, the son of a nail maker, who was a favourite at Henry's court. Another Paget was created Marquess of Anglesey for his gallantry at Waterloo, and it was the sixth Marquess of Anglesey who sold the southern portion of the Chase to the Forestry Commission. The remainder is leased from the Earl of Lichfield and from Lord Hatherton.

The gravelly soil of the Chase is useless for agricultural purposes but ideal for pine and larch trees. Heathers, bilberries and bracken provide the general ground cover and cranberries can be found on the peat bogs, by diligent searchers.

In the south west corner, surrounded by the Chase on three sides, is Castle Ring, a British hill fort built about 2,000 years ago and standing 800 feet above sea level. The wide views over the Trent basin compensate for the climb to the top.

The herd of fallow deer, shy and hard to find in the daytime, keep mainly to the northern part of the Chase, where there is plenty of bracken cover but walking at

Brereton Hayes, on the southern fringe of Cannock Chase. The inn, now a shop, is a relic of mining days.

Like Wren's Nest, one of the big assets of the Chase is its accessibility—it is less than ten miles from the industrial districts of Wolverhampton, Walsall and Cannock. The Chase, preserved for centuries for the sport of the nobility who inflicted diabolical punishments in the name of the Forest Laws on anyone found trespassing, can now be enjoyed by the general public. Hundreds of acres of the Chase are available to walkers, motorists and naturalists and the great expanse of Chase Water offers excellent boating facilities.

South of Walsall, in the crowded county borough of West Bromwich, nearly 1,000 acres along the Sandwell Valley have recently been purchased for use as a country park. The land follows the western boundary of West Bromwich and is bounded on the north by the River Tame.

Dartmouth Park and Sandwell Park Golf Clubs already constitute a large, well wooded open space in the southern corner. The M5 motorway divides the remainder of the site in half, cutting through from North to South. The area of the new Sandwell project nearest to West Bromwich, is to be split up into sections for organised recreation, where every kind of sport will be catered for. There is already a riding school established in the stables of Sandwell Park Farm and the scheme pro-

dusk one evening, I disturbed three of them, which had strayed down to the Cannock end.

All kinds of moorland birds can be seen on the hills of the Chase, even an occasional pair of red grouse. Pheasants and partridge are fairly common, as are snipe and woodcock, if you know where to look.

125

vides for the preservation of this beautiful old farmhouse.

The wilder stretch of country to the east of the M5, is to be developed into a natural park. It is a plan which would have appealed to 'Billy My Lord', the fourth Earl of Dartmouth, one of the previous owners of the land, who lived most of his life at Sandwell Hall. A natural unaffected man, as his nickname suggests, and devoted to his family, he regarded his tenants and his workpeople as extensions of the family and was particularly kind to them during the great trade depression in the early nineteenth century. Like Job Garratt at Halesowen, he also enjoyed entertaining them in his own home.

The Hall was built on the site of Sandwell Priory, whose monks in their time, together with the monks of Hales Abbey and Dudley Priory, had cared for the well-being of the scattered Midland communities.

The Priory was dissolved about 1524 and in 1755, the lands passed to the Legge family, later to become the Earls of Dartmouth. When two collieries developed, one at Sandwell, behind the hall and the other at Hamstead, in front of it, they moved to Patshull near Albrighton, where the much loved 'Billy My Lord' died in 1853.

After the Dartmouths left Sandwell, the Hall was given by them for charitable purposes, until it was demolished in 1926. All that remains, is the long pool, an ornamental stretch of water which lay in front of the Hall. This large lake, which had to be drained, while the M5 was being constructed, is already being re-landscaped for the new park.

I was joined on my tour of the site by two brothers from Handsworth, one black and one white, aged about eight and nine, who had already walked a good three miles on their way to play in Dartmouth Park. Eager bird-watchers, they were delighted when we saw a flock of crested plovers feeding in one of the fields, watched by a brown owl from the top of a disused cable pole. Its camouflage was so perfect, only the occasional wink of a beady eye, gave it away.

We disturbed a stoat, as I helped them dig up one of the heavy iron casting boxes, which together with loads of old bricks had been sunk into one of the boggy paths. They knew all about the casting boxes, as their father worked in a local foundry.

By this time, we were friends and I was taken to see their 'Eskimo's House', hidden in the woods. This turned out to be a brick-built ice house, about six feet in diameter, with much of its dome shaped roof intact—a last relic of life at the hall. This is carefully marked on the plan for preservation. In the meantime it made an ideal defensive post for playing soldiers.

The boys talked about the Civil War, the battles fought at the castles at Dudley and Rushall and at Sandwell Hall and Moseley Hall. Their facts and their kings were a little mixed but their enthusiasm was unbounded, as they leapt down into the ice house and defended their castle, against all comers shouting loud bang bangs behind their imaginary guns.

Forgotten by the young warriors I walked across to Forge Farm and Old Forge Mill, sites of sixteenth-century iron workings. What is left of the mill was filled with bales of hay and eager young people were getting their ponies ready for a Saturday afternoon treck.

The owner at Forge Farm was more leisured and showed me one of his outbuildings, which once had had a forge at one end, a chapel in the centre and a pigsty at the other end. This building had been altered in his time, as he remembered the wooden crucifix being removed from the chapel. Though the premises are now given over entirely to his pigs, he still gets parties of American Methodists asking to see the site where Francis Asbury is thought to have preached. Asbury, who was made an American Methodist Bishop in 1784, was born nearby at Hamstead and apprenticed to an ironmaster in West Bromwich. He became a leader of Methodism in his home town, being supported by William, second Earl of Dartmouth, before being sent to America by John Wesley in 1771. It seemed incongruous that the bricked-up door of his chapel should be hidden by a cartload of stale loaves awaiting the pigs.

It is proposed to preserve the farms and the agricultural land on the banks of the Tame, with suitable rights of way for nature trails. Swan Pool, to the south of Forge Farm, is to take in all the surrounding marsh land and be extended to create a large sailing lake. The spoilbank of Jubilee Colliery, behind this, is to be levelled to make a car park and the existing colliery buildings converted into a park centre, which will house the warden's information office. The Sandwell Valley scheme is an excellent one and it is hoped that it can be speedily completed with the £200,000 allotted to it.

The sunshine had lured me away from the streets of West Bromwich but I returned to visit the town's two historic houses.

It was a long struggle to save The Manor House from demolition and a hard grind to provide the money for its restoration. The half-timbering was covered with plaster, it was let off as tenements and surrounded by property, in as poor and dilapidated a condition as the house itself. It was aptly known locally as the old hall.

It is interesting to see the photograph of the plastered tenements, on view inside, and to realise the mammoth task which must have faced the restoration architect, James Roberts and the dedicated craftsmen who worked with him for three years.

The house was completed in 1960, at a cost of £24,000 and the Corporation were faced with the problem —how to use the house to the best advantage, as they already had a period museum at The Oak House.

The dilemma was solved by Ansell's Brewery and The Manor House is once more lit up at night and splendid meals are served in the original dining hall.

The Manor House does great credit to all concerned, as it is a rare example of a timber framed medieval hall and few examples of this early type of architecture have survived, as the Great Hall is dated 1290–1310. The north solar wing, the south wing, chapel, kitchen block and gatehouse have been faithfully restored, the moat cleared, the surrounding cottages demolished and the land beyond the moat laid out as lawns, with a large car park discreetly out of sight.

The Oak House has had a less turbulent history. The first documents relate to Thomas Turton as owner of "The Oak" in 1634 and the brickwork on the west front dates from that time. Other parts of the house are thought to be at least a hundred years earlier.

Although the fabric of Oak House suffered in the early nineteenth century, when it was used as a farmhouse, it was rescued by Alderman Reuben Farley before it had become as bad as The Manor House and was presented to the town in 1898, for use as a museum.

After the second world war, alternative accommodation was found for the museum collection and in 1951, the Oak House was opened as a period house. Like Aston Hall, it is beautifully maintained and a joy to visit. The furniture is, in general, early seventeenth century, although some pieces are earlier and great care has been given to the choice of carpets. The staircase, panelling and floors, were carefully restored for the opening in 1898 and have had many years of care lavished on them since then.

The oak tree, from which the house took its name, stood in front of the house until 1846, when, hollow and rotten with age, it was destroyed by fire. Although there is no longer an oak tree, the Oak House stands in a large and well kept garden, with plenty of seats from which to contemplate its handsomely gabled exterior.

It was a lovely afternoon, so I crossed the River Tame and the Tame Valley Canal, for a walk round Red House Park at Great Barr. This is a semi-wild park with large pools and well established trees and some more formal grounds round the house. Red House was thought to have been built in the early nineteenth century, by Robert Wellbeloved Scott, a Stourbridge industrialist and Member of Parliament for Walsall from 1841 to 1847. It was the home of the Bagnalls and later the Mar-

West Bromwich. The Manor House, where you may dine in the great hall, built in 1290.

shalls, well known local iron-masters, before it was taken over in 1929 by the West Bromwich Corporation and with its extensive grounds, opened as a public park. It is a hilly site with some beautiful walks.

The road through Queslett passes the grounds of Barr Hall, now occupied by St Margaret's Hospital. The Hall was the home of the Scott family, whose most famous son was Joseph Scott, Member of Parliament for Worcester from 1802–1806. It was during his time that the Hall was let to the Galtons, the Birmingham gunsmiths, and a number of meetings of the Lunar Society were held there, faithfully recorded by that prolific writer Mary Ann Galton.

On the opposite side of the road is Booth's farm and recreation grounds, one-time home of Booth the forger, whose villainy is remembered, while the Scotts and the Galtons are forgotten.

The Scott Arms, a well known hostelry on the Birmingham Walsall Road, built in 1800, was the headquarters of the Great Barr Society for the Prosecution of Felons, formed in order to deal with the sheep and cattle thieves, the highwaymen and other rogues, like Booth. The magistrates' court was held at the Scott Arms and, until recently, the cattle market site was behind it.

I drove up Beacon Hill, just east of the Walsall boundary and then on to the top of Barr Beacon, to watch the sunset. Thanks to a good approach road and an adequate car park, it is possible to drive to the summit of the beacon and from the wind-free comfort of a car, to identify the distant hills, from the Wrekin and Wenlock Edge round to Frankley Beeches. The Birmingham Post Office Tower appears misleadingly near.

What a view of the West Midlands can be seen from this famous Beacon Hill—said to have been used for sacrifices by the Archdruids.

The hill, whose beacon flashed the warning of the approaching Spanish Armada in 1588, was similarly prepared during the Napoleonic wars to announce the landing of Napoleon's troops, which, like the threatened landings of Hitler, never materialised.

The gigantic beacon lit in 1897 was for a more joyous affair—the Diamond Jubilee of Queen Victoria. Today, the site of the old beacon is occupied by an elegant columned memorial, erected to the memory of the Staffordshire men and women who died in the 1914–18 war and in gratitude to Lt. Colonel Joseph Henry Wilkinson, who presented "Barr Beacon to the people for ever."

As the crow flies, it is a short distance from Barr Beacon to Sutton Park, which was a favourite haunt during my school holidays. In those days, if we wished to go anywhere, we walked. What few cars there were in my family circle, were kept exclusively for grown-ups

Sutton Coldfield. Its benefactor, Bishop John Vesey, paved the streets, founded a school, built a market hall and gave the park to the town.

—there was no second car and no mother's taxi service to transport the young to school.

The Royal Borough of Sutton Coldfield, given its charter by Henry VIII, has always remained a separate authority, although many people regard it as a suburb of Birmingham. No matter how much the commuters fill its acres with houses, no one can encroach on the 2,400 wild acres of Sutton Park.

John Vesey, Bishop of Exeter, a native of Sutton, distressed at the poverty of its people and the ruinous condition of the town, procured a charter of incorporation in 1529, under the title of the "Warden and Society of the Royal Town of Sutton Coldfield". The charter granted the park and town to the corporation and the inhabitants were allowed to graze their cattle in the park.

In my youth, going to Sutton Park was a long day's outing. It was only after we had left the tram at the terminus at Erdington and walked down Chester Road, to enter the park at Banners Gate, that the outing really began. We tracked through the woods, walked along the old Roman road, picnicked and sunbathed on the open stretches of moorland and revelled in our day out.

If we were in the money, having increased our pocket money by cleaning the knives with a potato and scouring the front steps with Gornal sand, we hired ponies from the local stables. The park was and still is a wonderful place for riding, with really fast, open gallops, as well as all the beautiful woodland rides.

Our money seldom stretched to paying for a swim at Keeper's Pool. We swam in Bracebridge Pool, which is well hidden by trees and bushes and gave some cover for undressing. We enjoyed every moment we spent there, although the homeward stretch of the Chester Road seemed endless. The children of today, who are brought to their favourite stretch of park by car and are served with elaborate picnics from the car boot, cannot possibly enjoy the park more than we did.

I hope the good bishop, whose tomb is in Holy Trinity church, knows what pleasure his park has given to countless generations of young people and particularly to boy scouts from all parts of the world who have been allowed to hold their rallies there.

Wednesfield, Willenhall and Wednesbury are small industrial centres which lie between the two important Ws, Wolverhampton and Walsall. As part of the West Midlands plan, they are to remain industrial, as are Darlaston, Oldbury and Tipton.

They are all places of interest to industrial historians and are the birth places of many famous men, from the Tipton Slasher, boxing champion of England 1850–57, to the Bridge brothers of Oldbury. Sir Frederick Bridge was organist at Westminster Abbey and his brother at Chester Cathedral and they are affectionately remembered in the Black Country as Westminster Bridge and Chester Bridge.

A drive through the centre of the Black Country back to Lightwoods Park, passes through Smethwick, which for years has been regarded as part of Birmingham, but is now included in the Borough of Warley. It has been a busy industrial area for several hundred years but fortunately possessed at least one industrialist who cared for his employees, in the person of J. T. Chance. In 1896, he not only gave 50 acres of land for a public park but also added £20,000 for its beautification, which included the development of a large boating lake.

The Chance family were glass makers who moved from Nailsea to Smethwick at the beginning of the nineteenth century. They developed the making of sheet glass, supplying the glass for the Crystal Palace in 1851. Their lighthouse lenses are famous throughout the world and the lens at Europa Point, Gibralta, is the original one supplied in 1864. The old house where the Chance family lived is now preserved within the great complex of the works at Spon Lane.

Members of the Albright family, chemical manufacturers, also gave land for public parks. Now that there is no longer any more land available for recreation,

Tipton. A section of the Old Main Line Canal, to be included in a new landscape scheme.

another great firm, Guest, Keen and Nettlefold, is trying to solve the problem by creating gardens among the factory premises. They have dredged and cleaned up a disused arm of the canal, now a pleasant stretch of water beside their medical centre and have paved and grassed all the available space on each bank. Seats have been sited

133

in sheltered corners and trees, shrubs and flowers improve the surroundings of the old brick buildings.

Other firms are following this excellent example. Joseph Lucas Ltd have given £70,000 towards the landscaping of 32 acres of land surrounding their factory in the Newtown Development Area.

Six hundred trees are to be planted, sports facilities laid out and a network of public footpaths provided to link the Lucas factory with adjacent residential areas and with public transport.

At the Guest, Keen and Nettlefold factory, the largest garden is opposite their Heath Street Mill, which is the original Nettlefold and Chamberlain Mill, started by them in the 1850s for the manufacture of wood screws. Hand-made screws had been used in England since the mid-sixteenth century but it was John Sutton Nettlefold, with money borrowed from his brother-in-law, Joseph Chamberlain, who finally launched a satisfactory machine-made screw on the markets of the world.

Smethwick Chapel, completed in 1728, is a simple brick building of great charm, with its round-arch windows. It stands in a large churchyard, which the present vicar has planted with flowering trees and shrubs. It is intended as a small bird sanctuary, since there are so few trees or even hedges in the vicinity—an owl has already made its home there.

The chapel is now re-named the 'Old Church', as it is a church without a saint. The name of the pub beside the church and built at the same time, has degenerated from 'The Hand of Providence' to 'The Old Chapel'.

Following a fire at the church, the opportunity was taken to make the interior of the church lighter by replacing the damaged gloomy Victorian glass window by a sparkling new one of fused glass, designed and executed by Claude Price of Yardley.

Away from the old church, in the extreme western corner of Smethwick, there is a green and shady little park called Black Patch. Flowing through this park is Hockley Brook, the small stream which provided so much power at Matthew Boulton's Manufactory. Beside the park is Soho Foundry, where many of Watt and Murdock's heavy machines were made, where the site of the first gasholder and Murdock's cottage are preserved and the original foundry clock is still in good ticking order.

The Black Patch was for many years a winter quarters for gypsies, who were finally turned off in 1909, when the land was acquired by the Open Space Society, for the then princely sum of around £10,000. It was opened as a public park in 1911 and is the only open space in the low-lying district, hemmed in by railway embankments, incongruously known as Merry Hill.

Smethwick. Galton Bridge, constructed by the Horseley Iron Company for Thomas Telford in 1826.

The gypsies, having squatted there for several generations, considered they had a legal right to their Black Patch. During the nineteenth century, when the surrounding heathlands became packed with streets of small houses, it was an ideal site from which to conduct their door to door trading. It was not surprising therefore that in the early 1900s, they fought a long hard fight to retain it.

Among the many gypsy battles fought at Black Patch, one of the fiercest was between the old-established gypsy families, the Smiths and the Claytons, against some foreign refugees, touring with a large troop of dancing bears. They too, saw the advantages of Black Patch and with the aid of the bears, thought to clear a place for themselves, but they were no match for Birmingham's gypsies.

Their feeling of security was further strengthened by the local sympathy aroused when Gypsy Queen Henty died in her caravan on Black Patch and crowds of non-Romanies attended her funeral.

The gypsies felt that they were at last part of the community but it was not to be, they were moved on and Black Patch was enclosed with stout iron railings.

The stout iron railings reminded me of Telford's Engine Arm Aqueduct at Smethwick Locks and of his Galton Bridge, a fitting place from which to bid farewell to the West Midlands. This bridge is the most important construction remaining in the Black Country, from the time of the industrial revolution.

In 1826, when Telford was asked to improve on Brindley's canal system, he designed a short cut from Merry Hill to Oldbury, with a second canal at a lower level than the existing Birmingham Canal. This new canal had to be crossed at a high level, by the road connecting Smethwick with West Bromwich and this necessitated a bridge.

Undaunted by the magnitude of the problem, Telford persuaded the Horseley Iron Co. to construct, what was at that time, the largest bridge in the world. It had a span of 150 feet and was 80 feet above his canal.

Because of their industrial setting, neither the aqueduct nor the bridge, have received the acclaim afforded to Darby's Ironbridge over the Severn.

The Ministry for the Environment has now taken over and when the new road is cut across the old Galton estate, which was enclosed by the two canals, the splendid old bridge will carry only pedestrian traffic.

It is hoped to landscape the wooded slopes, overgrown with coltsfoot amid the remains of rusting cars. The land which was once the garden surrounding the Galton's home, is to become a garden once more, after one and a half centuries of industrial turmoil.

The Engine Arm Aqueduct constructed by Thomas Telford to convey a branch canal off the Old Main Line Canal, at a height of three locks above the cruiseway.

CHAPTER SEVEN

The Centre of England

The American author, Henry James, writing nearly a hundred years ago, described Warwickshire as "the core and centre of the English world; midmost England, unmitigated England."

He was writing of the gentle countryside surrounding Meriden, and though the Meriden James knew has changed during the intervening years, it is recognisably the same place, particularly since the construction of a by-pass some years ago. Ducks paddle peacefully once again on the village pond, and the cross on Meriden Green, which for five hundred years has been regarded as marking the centre of England, is no longer rocked on its foundations by heavy traffic. This now quiet village, this midmost England, seems a suitable place from which to start our circular tour.

Our route from Birmingham to Meriden, passed through Solihull, which since my schooldays has become part of Birmingham's commuter belt. The cobblestones in the main street and the old shop fronts have gone. The pharmacist's on the corner, which had two beautiful bowed windows in which were displayed his sign, three enormous bottles of brightly coloured liquid, has been replaced by a functional building. One misses too, the rows of blue glass bottles and the pink china jars with mysterious Latin abbreviations in gold letters—an essential part of the old shop. These are now treasured by interior decorators and collectors.

Today, Solihull is a county borough. The shops are large and impersonal, and the customers are no longer greeted by name. In the stores and supermarkets, the old tradition of personal service has been replaced by machines. The old back lanes have disappeared to make room for acres of car-parks. However a small number of buildings have been preserved and restored. These include the Malt Shovel Inn, enlarged but unspoilt and the half-timbered Manor House, which after years of delay, was opened as a cultural centre. The oak-floored rooms are used once more and part of the walled garden has been saved from the encroaching car park. A row of restored Tudor houses complements the fine old church.

The village green has made way for the War Memorial and wider roads, but in the stones beside the west door of the church can still be seen the grooves

Solihull. A house with a preservation order — built in the late sixteenth century. Restored and converted into four dwellings.

made by the bowmen of old, who sharpened their arrows there before practising on the green. The central tower is part of the original church, thought to have been built between AD 1207–1220 by Hugo de Odingsell, who owned the manor of Ulverley (Olton). The main body of the church, with the exception of the south aisle, was completed by 1360. The only major building construction since that date was the addition of buttresses outside the south aisle, as the original foundations of the church were laid in the unsuitable clay of Miry (or muddy) Hill.

A rare feature of the church is the raised chantry chapel of the Odingsell family, built in AD 1277 by Sir William the Younger. Immediately beneath, is the crypt chapel, which was the sacristy used by the chantry priests. The fireplace, shutter hinges and the signs of the door having been barred from within, indicate a priest's lodgings. A list of priest's names, dating from 1287 to 1487, hangs on the wall.

Many local families are recorded on the church's interesting collection of funeral hatchments. These include the Greswoldes of Malvern Hall. Henry Greswolde was the vicar from 1660 to 1700. It is only a stone's throw from the churchyard of St Alphege to the peace of Malvern Park. The Hall, now a school, was once the home of the Greswolde family, who are reputed

to have bought the herd of deer from the Holte's park at Aston, Birmingham. In the park-lands, tennis courts and an adventure playground have replaced the deer and the park is linked with Brueton Park, with its large pool and walks beside the River Blythe.

By crossing the Warwick Road, the walk can be continued by field-path through the grounds of the old Berry Hall. This half-timbered hall has been considerably reduced in size and is now a farmhouse. The walk continues through the grounds of the Victorian Berry Hall, built by the son of Joseph Gillott, who made a fortune from the manufacture of steel pen-nibs, an idea which originated from a humble smith at Sedgley. The footpath continues across fields, returns to the Blythe in Ravenshaw Lane and meets the river again at Henwood Mill.

All that remains of the nunnery at Henwood are some mounds in a field at Henwood Hall, a farm on the site of the old hall. Henwood Nunnery was founded in the reign of Henry II and was an important Benedictine establishment until the Dissolution. Alice Waring of old Berry Hall, was Prioress at Henwood in the reign of Henry VI.

Although none of these past glories are to be seen at Henwood, the mill, with its wall dovecot and the River Blythe swirling beside it under the willows, is a delightful spot, barely a mile from Solihull's busy High Street.

The Grand Union Canal crosses the lane just above Henwood Mill and it is possible to walk along the towpath to Warwick, or to change over to the Stratford Canal at Kingswood Locks, and walk to Stratford-upon-Avon.

Both canals were cut through beautiful Warwickshire country and it is hoped they will remain completely navigable for pleasure boats, many of which leave from Gas Street Basin in Birmingham for the Avon at Stratford.

Just beyond Henwood, the canal passes behind Grimshaw Hall, one of the oldest of the Forest of Arden houses, and the home of the Grimshaw family until the eighteenth century.

Many of the Grimshaws are buried at their parish church at Knowle, which was built at the beginning of the fifteenth century, and which still retains its original roof timbers of Arden oak.

Walter Cook, Canon of Lincoln, Salisbury, York and London, but a native of Knowle, was responsible for building the church and founding the Guild of Knowle.

The Guild Hall, a half timbered building which stands beside the church, was used for a variety of purposes after the Dissolution, but it was restored and returned to the church in 1912.

Knowle Church, consecrated in 1402 and built of Arden sandstone, stands beside the Guild Hall. The Guild of Knowle was founded in 1412.

The road beside the church soon leaves behind the houses of Knowle and winds through farm land, crossing the Grand Union Canal to rejoin the River Blythe at Temple Balsall.

The perilous bend in the lane is apt to divert attention

141

from one of the historic quarters of the Knights Templar, given to them by Roger de Mowbray in the middle of the twelfth century.

The military-religious order from which Temple Balsall takes its name was founded to protect pilgrims to the Holy Land. The order was dissolved in 1312 and its successor at Balsall, the Knights Hospitallers, are believed to have built the chapel about 1320.

The Hospitallers, an order named after the hospital of St John the Baptist at Jerusalem, was dissolved in its turn in 1540. Today, the good work is continued as the St John Ambulance Brigade.

The hospital at Temple Balsall was endowed in 1678 by Katherine Leveson, a descendant of Wolverhampton's wealthy wool staplers and a grand-daughter of Robert, Earl of Leicester. The elegant hospital buildings, a pleasing mixture of brick and stone, with a central clock tower and sundial, surround a garden on three sides and are best seen from the walk which leads to the Knight's Chapel. This is not thought to be the original building, but it is a typical medieval chapel, which was carefully restored by Sir Gilbert Scott. The Knights' Hall, believed to have been contained within the brick buildings to the west of the church, is still used by the clergy.

The hospital was intended for poor women pensioners of Balsall and the school was for poor boys. The school has been completely modernised, but only the interior of the hospital has been altered and now provides 24 self-contained apartments, to which some married couples are now admitted. It is a charming setting, with a view across the rolling farmlands towards Chadwick End.

Berkswell, like Temple Balsall is easy to pass by unnoticed. One needs to walk in order not to miss the stocks on the village green, with their unusual five holes, and the ancient baptismal well beside the churchyard gate.

In 1972, Berkswell staged a festival to mark 1,000 years of Christianity in the village.

Alongside the church is a field path passing close to the lake in the Hall park and, skirting a wood, goes over the meadows to the pack-horse bridge, which crosses the Blythe near Hampton-in-Arden. Sitting on the bank beneath the railway arch and looking up-stream towards the bridge, there is a seasonal chance of seeing a kingfisher, as they favour the Blythe's dry, sandy banks as nesting sites.

Meriden used to be on the busy main road from Birmingham to Coventry but the new approach road leading to the M1, is well to the north.

In my art student days, when we spent our weekends

Meriden. The oft-disputed 'Centre of England'.

at a cottage at Fillongley, we left the bus at Meriden, to the clang of the bell and the bus conductor shouting, "Meriden Green, the centre of England!"

The village shop on the corner of the green and Fillongley Lane proudly displayed its 'Centre of England' notice. On Saturday afternoons, we called there to pack our rucksacks with provisions and give all our news to the old lady who owned the shop. Although only ten miles from Birmingham, she had never ventured that far, she told us, as with a knife, she cut thick slices of home-cured bacon, an exact pound of cheese with one pull of a wire and filled our basin with brown eggs.

The shop is now the inevitable self-service type, where the mass-produced bacon and cheese sweat in polythene packets.

At the time of the Domesday survey, the settlement on the hill was called Alspath (or Ailespede). Lady Godiva was the Lady of the Manor in the reign of Edward the Confessor (1042–66). Most historians believe she provided the church, although the earliest recorded vicar was Geradi de Alspath (1301).

When the highway from London to Chester was first developed, it skirted the hill, and a hostelry and some cottages were built in the hollow by the pool at Mireden, subsequently known as Meriden. It is here, in the centre of England, that cyclists converge on the village green beside their memorial, for a service of remembrance for cyclists who lost their lives in the two world wars. In recent years, it has been one of the stages in the Cyclists' Round Britain Milk Race—an event which draws teams from many European countries.

Meriden is also the headquarters of the oldest archery society in England. Meetings are held on the lawn at Forest Hall, the turf of which is said to have been undisturbed since the time of Robin Hood, whose horn, the archers claim, hangs in the entrance hall.

The lane leading up to the church is a good half mile from Meriden Green along the road to Coventry, and quite a stiff climb up to Godiva's church and the beautiful half-timbered houses which surround it. A mounting block stands by the church gate, a relic of the days when many parishioners arrived on horseback. In the churchyard, on the shaft of an old cross, is a sundial which showed them the time.

Students of costume go to the church to rub a rare brass. The thirteenth to fifteenth centuries were the main period for memorial brasses but the one at St Laurence Church of Elizabeth Rotton is much later. It shows her wearing a costume of the Charles I period and is dated 1638.

One of the effigies in the church is of Sir John Wyard, an Esquire to the Earl of Warwick, who was Mayor of

London in 1375. Standing by the church, looking down the lane towards Coleshill, one sees the beauty of the valley of the Blythe, Packington and Maxstoke, where "Parks, Meadows, Groves, their mingled graces join."

The ruins of Maxstoke Priory are now privately owned, as is Maxstoke Castle, the home of Lord Dilke. Both were built in the fourteenth century, and the Priory ruins can be seen from the churchyard of Maxstoke's fourteenth century church and the castle gateway, from Castle Lane.

As students, we thoroughly explored the sites of the two ruined castles at Fillongley, but modern mechanised farming has done much to level them and the path to Castle Yard is now across farmland. Castle Yard, was a fortress in the reign of Henry I and became the chief Warwickshire residence of the Hastings family. Like many of the old families, they intermarried and we find traces of them in many parts of the Midlands.

The Henry de Hastings who fought with Simon de Montfort against Henry III, married Joanne de Cantilupe of Aston Cantlow, the well loved sister of St Thomas de Cantilupe of Hereford.

The Hastings men married shrewdly and with their wealthy wives acquired the titles of Abergavenny and Pembroke. At the death of the fifth Lord Hastings in 1389, the Hastings title became dormant, the Pembroke

The ruins of the fourteenth-century Maxstoke Priory. Sir William de Clinton built Maxstoke Castle and is thought to have founded the Priory.

title reverted to the crown, but the Abergavenny title passed by marriage to the Nevilles, who hold it to this day. The most famous Neville was Richard, Earl of Warwick and of Salisbury—Warwick the King Maker.

The castles at Fillongley, like many fortified houses,

were destroyed on Cromwell's orders after the Civil War.

Townpiece Field, which is still held by the vicar, is believed to be land given to the church by Thomas de Hastings in 1260 to pay for two sanctuary lamps to burn in the church for the souls of his ancestors. The lamps still burn over the high altar in the church, which was largely restored in 1887.

Evenings at Fillongley were often spent reading George Eliot, a writer who has returned to popularity with the television productions of her *Middlemarch, Silas Marner* and *Adam Bede*.

The country between Fillongley and Arbury is George Eliot country, so well described in her books. Her father, Robert Evans, was a land agent for the Newdigates of Arbury Hall and Mary Ann Evans (pen name, George Eliot) was born at South Farm on the Arbury estate in 1819.

Her great joy was to drive through the surrounding country with her father and to visit her friend, the house-keeper at Arbury Hall. Her book, *Scenes of Clerical Life*, first published in 1857, is set in the Warwickshire she knew so well. Cheverel Manor is Arbury Hall and Sir Roger Newdigate, her Sir Christopher Cheverel.

Although Sir Roger died before she was born, his transformation of Arbury Hall from Elizabethan to pure

146

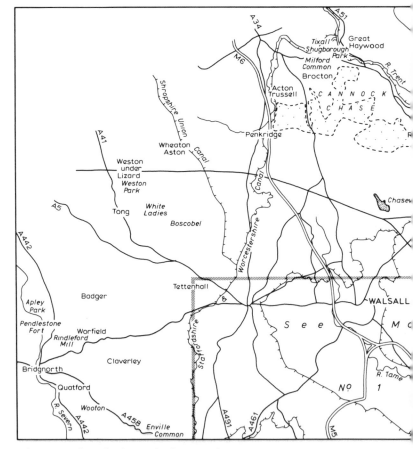

The Heart of England: North of Birmingham

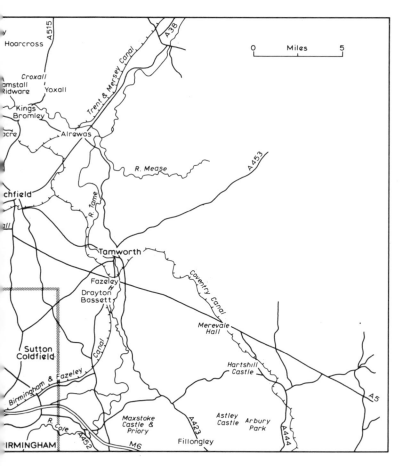

Gothic was well described to her by her friend the housekeeper. Whether or not we agree with her that "Cheverel Manor grew from ugliness into beauty" is a matter we may in part decide for ourselves, as Arbury Hall and its gardens are open to the public on Sunday afternoons during the summer.

The Gothic revival, which became so popular towards the end of the eighteenth century, is seen to perfection or *ad nauseam*, according to taste, at Arbury.

The usual approach to the house is through the magnificent iron gates at the main entrance but the back drive is also open. This leads through Arbury's beautiful woods, carpeted with flowers in the spring and russet with bracken in the autumn. From this entrance, there is a view of the lakes and, if on foot, a chance to see waterfowl of various kinds in the reeds. On my last visit, the young grebe had hatched and their heads were just visible as they rode around the lake on their mother's back, with father grebe beside them, crest upstanding in the breeze.

If the unending false fan-vaulted ceilings of the house are overpowering, the gardens are a delight. Sir Roger Newdigate was responsible for them at a time when formal planting was out of fashion. Wide lawns, spreading cedars, serpentine paths with well sited trees and a large lake adorn the gardens at Arbury.

147

Astley Castle. Parts of the building date from the twelfth century. The home of Edward IV's Queen and Lady Jane Grey.

tragedies. The church was rebuilt in 1343 by Sir Thomas Astley, who also established a college in connection with it. This was suppressed at the Reformation and much of the church fell into decay. Some of it was demolished in the early seventeenth century. But it is rewarding to get the key from the cottage at the churchyard gate, in order to see the rare high oak stalls, which have somehow survived the church's vicissitudes. There are nine stalls on each side of the nave, with delicately carved tops; the backs are painted with life size figures bearing scrolls—a ghostly choir in the silent church, appearing to reprove the visitor. It is suggested that those on the north side represent the apostles and those on the south, the prophets, but why 18? The paintings are in excellent condition, as are the early seventeenth century texts painted on the walls.

Astley Church is the Knebley of George Eliot's *Mr Gilfil's Love Story*. In her childhood, Mary Evans listened to many of the sermons of the Reverend Bernard Gilpin Ebdell, who became her Mr Gilfil.

An Astley heiress carried the estates to the Greys. In 1464, the widow of a Grey *née* Elizabeth Woodville, married Edward IV, and later, the tragic Lady Jane Grey was a proclaimed Queen of England in 1553, after the death of Edward VI. Her reign, if it could be so called, lasted only nine days before Edward's half sister Mary

After such well kept grandeur, the neighbouring Astley Castle is a sad little place, the moat choked with reeds, the sandstone of the house crumbling.

The castle, rebuilt as a battlemented house about 1550 and the church beside it, have a deserted, overgrown air, as though no-one was interested in their past glories and was declared legitimate and proclaimed the rightful heir to the throne. Jane's father, Henry, Duke of Suffolk, fled back to Astley, where he hid in a tree for three days before he was betrayed. Nothing saved the plotters from execution—nor did it save Jane, a girl of 16, hapless victim of the plot, who spent some of her girlhood at Astley and studied her books sitting at her favourite window which looked out on to the church.

To the north-east of Astley Castle, at Hartshill are the ruins of Hugh de Hardreshull's castle, which he built in 1125. Although overgrown, it is near the road and reasonably easy to walk round, to see the traces of the chapel and of the fourteenth century walls. It is surprising that these ruins remained through the nineteenth century, surrounded as they were by rows and rows of miners' cottages, many of which have not yet been replaced.

The lane beyond the Hartshill castle passes the ancient earthworks at Oldbury and goes on through Monks Park Wood to the Abbey of Merevale. The great gatehouse is in good repair but the few ruined remains of the Abbey, like those at Hales, are part of a busy farm. The path through the gateway leads to the church, with a view across the lake to the rising wooded hillside, with the tower of the Dugdale mansion high above the trees.

"According to Dugdale". How often one reads this in books on Warwickshire! He lived from 1605 to 1686 and was born at Shustoke, near Coleshill. After his marriage he lived with his wife's family at Fillongley, before he purchased the Manor of Blythe, near Shustoke. Interested in antiquarian studies, he went to London and was given a lodging at the Heralds Office. From there, he was commissioned to record the monuments in England's principal churches, and was knighted in 1607, when he was created Garter Principal King-at-Arms. He attended Charles I at Oxford and after witnessing the battle of Edgehill, made an excellent survey of the positioning of the troops. This survey was used some years ago when the battle was re-enacted.

His most important work, published in 1656, is the *Antiquities of Warwickshire*. It not only gives an accurate picture of the county at that time, but is most entertaining reading for those who know the Warwickshire countryside.

His diary, which contains references to his great friend, Samuel Pepys, was kept in the home of his descendants at Merevale Hall. The family have now moved to Coleshill.

The church is well below the level of the entrance and has worn steps immediately behind the door which can precipitate the unwary into the dark west end of the

Merevale, Gateway to Merevale Hall, home of the descendents of the Warwickshire historian William Dugdale.

church. This bare, seatless church, with a floor of red bricks, is lit at the east end by a flood of light, which comes through the rare Jesse window of fourteenth century glass which is thought to have been brought from the Abbey. The name 'Tree of Jesse' is applied to a design representing the descent of Jesus from the royal line of David.

In this window, the five good kings of Judah sit in the lower panels, the second row of kings shows David in the centre and the figure of our Lord is the centre of the third row of figures. Winding its way through all the figures to the top of the window with its angels and golden horse shoes, is the Tree of Jesse.

It is a wonderful window to find in a little church, hidden away behind the great gatehouse. A Jesse window is deemed a treasure, at Chartres and Wells Cathedrals.

The dark west end of the church is part of a chapel built in the thirteenth century and is divided from the rest of the building by a stone arch. The chapel contains a massive piece of ancient carpentry, a gallery standing on eight pillars—rough hewn and sturdy. It may have been a rood loft but, standing as it does, with its back to the wall, in a dark chapel, it resembles a treasured piece of furniture stowed away in an attic.

The effigies in the church are believed to be of the Fer-rers. The one with decapitated head and feet is perhaps the earliest armoured figure in Warwickshire—possibly William Ferrers, Earl of Derby. Judging by his chain mail, he may have fought with the Barons against King John. Many of the Ferrers were buried at Merevale before the days of coffins, when the dead were carefully wrapped in oxhides.

We enter Staffordshire at Fazeley, a small town largely developed by the Peel family, who built their money-making cotton mills there and streets of depressing houses for their workers. Although Fazeley has existed since Roman times, there is little to recommend it to modern visitors, but in 1843 it had three glorious days, when England's Prime Minister, Sir Robert Peel, enter-tained his Queen at Drayton Manor. The mean streets were bedecked with flowers and triumphal arches, with Sir Robert's loyal but poor workpeople lining the road to welcome their Queen and the Staffordshire Yeo-manry, in their smart dress uniforms, standing firmly in front of them.

The Royal party arrived at Tamworth Station, to be met by Sir Robert, suitably supported by members of the nobility—a proud day for Tamworth, which had been forgotten by Royalty since Stuart times.

The party drove around the town and received a loyal

151

address from the Mayor and Corporation before driving with their cavalcade of Yeomanry to Drayton Bassett, where they were joined in the evening by the Duke of Wellington.

Here, in the Elizabethan style manor house, built by Sir Robert's father in 1790, the Queen and Prince Albert were given a royal suite of seven rooms, specially decorated for the occasion, with the royal bed hung with chintz and lined throughout with pink silk.

The state visit lasted three days and three great dinner parties were held at the manor. The Queen graciously received the local aristocracy not forgetting 'Billy My Lord', Earl of Dartmouth, or her members of parliament and the Mayors of Staffordshire.

The only blot on Sir Robert's magnificent hospitality was the behaviour of his ducks. They failed with two exceptions to rise to be shot by the Prince from his boat at the end of the lake, which is still called the Duck Shoot. The party had to resort to Sir Robert's well stocked preserves for pheasants, hares and woodcock.

Meanwhile, the people of Fazeley and Tamworth were hastily changing their triumphal arches from a 'Welcome' to a 'God Speed' and the school children were preparing to line the streets for the royal departure. Their Majesties, followed by the Iron Duke, left for Chatsworth, while Adelaide, the Queen Dowager and Prince Edward of Saxe Weimar, left with Earl Howe to be his guests at Keddlestone.

It is hard to visualise all this gracious splendour at the Drayton of today. The great house has been demolished, select small houses have been built among the silver birches of the preserves, and the remainder of the park is open to the public. They walk on the terraces in the footsteps of the famous, boat on the lake, play golf and generally enjoy the beauty of the tall trees and the parkland.

Only one of the cotton mills remains and the workers' houses are being replaced by high-rise flats—the first named Peel Court. In a sprawling way, Fazeley is almost reverting to its description in Roman times—a place clustered around the bridge which carries Watling Street (now the new A5), across the River Tame.

The only relic of the Bassetts, of whom Turstin the Norman was the first Lord Bassett, is the site of one of their boundary stones. This was set up before the signing of the Magna Carta in 1215. The present war memorial marks the site.

Opposite the entrance to Drayton Manor Park, with its grey stone lodge, the Fazeley Canal runs alongside the road. The old canal footbridge is reached by circular steps contained within two castellated towers, a relic of the days when a humble canal bridge had to match the

Drayton Bassett. A footbridge above a swingbridge on the Birmingham-Fazeley Canal.

J. PRIDDEY.

style of the Lodge opposite.

Approaching Tamworth from Drayton Bassett, the glowing pink stone of the castle rises out of the trees on the castle mound planted by the last private owner of the castle, the Marquis of Townshend. He also built the lodge in 1810.

Contrasting with the pink of the castle, is the grey stone tower of St Editha's Church rising behind it, but on the immediate left, totally dwarfing them, are six high-rise blocks of flats. The recommendation of the planners to restrict building in the town to a height of four storeys has come, as is often the case, too late.

On Lichfield Street, the beautiful Moat House, where Prince Charles stayed when his father James I was staying at the castle, is dwarfed to insignificance by the towering flats.

Like St Editha's Church the Moat House has been denuded of its lands and is hemmed in by new buildings. After seeing the paintings and prints of old Tamworth in the castle museum, it is distressing to see how the whole appearance of the town has degenerated in this century.

Among the good things in the town are the castle gardens and the river walk intended eventually to link the flats at Bolebridge with the new residential area at Lady Bridge.

It was extremely pleasant to sit under the trees on the river side, one's back to the offending flats, watch a line of stately swans swim past at the confluence of the Rivers Tame and Anker, and get a good view of the stone bridge. The river walk crosses this and continues through the castle gardens, along the bank of the Anker. Beyond, are the old flood meadows, now converted into playing fields by raising the land level, using waste from local colliery mounds. Lawns and a bandstand are on the site of the castle outbuildings and the Tudor stables.

The castle, which contains a Tudor-Stuart house behind the Norman walls, has been well preserved, owing to the fact that, except for short periods, it was occupied, until in 1897, when it was bought from the Marquis of Townsend by the corporation, for use as a museum. It was formally opened by the Lord Lieutenant of Staffordshire, in commemoration of Queen Victoria's Diamond Jubilee.

When Offa became King of Mercia in 757, he chose Tamworth as his capital and here he had his palace and his mint.

It was Offa who minted coins about the size of our new 2p piece—they were known as pennies but were made of solid silver. According to Matthew Paris, a chronicler monk at St Alban's in the early thirteenth century, Offa was the originator of Peter's Pence, but Layamon, the poet priest, says the idea originated with Offa's predecessor, Ini, King of Wessex.

Peter's Pence was a tax on every hearth, paid annually to the popes. During the tenth century, it was squeezed out of Poland, Prussia and Scandinavia, and attempts were made by Pope Gregory VII to obtain it from France and Spain. It provided an extremely handsome income and we have reason to be thankful that it was abolished in this country in 1534 by Henry VIII.

In the museum, there is a well displayed collection of coins from the Tamworth Mint covering a period from the coins of Eadwig (955) to those of Henry I (1135). The Mint ceased to operate when Henry II reorganised the coinage in 1154.

Tamworth Castle was well known to us in our school-days, when we had to learn by heart Sir Walter Scott's poem 'Marmion'.

> They hail'd Lord Marmion:
> They hail'd him Lord of Fontenaye,
> Of Lutterward and Scrivelbaye,
> Of Tamworth tower and town.

Robert de Marmion, a baron from Fontenay-le-Marmion, came into possession of Tamworth Castle and the Manor of Scrivelsby in Lincolnshire, after the Norman Conquest, but the male line ceased in 1294. The castle was granted to Sir Alexander de Freville by Edward I and when that male line died out in 1423 the castle passed to Sir Thomas Ferrers, who had married a Freville. The Ferrers we have already found at Merevale and there are more of their tombs, together with those of the Frevilles, in St Editha's Church.

The only relic of the Marmions is the Marmion Stone, by the entrance to the castle keep. This formerly stood on Lady Bridge and bore the arms of the Marmions and the Bassetts. It probably served as a boundary stone, when the Manor of Drayton reached as far as the bridge.

We are reminded of the Saxons by the well on the lower lawn. It is known as the well of St Ruffin (slain by his father, Wulfhere, pagan King of Mercia 657–675), for his conversion to christianity by St Chad, then Bishop of Mercia. The surroundings of the well were improved in 1960, when Tamworth commemorated its twelve-hundredth anniversary.

The great Æthelfleda, warrior daughter of Alfred the Great,—the 'Lady of the Mercians', is remembered in Tamworth through her niece Editha, to whom the parish church is dedicated. The hospital too, was named after her but is was her aunt who rebuilt Tamworth after the first Danish invasion and who died at Tamworth in 918.

The exit from the castle is in Market Street, opposite the old town hall, built in 1701 from a bequest by

*Tamworth. Gardens
on the castle mound,
which was constructed
by the Saxons.*

Thomas Guy, who spent his schooldays in Tamworth and who from the fortune he made from the sale of Bibles, founded Guy's Hospital in London.

The statue in front of the Town Hall is of the first Sir Robert Peel, father of the statesman. As Mr Peel, he rented the Banqueting Hall in the castle in 1790 for two years to use as a blacksmiths' forge in connection with the factory he built by Lady Bridge. Fortunately for Tamworth, there was no disastrous fire, as there was at Dudley, when the castle was rented to smiths.

The best view of the Town Hall, with its stone arches and cupula, is from Silver Street, looking along Market Street. There is no vantage point from which to view St Editha's, cluttered as it is with shopping precincts and car parks, but the interior is a peaceful contrast. It is the fourth church to be built on the site since the eighth century and contains a variety of styles—traces of Norman, fourteenth century, sixteenth century and several windows of the nineteenth century. These were made by William Morris. The three relating to the history of St Editha, were designed by Ford Maddox Brown, who was greatly influenced by the work of the Pre-Raphaelites. His windows at St Editha's are more interesting than those designed by Burne-Jones, which are not his best work.

Under the fourteenth century arches are the ancient tombs of the Frevilles and the Ferrers and a flamboyant seventeenth-century marble memorial to a later Ferrers at the foot of the tower.

A direct road connects Tamworth with Lichfield but it is far pleasanter to make a diversion along the lanes through Wiggington, to see the villages of Clifton Campville and Elford and travel to Lichfield along the valley of the River Mease.

About 100 yards from the junction where the Wiggington Road leaves Tamworth, there is a small passageway on the right hand side which connects with the Ashby Road. Half way along the path hidden by the houses, but standing in its own small garden, is Spital Chapel.

This fascinating little Norman Chapel, beautifully kept and used for worship, is one of Tamworth's oldest buildings. It was part of the hospital of St James, granted to the Marmions and later to the de Combreys, until the Dissolution in 1534, when the greater part of the hospital buildings were destroyed. What a treasure to have by one's garden fence!

*Temple Balsall. The chapel of the Knights Templar. Built on
land given to them circa 1150.*

CHAPTER EIGHT

Literature and Landscape

I knew Lichfield during the last war when petrol ration-ing kept the streets moderately free from cars. Now that the new tree-lined ring roads encircle the town, it is once more a peaceful place to walk around—to watch the sailing boats on Stowe Pool or to sit by St Chad's Well or by Minster Pool and watch the mallard ripple the reflections of the cathedral's three spires.

St Chad, to whom the cathedral is dedicated, was one of four brothers who were taught at the Christian settle-ment in Lindisfarne. After previously working around Lichfield, he became Bishop of Mercia in 669 and chose Stowe as his See, this being within easy reach of the royal court at Repton. His predecessor, Jaruman, had already established a church at Stowe, surrounded by the fields in which hundreds of early Christians had been slaughtered, as they fled the warrior hordes from Wales.

At the well near the church, Chad baptised his con-verts, and brought together for the first time into one church Angles and Britons. He became known as 'The Apostle of the Midlands'.

Except for Stowe Pool and the Georgian Stowe House, St Chad's small church and the well are now sur-rounded by a housing estate and Stowe is a suburb of Lichfield. The well is in a small garden by the church-yard, where a small flock of goldfinches flew out from the tall grass to the gravestones and then darted over the well, as if they were the spirits of the martyred Chris-tians, their red caps resembling spots of blood.

Stowe Pool and Minster Pool, fed by Curborough Brook, are older than the Cathedral, which was first built by Bishop Hedda in 700 as a shrine to St Chad. Pilgrims flocked to the shrine, and the town separated from the Cathedral by the pools, developed to accom-modate them. With the Roman roads, Watling Street and Icknield Street so near to Lichfield, the pilgrim trade flourished, as does the tourist trade today.

The land slopes up towards St Chad's from Beacon Street and you see the full beauty of the cathedrals' west-ern front as you enter the Close. Ornate carving forms arcades and panels above the magnificent doors, rising row upon row to the base of the western spires. Within the panels are no less than 113 figures. Immediately above the doors are those of the Apostles; above them, a

Lichfield. Minster Pool garden.

group of English kings on either side of St Chad. Higher still are saints, bishops, archangels and prophets and, in the centre gable, above the great west window, is the figure of Christ.

The glory of this western front, carved in red sandstone, glows in the light of the setting sun.

The Cathedral has always been protected from encroaching buildings on its south side by the Stowe and Minster pools. In medieval times, their abundant waters held a plentiful supply of fish for the towns folk and were used by many local industries for the dyeing and fulling of cloth, parchment-making, tanning and also for powering several mills, including the Bishop's corn mill, which stood at the eastern end of Minster Pool, by Dam Street.

Dam Street and Bridge Street are on the sites of the two causeways, which, centuries ago, were built across the pools to connect the town with the Close, but which eventually caused the silting up of the pools.

The Bishop's fish pool on the west side of Bridge Street silted up completely and a far-sighted Corporation converted it into the Museum Gardens. Minster Pool and Stowe Pool were dredged and their surroundings now provide tree-lined walks and open spaces within the rapidly developing town.

In Dam Street, where Samuel Johnson was first taught English in Dame Oliver's school in 1714, ancient and modern art are both represented. In Quonian's Yard, in the half-timbered buildings, are the work shops of the old-established ecclesiastical wood carvers and stonemasons who attend to the traditional work required at the Cathedral. Opposite, in one of the small Georgian houses, is a modern art gallery, showing the work of contemporary artists, including the lively sculpture of Liverpool's Arthur Dooley.

The statue of Dr Johnson which sits in Market Square is one of the few commemorative works remotely resembling all one has read of the original—a heavy, uncouth and slouching figure, which belied the brilliance and wit of his conversation. There he sits, brooding, in the market place, opposite the house where he was born.

"Parents we can have but once; and he promises himself too much, who enters life with the expectation of finding many friends." His caustic wit offended many who would have been his friends.

His father's house and bookshop, on the corner of Market Street, is now a museum containing many of his son's books, writings and personal belongings.

The statue to the great man's trumpeter, Boswell, also stands in the market square, a trim and lively figure.

Between the statues grows a tree, which marks the

Dr Johnson's statue faces his father's book shop in the market square at Lichfield.

walking the country preaching his new ideas, when he was not in prison for so doing. After his release from Derby prison, he walked to Lichfield and cried out in the market place, "Woe to the bloody city of Lichfield!" He felt strongly about the massacre of the early Christians and even more strongly about the burning at the stake in 1555 of Joyce Lewis, a woman from his mother's village near Mancetter.

Lichfield has been a market town since 1161 and Market Square is still bustling on Fridays, with the buyers and sellers of local produce. After the crowds in the square, the Friary Gardens offer a quiet respite. The Friary Church was destroyed at the Dissolution but in 1933, when the road was being widened, excavation disclosed the working part of the Friary. Following this, the Friary Church beyond the road was also excavated and the ground plan of the church was laid out with paving stones in the lawn of the gardens.

Beyond the Friary Schools, is the Hospital of St John the Baptist, which was founded in 1192 by Roger de Clinton, Bishop of Lichfield. The present building dates from the fifteenth century and is one of the earliest houses built after chimneys were introduced into domestic architecture. The eight tall chimneys are a striking feature, as they rise from pavement level to chimney-pot.

Taking a casual glance down the street, the building

spot where Protestants were burnt in Queen Mary's reign. Edward Whitman of Burton on Trent, burnt there in 1612, was the last to suffer this barbaric punishment.

There is also a plaque to George Fox, the Quaker and founder of the Society of Friends. He spent his early life resembles a Victorian factory, until you see the elegant Tudor doorway, recessed between the centre chimneys. The Hospital has suffered many vicissitudes since its endowment and even today the Welfare State poses the Warden many problems in administering such an ancient charity.

The Tudor doorway opens into a quadrangle of old buildings, including the chapel, which served as a grammar school in Samuel Johnson's time and was also attended by Elias Ashmole. Elias studied law, married a wealthy second wife and was a court favourite of Charles I. He charmed Cromwell and became successively, Windsor Herald, Commissioner, Comptroller General and Accountant General of Excise. He refused the offer of Garter King of Arms, in favour of the father of his third wife, Sir William Dugdale.

Elias was a keen antiquarian and is best known for his collection of curios, which he presented to the University of Oxford on condition that it was housed in a suitable building. Hence the Ashmolean Museum became the first museum of curiosities in England.

In eighteenth century Lichfield a well known figure was Dr Erasmus Darwin, grandfather of Charles Darwin. Dr Erasmus practised medicine from his house in Beacon Street, which backs on to the houses in the Cathedral Close. He had a large practice and did much to help the poor of Lichfield—especially to help them overcome drunkenness, which in those days was as great a social problem as drug addiction is today.

He was a member of the Lunar Society of Birmingham and entertained in Lichfield many of its members, along with other eminent men of his day.

He also found time to help Anna Seward, writer and poet, who basked in much reflected glory as she was the daughter of a canon and resided in the Bishop's Palace. She wrote the memoirs of her neighbour Dr Darwin, and was fortunate enough to have Sir Walter Scott edit her poems. Like most leisured women of her time (1747–1809), she was a prolific letter writer and from the age of 37 kept copies of her letters. Many still make entertaining reading. This beautiful daughter of the canon was the centre of Lichfield's intellectual set. She talked with the 'old growler' Johnson, wrangled with Boswell over Johnson's childhood and read aloud her contemporary poets, William Cowper, Wordsworth and Southey. With bosom suitably heaving she recited her own poems to various members of the aristocracy, to distinguished men such as William Wilberforce and General Eliott, the defender of Gibraltar against the Spanish.

Although Sir Walter Scott corresponded with her, called on her for an hour and stayed two days and edited her poems, he privately described them as "absolutely execrable".

While staying at Barmouth, she met those rare characters, 'The Ladies of Llangollen', Lady Eleanor Butler and Miss Sarah Ponsonby, with whom she corresponded for many years.

Her letters give a sincere description of her friends and contemporaries and of the Lichfield of her time. I doubt if some of our *son et lumière* performances bettered Lichfield's Feast of Light, described by her in 1789: "Every window shone, many with transparent paintings, whose emblems were well imagined, while loyal, enwreathed thanksgivings glowed in phosphorus."

She was a great lover of the theatre and gives lively descriptions of the performances of Mrs Siddons and David Garrick.

David Garrick, who for many years was the owner of the Theatre Royal, Drury Lane, spent his childhood at Lichfield. His father, a captain in the army, married Arabella Clough, the daughter of a Vicar Choral at the Cathedral. They had a large family and, as the captain was abroad so much, they made their home at Lichfield. Their house was on the site now occupied by the museum in Bird Street. David Garrick attended Samuel Johnson's school at Edial near Burntwood, about three miles from Lichfield. There at an early age he displayed his talent for acting, amusing his fellow-scholars with his impersonations of their newly-wed, love-sick teacher and his fat middle-aged wife.

The school was a dismal failure and Johnson and Garrick left to conquer London, with only a few pence between them.

About one mile south of Lichfield, on Watling Street, was the small Romano-British town of Letocetum, now Wall.

The new A5, (old Watling Street) no longer passes through Wall, so it is possible to stop beside the village green and walk up the lane to the excavated site of the bath house and to look round the small museum.

Watling Street was used by the Roman armies for their advance into Wales. Only the bath house of their posting station is exposed, but it is known that the settlement which developed around the post, covered about 20 acres.

The native Britons would congregate around the station for the sale of local produce to the soldiers and to the Gallic traders who followed in their wake.

The excavated bath house, now in the care of the Ministry of Works, is beautifully maintained. It is sobering to see the Roman drainage systems and the underfloor heating and think of the dark ages which elapsed before our houses were built with indoor sanitation, heating and baths.

The country north of Lichfield is mostly agricultural land, well watered by the rivers Trent and Blithe. The Trent and Mersey Canal between Handsacre and Alrewas, and beyond Barton-under-Needwood, up to the outskirts of Burton on Trent, offers good cruising and tow path walks through that delightful country.

Alrewas is a village with many half-timbered houses along the wide street, which was part of one of the old Salt Ways going from Cheshire through Kings Bromley and Alrewas, en route for Lincoln.

The thatched and half-timbered houses in their unique groupings, are well preserved and as yet, unspoiled by tourism. They are small, square-beamed cottages, the homes of ordinary people. The River Trent, joined by the Swabourne, winds its way around, rather than through the village and is joined for a short distance by the Trent and Mersey Canal. For flood reasons, Brindley disliked his canals to have to use a river but at Alrewas he had no alternative. The cost of crossing the Trent marshlands with a long aqueduct would have been prohibitive. Consequently the three waterways flow alongside each other—the canal, its lock by-pass and the river—as they make their way to Wychnor Bridges. Here, the canal

Alrewas, on the old saltway from Chester to Lincoln. An unspoilt Staffordshire village beside the River Trent.

leaves the Trent and follows the Roman Ryknild Street as far as Tatenhill Locks.

The name Wychnor Bridges relates to the bridges and flood arches cut in the causeway built by the Romans across the marshy wastelands of this flat plain.

The Saxon Leofric, Earl of Mercia, died at Kings

Bromley, to the west of Alrewas and although his body was taken to Coventry for burial, old historians claimed that his wife, Lady Godiva, was buried at Kings Bromley. It is now known that the ancient cross, believed to have been erected to her memory, is a medieval preaching cross. There is a fine Norman cross at Armitage, which, with Handsacre, is rapidly becoming part of the growing town of Rugeley.

But cross the Trent at Handsacre by the 100-year-old iron bridge, with its span of 140 feet and the factories and the traffic of Rugeley are left behind and you can take the lanes to the Ridwares. The name Ridware comes from *rhyd,* meaning river and *wara,* meaning 'dwellers' and the Ridwares (homes of the river dwellers), lie between the River Trent and the River Blithe. The lane to Mavesyn Ridware makes a horse-shoe bend to and from the 5014 road and on the bend is a group of historic buildings.

St Nicholas Church contains rare tombstones of alabaster, which was mined nearby at Burton-on-Trent. The Mavesyn tombs have full length figures, the drawing incised on the alabaster and filled with black. The figures wear the costumes of their period, beautifully drawn—each a work of art. The alabaster slabs are arranged vertically around the walls of the small chapel, so their full beauty may be appreciated. Considering

their age, they are in excellent condition.

The stone to Malvoisin Sire de Posny, is the earliest. He fought at the battle of Hastings—

Armed Henry Mavesyn with Duke William to land in Pevensey Bay
And aid his liege lord with the crown at Hastings battle day.

Another treasure in this strange little church is a small collection of encaustic tiles from Caen in Normandy, believed to have been brought to Mavesyn at the time of the Conquest.

The fortified home of the Mavesyns stood between the church and the River Trent. The gatehouse still remains and is probably thirteenth century. The long top room, which may be seen on request, contains massive timbers and crude decorations. It is thought to have contained the family oratory and to have been used by Cromwell as a council room before advancing on Lichfield.

The half-timbered rectory, the gate-house, the tithe barn and the group of barns on the roadside, though hundreds of years older, are strangely enhanced by their distant background of the giant water coolers of Rugeley Power Station.

The lane from Hill to Pipe Ridware leads to a walk over Hunger Hill to Hamstall Ridware. From the hill, you look down on the church and the two-towered

Tudor gateway, once the entrance to a mansion—now a farm. The round capped pillars of the gateway have been used at some time as a dovecot. Another dovecot, a square brick one in excellent repair, can be seen near the church at Croxall a village to the west of Alrewas.

The small church of St John the Baptist, approached by a field path, stands on high ground overlooking the river Mease and Croxall Hall. This brick-gabled house, with its tall chimneys, sweeping lawns and the dovecot beside the entrance gates, was the home of the Curzon family. The tombstones of the early Curzons and of the Howes, may be seen in the fourteenth century chapel.

The wall monument to Sir Robert Wilmot-Horton and his wife Anne is famous in literary circles. Sir Robert's mother was the daughter of Admiral Byron and Robert was a cousin of the poet. After Byron's unhappy marriage, it was Wilmot-Horton who was instrumental in burning Byron's journals and memoirs, which before publication had been declared by discreet readers to be gross and scandalous.

Byron first met Sir Robert's wife at a ball, when she was wearing a black dress. He was so struck by her beauty it was the inspiration of his poem 'She walks in beauty, like the night'.

Another mother church which in its own way compares with Lichfield Cathedral, because it was built as a shrine to a much loved man, is the Church of the Holy Angels at Hoar Cross. It is hidden in the trees, north of Hoar Cross park, facing the tree-covered Hawk Hills —some of the remaining woods of the great Needwood Forest. The church was designed in 1872 by George Frederick Bodley, an admirer of fourteenth century English Gothic and the leading ecclesiastical architect of his time. Whether one likes the style or not, the great attention paid to the design of every small detail is impressive. The whole building gives the impression that it was as beautiful as the architect and his patron the Hon. Emily Charlotte Meynell Ingram, could make it. The church is more than a mile from the village of Hoar Cross in the valley below, but is on the lane which leads to Abbots Bromley.

This old village, the Bromley of the Abbots, with its wide market street and variety of buildings, grew around the Benedictine Monastery, which belonged to Burton Abbey. At the Dissolution, the lands were sold to Sir William Paget, whose descendant became the Marquis of Anglesey. In 1932, the Marquis gave back to the village the Butter Cross, the Pound and the Green.

The Green and the old Butter Cross, backed by the carefully restored Goats Head Inn, are the scene of the famous Horn Dance, which is performed there on a

Monday early in September. The dance is believed to mark the right of the villagers to privileges in Needwood Forest. In the days when the Staffordshire forests belonged to the king, and especially when the forest laws were administered by John of Gaunt, punishments were unjustly severe and privileges were carefully guarded.

The horns are held by the vicar and hang in the church, a relic of the days when the forest rights to food and fuel, were important to priests and laity alike.

Abbots Bromley clings to other old customs. At eight o'clock in the evening, curfew is rung from 13th October until Shrove Tuesday, the Angelus is rung at six o'clock from 13th November until Christmas Eve and a Shriving bell is tolled on Shrove Tuesday.

The village retains great charm, largely due to the width of the street, wide to accommodate market stalls rather than parked cars. The grey-roofed Butter Cross is a reminder of the many markets which were held beside it and there is an air of elegance about the old brick houses, as they stand among the more spectacular black and white half-timbered ones.

Schemes for making reservoirs in beautiful unspoiled country always cause a storm of protest, but when the letters to the newspapers are a thing of the past, the great expanse of water is usually appreciated by the public.

Blithfield Reservoir is no exception. If it were not for the Staffordshire Water Board notice, future generations would assume this to be the lake belonging to the Hall.

The small River Blithe feeds the vast expanse of water and there are a number of lanes and field walks leading down to the lake, now so well established, that herons, no doubt visitors from the heronry at Bagot's park, fish at the water's edge.

From the woodland walks in Blithfield Park on the hill by the church, the full beauty of the reservoir can be really enjoyed, as it complements the warm colour of the stonework of the great Hall.

Although the reservoir was opened only twenty years ago, few can visualise the hall as it used to be, perched high above the deep valley—it appears always to have been beside the beautiful lake. Nor could anyone have enjoyed the view of the distant crest of Cannock Chase to be seen from the causeway, or the lively sails of the boats, which race on this excellent three mile stretch of inland water.

It is not only the herons and the Bagot goats which share the two parks. In 1360, Ralph Bagot married Elizabeth, heiress to Blithfield. They gave up the Bagot home at Bagots Bromley to live at Blithfield but Bagots Park was not deserted.

The famous herd of goats, a long-haired black and

Abbots Bromley. A village where the medieval horn dance and other ancient customs survive.

white breed, which was presented to the Bagots by Richard II, in appreciation of the hunting he had enjoyed in their park, has lived in Bagot Park ever since. They are now in the care of the naturalist, author and Black Country historian, Phil Drabble.

The crest of the Bagots carries the emblem of a goat's head and can be seen in many parts of the hall buildings. The Crusaders originally brought this breed of black-necked Schwarzhal goat to England from the Rhône valley.

There is no trace now of Blithfield village except for the parish church, with its ancient cross in the church-yard, which adjoins the gardens of the hall. The church contains the Bagot memorials, including two in alabaster, similar to those at Mavesyn, but here they lie flat on the raised tombs and the full beauty of the drawing is not so easy to appreciate as in those standing vertically at Mavesyn.

In an arched recess on the outer wall is the tomb and effigy of Alfred de Blithfield, who preached there 700 years ago. The soft and crumbling stone was obviously welcome grit for one of the peacocks, which was pecking away at poor Alfred.

The hall has had many alterations and the present building is largely the romantic Gothic of the 1820s. It is open to the public, is beautifully decorated inside, and houses, among other treasures, a comprehensive toy museum. There are dolls' houses, toy theatres, basket-work dolls' prams in the shape of swans and a true toy of the Black Country—a cast iron money box. These took the form of black-boy busts with open, smiling mouths. Coins were placed in the hand of the boy, which then transferred them to the mouth, whence they were apparently swallowed and disappeared into the money box. They were made by the thousand in Victorian times but are now difficult to find.

There is an elegant orangery in the garden and a rare little octagonal building by the stable block. Built as a game larder, this has been converted into a dovecot and a flock of white fantail pigeons was very much at home.

A short distance along the lanes from Blithfield, are the two Haywood villages on the northern edge of Cannock Chase. They have no particular charm, but when you reach the massive grey stone railway arch at Great Haywood, there is a path leading to Essex Bridge. This is one of the longest and most beautiful pack-horse bridges in the country. Looking northwards from one of the triangular niches which enabled the pedestrian to avoid the loaded packhorses, there is a view of the weir, which lowers the two branches of the River Sow to the level of the Trent, before they flow under the bridge.

Essex Bridge. A pack-horse bridge which crossed the rivers Sow and Trent at Great Haywood.

Look back at the bridge either from this walk or from the path on the opposite side of the bridge, which leads into Shugborough Park.

The present stone Essex Bridge was built about 1630 to replace a wooden one. Originally the bridge had 43 arches, according to Chetwyn, writing in 1679, and served as a causeway to the Bishop's palace. There is no trace of the palace but the ornamental ruins built in the gardens of Shugborough in 1750 and now a ruin in ruins, contained fragments brought from the Bishop's Palace. Pictures in the house show the decorative ruins as they were originally with their colonnade on the far bank of the Sow.

Essex Bridge with its 14 arches, spans a distance of 100 yards and over each cutwater provides an essential recess for pedestrians. Only 4 feet wide, it is a narrow, bridge even by packhorse standards. A strong well laden horse, possibly with large paniers of coal on either side, would have occupied more than its 4 feet and any pedestrian caught halfway across would have had to squeeze into one of the angular recesses to avoid being hit by the passing load.

To the north-west of the bridge stood the famous house at Tixall, home of the Astons.

Trent by Tixal graced, the Astons' ancient seat,
Which oft the Muse hath found her safe and sweet retreat.

Between the two branches of the Sow, one sees the magnificent trees and flowering shrubs in the gardens of Shugborough Park. Looking south from the bridge, the two rivers have become one, and beside them flows the Trent and Mersey Canal. Between the two waterways is a tree lined walk, which leads back to Little Haywood.

171

Tixall. The gateway of the historic home of the Aston family.

Thus wrote Michael Drayton, the Elizabethan poet born at Hartshill in 1563, who was esquire to the Queen's distinguished ambassador, Sir Walter Aston.

Mary, Queen of Scots, who rode past Tixall in 1586 after the Babbington Plot, was lured into the house by a trick and held prisoner there for 17 days.

Lord Aston and his friend Lord Stafford, were involved in an even more infamous plot formulated by Titus Oates against the Catholics. Although both were innocent of the plot to murder Charles II, Lord Aston was imprisoned in the Tower for seven years and Lord Stafford was executed on Tower Hill.

All that remains of the old house, is the great three-storey Tudor gateway, with its four domed towers. It stands deserted, roofless and decaying in the centre of a field. Cattle have replaced the distinguished visitors who once passed through the archways.

I stood in the massive grey gateway to look over the hill across to Tixall Broad, gay with brightly painted craft. This section of the Staffs. and Worcs. Canal, opened in 1772, was widened and disguised as a lake in sight of Tixall Hall. The landed gentry of those days did not wish to be offended by the sight of Brindley's "stinking ditches" but were not averse to cashing in on the profits.

On the green at the entrance to the village, is the Tixall Obelisk, one of three remaining in Staffordshire. It is dated 1776, gives the mileage to Lichfield, London and Stafford, and belongs to the era when wealthy landowners added architectural features to their landscapes.

Fine, or misplaced (as your taste decrees) examples of this fashion are to be found in Shugborough Park. The park is part of the 2,100 acres given to the county by the Earl of Lichfield in 1957 and forms one of the most delightful parts of Cannock Chase. It is possible to motor along the farm tracks within the park, leave a car in the central car park and from there, walk around the wild garden and along the banks of the Sow to the charming Chinese summer-house beside the elegant iron bridge. This building and the Doric Temple, beautifully sited to become part of the landscape, are infinitely more beautiful than the elaborate architectural features which now stand starkly in the middle of farm land.

The Tower of the Winds, the Triumphal Arch and the Lanthorn of Demosthenes, are the work of James Stuart. Stuart and his friend Nicholas Revett spent many years measuring the Hellenic remains in Greece and when the first volume of their book *Antiquities of Athens*, was published in 1762, it started a great vogue among architects for 'the Greek Taste'.

According to Boswell, when Dr Johnson visited Shugborough, he had no liking for Admiral Anson or the

Shugborough. The Chinese House, completed in 1747, was copied from the original in Canton, by Sir Percy Brett, an officer with Admiral Anson in the Centurion.

Tower of the Winds. The Lanthorn of Demosthenes is the most happily placed of the park monuments. It stands on a knoll, with a background of trees and was originally intended to carry a metal bowl on an iron tripod, which was cast by Stuart's friend Matthew Boulton. The bowl proved too heavy for the slender stone temple and was replaced by a pottery bowl supplied by Matthew's friend, Josiah Wedgwood. Both tripod and bowl have now been replaced by a faithful replica in fibreglass, light in weight and more suited to the strength of the ageing temple.

The half-inch Ordnance maps give the overall position of Cannock Chase but for real enjoyment, the detailed map issued by the County Council Planning Department shows every section of the Chase—where to walk and where to motor, together with all items of historical and industrial interest.

The area south of Milford Common and Seven Springs is crossed many times by public footpaths, bridle paths and nature trails and is a motor-free zone.

The path from Seven Springs along the edge of Haywood's Warren, south to Parrs Warren, turns north along the Sherbrook Valley, one of the choicest parts of the Chase.

> Oh have you seen on Cannock Chase,
> The birches, queens of silver grace?

The Sherbrook winds its way through silver birches, the haunt of a great variety of tits,—the common blues, the great, the long-tailed, coal tits and sometimes the rarer willow tits.

If you are looking for badger setts or for fallow deer, leave the brook at the Stepping Stones and return to Seven Springs, along the edge of the Black Hills.

The walks on the other side of the Stepping Stones go up over Broc Hill, Oat Hill and Spring Hill, all of which offer wonderful views of the Clee Hills and Shropshire, before they drop down to the small village of Brocton or to the wide common at Milford.

The north-west part of the Chase is wilder and more natural than the coniferous wooded parts near Cannock which are controlled by the Forestry Commission.

There is a pleasant drive into Shropshire from Milton via Brocton, across to Acton Trussell and along the valley of the River Penk to Penkridge, then through Wheaton Aston to Weston-under-Lizard.

"The best things in life are free" is an old proverb, but some best things are worth paying for. I would always pay for the pleasure of walking in beautiful parks and gardens and Weston Park, at Weston-under-Lizard, is such a place.

Under the trees is a seat, in memory of a head gardener

—the inscription is simple: "He loved these gardens". Weston Park has an air of having been loved for centuries.

The woods, with their magnificent trees, are no haphazard plantings, nor is the ground cover of rhododendrons, azaleas and tall primulas.

There are beautiful vistas everywhere, whether from the Temple, surrounded by the scent of honeysuckle —looking over the perfect English parklands towards the house—or viewing the Temple and the house from the parklands. The landscaping was the work of Lancelot ('Capability') Brown, whose vision of future beauty was undaunted by the sight of hundreds of unpromising acres. He adhered to Alexander Pope's advice—

> To build, to plant, whatever you intend,
> To rear the column or to arch the bend,
> To swell the terrace, or sink the Grot,
> In all, let nature never be forgot.

This he did so well, we are apt to forget that many acres of English parkland are man made. Perhaps that was Brown's great gift—what he has left for posterity looks perfectly natural. Trained as a gardener in his native Northumberland, Lancelot moved south in search of work and had the good fortune to find it with Lord Cobham, at Stowe, in Buckinghamshire.

Weston Park. The house was re-built in 1671 and the grounds landscaped in 1762 by 'Capability' Brown and James Paine. Described by Disraeli as "Weston and its scenes so fair."

At that time, 1740, the famous architect and designer of gardens, William Kent, was re-designing the grounds at Stowe. He was quick to appreciate the work and vision of the young Lancelot, who soon rose to become head gardener. Kent died before the work at Stowe was

176

completed but Lord Cobham realised his head gardener was no ordinary man and left the work in his capable hands. He went further—he allowed and encouraged Brown to design parks and gardens for his friends.

After Lord Cobham's death in 1749, Lancelot moved to London to work on his own, sure of a wealthy clientèle, and was offered work all over England. He had great vision and before the days of bull dozers had no qualms about moving mountains or creating them. He would cut into a hundred acres, with as sure a hand as a master sculptor into a block of stone. He would ride around and across his sites. He looked. He observed, as all skilled artists do, before he committed a single line of his plans to his thick vellum paper.

He trained as an architect but he worked equally well with other architects. Weston Park is an example of the rapport which existed between Brown and his friend James Paine.

His vistas are enhanced by the architecture of James Paine, whether it is the Georgian proportions of the large temple or the simple, perfect proportions of the small one. This is an excellent place from which to appreciate the subtlety of the tree planting along the banks of Temple Pool and Paine's Roman bridge, which spans the pool at the narrow end.

The oriental plane tree on the lower terrace of the gardens, thought to have been planted when the house was built in 1671, has been enhanced by the stone balustrade. This follows the sweep of the tree's great branches, which cover an area 400 feet in circumference.

In a park as beautiful as Weston, there is no lack of birds, from the magnificent peacocks on the lawns, to the tiny tree-creepers working busily up the woodland trees and the variety of water fowl on the Church Pool. By the stable block, there is not only a plan of the walks in the park but excellent coloured photographs of the birds one could expect to find there.

In the house, (open to the public) there is a collection of bird paintings by the meticulous eighteenth-century Irish artist, William Hayes. These are in relief—the form of each bird has been delicately built up in papier mâché before painting in water colour and the result is breathtaking. Also on display are three bird books, superbly illustrated by Gould,—perhaps the finest of all bird artists.

The parish church of St Andrew, which stands beside the church pool, was re-built in 1700, with the exception of the tower, which is part of the medieval church. It contains monuments to the original Lords of the Manor, the de Westons and to the subsequent de Pershalls, Mytons, Wilbrahams, Newports, down to the Bridgemans, the present Earls of Bradford, whose earldom was revived in 1815.

When Brown was designing the park at Weston, which lies along what in his time was a busy Watling Street, he realised the property must be protected from the noise of the road. Temple Woods to the east and Shrewsbury Walk to the west, were his deceptively simple answer. The trees have had 200 years to develop and now form an effective barrier against the roar from the A5. Along Shrewsbury Walk, fallow deer move, oblivious to the freight-liners, long tankers and cars.

There are few more rewarding and pleasant stretches of country, for those interested in treading the paths of history, than the lanes south of Weston Park.

The story of Charles II's escape after the battle of Worcester on September 1651 and of the day he spent hidden in the oak tree at Boscobel, is well known. Not so well known perhaps, is that it is still possible to trace his wanderings.

One is apt to forget, too, that in Charles's time, the country was thickly wooded. Travelling unseen, even on horseback, would have been much easier than today, when the trees have given way to agricultural land.

Charles arrived at White Ladies near Boscobel in the early hours of the morning. At this house close to the Priory, he was met by George Penderel, the servant in charge of White ladies, the owner Francis Cotton not being in residence at the time.

Though the house at White Ladies is no more, the ruins of the adjoining Priory are well kept as an ancient monument. It is easy to visualize the tired king's relief on arriving there and meeting the friendly Penderels, some of whom are buried in the churchyard. Two Penderel stones stand against the wall of the Priory, one to William, who died in 1707, son of the William who looked after Charles at Boscobel; the other is a nineteenth-century replica of the stone erected to the memory of Jane Penderel, whom the king deemed his friend and called 'Dame Joane'. She was the mother of the five Penderel brothers who took a prominent part in the king's visit, but, who, unlike Francis Yates, the King's guide from Kinver to White Ladies, who was executed at Oxford, managed to escape punishment. George Penderel was caretaker at the house at White Ladies, his brother William holding a similar position at Boscobel. Brother Richard, who lived at Hobbal Grange, was called in to remain with the King. Another brother, Humphrey Penderel went into Shifnal ostensibly to pay taxes and although questioned by Commonwealth officers, returned safely to the king with valuable news of their whereabouts. John Penderel, who had already escorted Lord Wilmot to Moseley Hall and on to Colonel Lane's home at Bentley, returned to Boscobel to inform the King of Colonel Lane's plan for his escape to Bristol.

It is a pleasant walk through the small wood beside the Priory ruins, out to the field path beyond, to find the few remains of Hobbal Grange, home of Richard Penderel.

Boscobel House, is now in the care of the Ministry of Works and contains many prints and relics of the King's stay. Although there were good hiding places in the house, the Penderels decided that Charles would be safer hidden in an oak tree.

The present oak is reputed to have grown from an acorn of the original, which was destroyed by Stuart souvenir hunters when the story of the escape was eventually made public. Behind Boscobel House is Spring Coppice, the surviving part of the larger wood which was searched by the Commonwealth soldiers while the King was safely hidden in the oak tree.

Spring Coppice is an appropriate name. It is carpeted with bluebells and many spring flowers and there is a path through the wood, from which one can look back at Boscobel. From Boscobel the King rode on Humphrey Penderel's mill horse to Moseley Hall, complaining that she was "the heaviest dull jade he ever rode on."

Tong. A quiet village between Weston Park and Boscobel.

CHAPTER NINE

A Preacher and a Poet

The agricultural country between Boscobel and Bridgnorth, distinguished by winding lanes and field-paths and groups of cottages, includes the quiet villages of Ryton, Beckbury and Badger.

Farmyard hens roam free and drink from a century-old elm horse-trough, on the way to Badger. Ducks and geese share Badger Pool with the coots and moorhens, which swim among the kingcups and water lilies, yellow iris and tall bullrushes. They join the hens to peck for grit between the gravestones near the water's edge, watched by the swallows nesting in the church porch.

Over the dormer windows of a row of cottages dated 1500, the thatch is so thick it lies in great curves like a warm petticoat.

Badger Dingle is for walkers. Paths lead between the steep sandstone banks, where ferns grow in the clefts above the stream which feeds the mill pool. The mill has gone, but an old millstone helps to support a crumbling stream bank. The Dingle is a quiet place for watching the many birds and small creatures which drink at the water's edge and for trying to identify the songsters high in the trees.

For a contrast to the shade of the Dingle, there are fresh wind-blown walks on the heights of Castle Hill, before dropping down to the water meadows beside the River Worfe, as it twists and turns to reach the Severn.

Beside the gate to Worfield Church a large yew tree encircled by a seat invites visitors to enjoy a charming view of the village. First a street of black and white cottages, then Lower Hall, that magnificent example of Tudor architecture, leading the eye upwards beyond the slender spire of the church to the ridge of a steep escarpment. Back in the churchyard, a small stone lion, a fragment of an ancient tomb, peers through the grass. Nearby, an old sundial shows the time not only in Worfield but, suprisingly, in Jerusalem and Mexico!

After Worfield, passing through Wyken, comes Claverley, where the hidden beauty of the interior of the church was revealed only when the plaster was removed in 1902. The unique frescoes then uncovered are thought to date from AD 1200. The frieze, which is 50 feet long, is painted in the style of the Bayeux Tapestry, but autho-

Worfield. One of the gentle Shropshire villages.

rities on English wall painting believe it illustrates the medieval poem 'Pyschomachia', which tells the story of the seven virtues and the seven deadly sins.

Enhancing the red sandstone of the church is the vicarage, a fifteenth century refectory house, built for the Prior at Wenlock.

Refectory houses in such good repair as this are rare. They were used by monastic dignitaries while on tours of inspection of their properties and mostly fell into decay after the suppression of the monasteries.

The full beauty of the vertical and herring-bone timbering is best seen from across the road, where the vicarage, the lychgate and the old cross form a painterly group in front of the church.

Another walk out of Worfield follows the Worfe to the ford at Rindleford Mill. The millwheel is no longer turning, but the group of farm buildings and cottages, with the turn in the lane and the tall trees on the hill behind, are worth a backward glance. All this and the fork in the river, can be enjoyed from the footbridge, which now spans the ford.

The main road from Rindleford Mill into Bridgnorth passes a rich man's folly, built by William Whitmore of Apley Park, in the style of Apley Hall. It is known locally as Pendlestone Fort and is reputed to have housed

Claverley (clover pasture land) was given in 1071 to Roger Montgomery, cousin of William I.

Napoleonic prisoners. If so, they must have been housed in the old mill which was destroyed by fire in 1854. The present building was built on the site of this mill from stone quarried on the other side of the road, under Pendlestone Rock.

The rock rises 50 feet above the road and one source

attributes the name Pendlestone to one of a number of glacial boulders which were once on top of the sandstone ridge. Another source says it derives from Penda's Stone —Penda was a King of Mercia.

For a time the mill was used by Brintons, the carpet weavers of Kidderminster, which no doubt accounts for the tall factory chimney.

The warrior lady, Æthelfleda, Lady of the Mercians, fortified Bridgnorth against the Danes in 912. After the Conquest, the manor was granted to Earl Roger of Shrewsbury and it was his son, Roger de Belsmere, who transferred his borough from Quatford across the river and built his castle at Bridgnorth in 1101.

Neither the folly of a 'fort' nor the high Pendlestone Rock quite prepare one for the alien town of Bridgnorth. Hill-top towns are the exception, rather than the rule in England and Bridgnorth comprises two towns—Low Town along the west bank of the River Severn and High Town, perched on a sandstone rock a hundred feet above. A cliff railway, with a gradient of two in three, takes pedestrians from the river bridge to High Town and is a totally unexpected means of transport to find in a Shropshire market town.

The leaning tower of the castle ruins is not classed as one of the seven wonders of the world, yet it is 17 feet out of vertical, as against the latest figure of 15 feet for the leaning tower at Pisa.

At the foot of the cliffs along the riverside are cave dwellings, which were old when the castle was built above them—and what a magnificent site for a castle! It was unassailable on three sides and commanded a strategic view of the Severn valley. The castle withstood all comers until the Civil War, when it was destroyed after a fierce battle which raged through the town, during which Colonel Billingsley, commander of Bridgnorth's Royalist forces, was slain in the churchyard of St Leonard.

The castle site is now a memorial garden, with a view of the valley below. It contains a brilliantly placed statue of a soldier of the Great War, his hand outstretched towards the England he defended.

The churchyard of St Mary Magdalene adjoins the memorial garden. The church, with its curious dome-capped tower, is another unusual feature of Bridgnorth. It was built on the site of the castle chapel and was designed not by an architect, but by that great engineer and road builder, Thomas Telford.

From the church the path around the edge of the cliff leads to the top cabin of the cliff railway and to Stoneway Steps. These are cut out of rock and for those young enough, provide an alternative route between the upper and lower town. It is also the only route to the

Bridgnorth. A high town and a low town by Severnside.

Theatre-on-the-Steps. This former chapel, built on a shelf of rock, has been converted into a repertory theatre, where plays are performed and art exhibitions held.

In the centre of the High Street a converted barn, standing on stone arches, served as the Town Hall. This replaced the Hall burnt down during the Civil War siege and originated in Much Wenlock. It makes an unusual but charming building, with a clock set in the gable and its windows displaying the portraits of 14 English Kings.

Such an ancient town has had many renowned citizens and the oldest house, built in 1580, was the birthplace of Bishop Percy. Thomas Percy is remembered for his lifelong search for old manuscripts and for the ultimate publication of his *Reliques of Ancient English Poetry*. On one occasion, he was just in time to save a precious manuscript from being used as a firelighter.

Bridgnorth High Town has many steps and archways which eventually lead to the north gate and the church of St Leonard, beyond the half-timbered houses of Whitburn Street.

A humble cottage in St Leonard's Close, was the home for two years of the preacher, Richard Baxter.

His statue stands in Kidderminster where, in 1641, at the age of 26, he preached a brillant sermon, was elected minister and stayed for nearly twenty years.

In the basement of one of the houses behind St Leonard's church, a young potter has set up his wheel and kiln, and is producing items of excellent design. In some converted out-houses at the other end of the town, an enterprising modern art gallery shows paintings, sculptures and fine examples of Shropshire craft work.

First an early settlement, then a medieval fortress, Bridgnorth now has a more settled way of life as a market town. Rows of stalls line its wide street, while the variety of buildings on either side give substance to the story of its past.

On the opposite side of the Severn, towards Bewdley, on the high sandstone rock, is Quatford. This is where the Danes made their camp in AD 894, providing a good vantage point from which to command the river crossing below, appropriately at Danesford.

To this remote spot, more than a hundred years later, came the Norman, Roger de Montgomery, Earl of Shrewsbury, cousin of William the Conqueror. He rode out from Shrewsbury to welcome his second wife, the Countess Adelina. Their entourages met at Quatford and in gratitude for the safe arrival of his betrothed, after crossing the storm-tossed Channel he built a church on the rock at Quatford.

The old road to the church has been kept as a parking and picnic area, while the new road has been routed nearer to the Severn. The steep flight of steps leading up to the church, cut originally in the sandstone, became so worn with age that it had to be levelled with concrete.

Quatt. One of the smallest Shropshire villages – near Quatford.

The churchyard on the high rock commands a wide view of the Severn valley and the church retains much of the original Norman building.

The ideal way to see the beauty of the countryside between Bridgnorth and Worcester, is to travel along the River Severn by camping canoe, stopping whenever the fancy takes you, to enjoy the many river walks and variety of interesting places on either bank. Such travellers may see the Hermitage at Blackstone Rock or Quatford Church, towering high above the river, or watch the birds in the Long Covert above Hampton Loade, and drift down to Upper Arley and the Wyre Forest.

The Severn leaves Shropshire for Worcestershire just north of the historic village of Upper Arley, the home of Sir Robert de Burgh, the Earl who saved England for the English. He held the manor of Arley in the reign of King John, for whom he defended Dover Castle. He defeated the French in the Straits of Dover and also urged his king to sign the Magna Carta.

He died, a much loved man, in 1243 and is remembered by theatre-lovers as a great character in Shakespeare's *King John*—and again, in lighter vein as the crusader, in *1066 and All That*.

For many years, Upper Arley was no more than a small group of stone houses at the end of an arched road alongside the river, with the church and the castle on the hill. Now, the modern battlemented castle which stands on the site of the earlier Manor House, is occupied by a school. Upper Arley is expanding but the modern flats being built are long and low and harmonise with the contours of the land. Unchanged however are the various lanes leading down to the river—cars are better

186

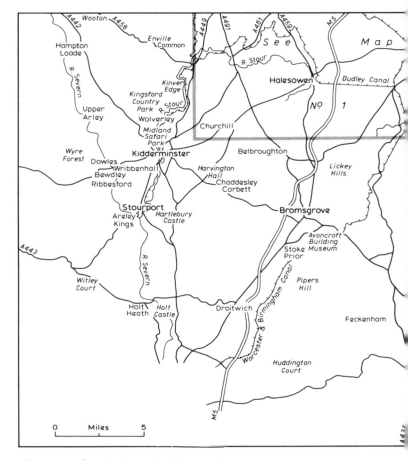

The Heart of England: South of Birmingham

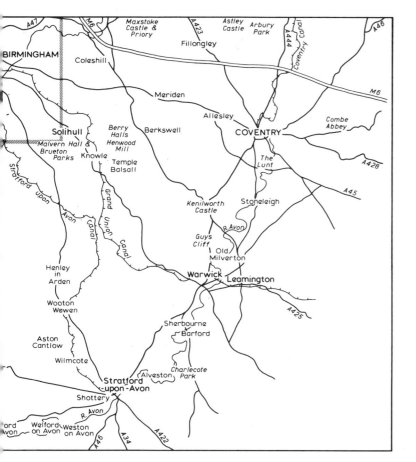

left on the higher ground.

The river can be crossed at Upper Arley by chain ferry, reputed to be the last of its kind in England. By adjusting the tiller, the force of the rapid current carries the ferry from one side to the other.

Rewarding views of Upper Arley are provided from the lane on the west side. This leads to a handsome sandstone barn and a pleasant pub, with seats in the garden from which to view the beauty of the Wyre Forest.

Further down the river, on the east bank, is the small village of Wribbenall. From here, it is easy to see why the Normans named the opposite bank 'Beaulieu' (Bewdley)—beautiful place. Seen now, it is Worcestershire's most charming Georgian market town, rising up the hillside from the old river wharves.

Telford's bridge, with its three elegant main arches and small land arches, was completed in 1798 and carries the road from Wribbenall across the river.

To appreciate Bewdley's buildings, walk around the town, starting with Severnside, a charming river-bank street, with its River House, rows of cottages and timber-framed gable house, and look across to the equally attractive buildings on the wharf side at Wribbenall.

Severnside, like the town of Bewdley, was a busy place in Tudor times, a flourishing inland port among the wooded hills of the Midlands. In the great days of

187

sail, Bristol was already an important port, and many Bristol merchants had warehouses on the wharves at Bewdley and Wribbenall. In those days, using timber from the Wyre Forest, Bewdley men were building long boats called Trowes. These were hauled by horse and by hand, along the river between Bristol and Bewdley. Wine, spices, silks and sometimes slaves, were the cargoes coming up the river, with return loads of caps, horns, leather, small metal goods and all kinds of besoms,—brooms made of twigs or heather.

Cap-making was established in Bewdley as early as 1446, when Richard of York, a descendant of the Mortimers, obtained a license for the town to hold a weekly market.

The manor of Bewdley, with Tickenhill, its manor house on the hill, was given to Roger de Mortimer after the Conquest. When a descendant of the powerful Mortimers was crowned Edward IV, Tickenhill became one of the royal palaces. Edward constituted Bewdley a corporate town, which remained important until the development of the Black Country and the building of the canals in the eighteenth century.

King Edward's town was high on the hill by Sandy Bank and Wyre Hill, with its centre of commerce, the inn, now called 'The old Town Hall'. Here, the loaded pack-horses assembled, before passing through the Welch gate, on their way to Ludlow and the west.

Henry VII enlarged the palace of Tickenhill for his eldest son, Prince Arthur, and it was there that the boy's marriage by proxy to Catherine of Aragon took place.

Bewdley's trade in caps flourished, thanks to the action of Henry VIII in forbidding the import of caps and later, to the ruling of his daughter, Queen Elizabeth, that caps must be worn on Holy Days and Sabbaths. It was of no avail—French Protestant refugees introduced wide brimmed hats with sweeping plumes, which became the rage with the Stuart kings and the cavaliers.

In the first half of the eighteenth century, Bewdley, like Bath, developed into a fashionable society town. Balls and assemblies were attended by the wealthy landowners of the surrounding countryside and young Miss Kemble, later to become better known as Mrs Siddons, acted at the Angel Assembly Rooms in Load Street.

Small wonder the corporation refused permission for Brindley to bring his canal, or 'stinking ditch', to join the Severn at their beautiful town. Brindley's answer was the creation of Stourport, lower down the river and, as Stourport grew and flourished, so the trade of Bewdley dwindled and died, forcing the inhabitants to leave and seek work in Kidderminster and Stourport.

In addition to the charm of Severnside, Bewdley has many interesting buildings. Lax Lane leads up the hill to

High Street and on the corner is the house where Stanley Baldwin was born in 1867.

He spent his childhood at Wilden, near the banks of the Stour and his later life at Astley Hall, by Dick Brook. His birthplace boasts a blue plaque but the house is not in good repair, nor are the Sayers Almshouses, founded in 1763. The remainder of the street, leading to St Anne's Church, is lined on either side by charming houses, which include the Manor House (1607) and the half-timbered Bailiff's House, well cared for by a brewery.

St Anne's Church, isolated by the one-way traffic lanes at the top of Load Street, is plain and simple. It was built in 1745 on to a tower which was already fifty years older.

Whether you look down Load Street from St Anne's or up from Telford's bridge, it is a wide and pleasant street, with a variety of building periods, not too spoilt by the modern shopfronts. A three-storey sixteenth century house of timber framing, has recently had its timbers uncovered and its façade restored by the Council.

There are many walks leading out of Bewdley—one footpath from High Street leads to the old parish church of Ribbesford, passing close to Tickenhill, now privately owned.

Henry VIII added to Tickenhill for his daughters.

Bewdley. A country seat of the Tudors.

Later, it was the home of Sir Henry Sidney, Lord President of the Marches, and it was used by a royalist garrison during the Civil War as a base from which Charles I sent troops to besiege Dudley Castle.

189

In the heyday of Georgian Bewdley, a great deal of building took place and the present Tickenhill with its Georgian façade, dates from that time.

Although much altered since the time of the young Prince Arthur's strange marriage ceremony, it is romantic to walk past the site where so many members of the royal families spent their more leisured hours enjoying the beauties of Worcestershire.

The walk passes along an avenue of sycamores planted by one of the Herberts of Ribbesford Hall and then crosses the fields to Ribbesford church.

Like Bewdley, the Manor of Ribbesford belonged to the Mortimers and was held under them by a knightly family, who took the name of de Ribbesford. Many owners followed—the Beauchamps, the Actons, and when the property reverted to the crown, Charles I gave it to three famous brothers—George Herbert, whose poems consoled him during his imprisonment—Edward Herbert, philosopher and historian—and Sir Henry Herbert, who was Master of the King's Revels and Lord of the Manor of Ribbesford in 1627.

The present house, with its gables, turrets and domes, is thought to stand on the original site.

The Norman church of St Leonard, beside the walled garden of the Manor House, was altered in the fifteenth century and retains an arcade of roughly hewn oak arches and pillars. The church is associated with five attractive sisters, the daughters of a country parson who is buried with his wife at St Leonard's.

Two of the girls married famous men and two had famous sons. Alice Macdonald on a picnic in the Potteries by the side of Lake Rudyard, met, and subsequently married and went to India with John Lockward Kipling. They named their son Rudyard, after their first romantic meeting.

Louisa married a local manufacturer, Alfred Baldwin, whose works and house were at Wilden on the Stour, where their son Stanley, was brought up with an enduring love for Worcestershire.

Georgiana married Edward Burne-Jones, and Agnes married Edward Poynter, who became President of the Royal Academy—both these men received knighthoods.

Edith looked after her parents until she went to live with her sister at Wilden House, where she spent ten years embroidering an altar cloth designed by William Morris for Wilden Church.

The memorial window to the Macdonald parents in Ribbesford Church was designed by Sir Edward Burne-Jones and made by William Morris.

On the other side of the Severn, on the high ground above Wribbenall, lies the romantic estate of Spring

The ford at Wotton, Shropshire.

Some day, he would buy the hill and build himself a finer house than Tickenhill, with a handsome columned portico, surround it with beautiful gardens, a lake and fine trees. He would build a stable block with a clock tower and stalls for a dozen horses. He would have carriages in which to drive to his own works on the banks of the Severn. He would have a farm on his estate and good cottages for his workers.

I sat on the steps of Skey's dream house with another visionary and looked across to Tickenhill—across Skey's matured parkland, past the great copper-beech trees standing beside the lawns which sloped down to the lake. Here the grebe and the herons were at home amid the reflections of the rhododendrons and wild yellow iris. Spread out at our feet, was a detailed plan of the 250 acres of the Spring Grove estate, showing six miles of winding drives between newly created slopes, ingeniously designed so that the cars of the visitors driving into the future West Midlands Safari Park, would not see those driving out.

> He gains all points, who pleasingly confounds,
> Surprises, varies and conceals the bounds.

With this vast project under way, only two of the hundreds of beautiful trees have had to be felled. Conservation is the watchword for the buildings, the park and

Grove—romantic because it was a dream come true, the dream of Samuel Skey, a poor boy who worked his twelve-hour day for a drysalter in Bewdley in the early eighteenth century. He went on errands to Kidderminster, climbing the hill out of Wribbenall and resting on the hill's crest to look back across the valley of the Severn to the great house of Tickenhill.

191

the excellent vistas, for it is an estate covering several low hills. The most suitable areas have been allotted for the many species of wild animals which will roam in the park. Soon giraffes will be nibbling at the tall trees and prides of lions will be at home under the spreading oaks.

There will be boating on the great lake but the three small lakes are to be preserved for birds. Monkeys and baboons will live in one spinney, the other is for the pheasants, foxes and badgers, squirrels, weasels and stoats already at home on the estate.

Samuel Skey was a great animal lover and his pride and joy were his beautiful white mules, which he bred at Spring Grove. It was behind these handsome creatures that he drove down the hill and across the bridge into Bewdley to attend to his many businesses.

In addition to the acres of Samuel Skey's country estate above Wribbenall preserved for public enjoyment, there are the 6,000 acres of Wyre Forest on the other side of Bewdley. They stretch from Cleobury Morimer in the west and covering the valley on the north side of the town, reaching the Severn by the forgotten village of Dowles.

Dowles Brook flows through the woods—forest alas, no more, after the depredations of two world wars. The prettiest walk is along this brook, starting from the A456, just before the brook joins the Severn. Following the

Spring Grove. Samuel Skey's dream house, now the headquarters of the Midland Safari Park.

brook, one comes to Knowles Mill, which, with four acres of orchard, was given to the National Trust by Mr Paul Cadbury. The mill house is tenanted, the garden gay with flowers. Like many other houses in the forest, it has a stone grinding wheel serving as a garden table. The river bank here has been built up with gabions. These are

192

wire baskets filled with stones and are stacked one above the other to form a wall, rarely seen these days but quite in character with the old mill. The working gear of the mill is still there and it is hoped eventually to have it fully repaired and in working order.

It was on the stretch of the brook between Knowles Mill and Cooper's Mill that I saw a pair of kingfishers on their constant trips from the stream to their nest in the bank. Spotted flycatchers were darting about and the spotted grizzled skipper butterflies were flying over the stream meadows, difficult to distinguish from the wind-blown gorse petals.

The site of Cooper's Mill has a recently built hostel for boys, but the mill gearing is displayed in the field and can easily be seen from the path.

For a round walk, take the path through the Chamber-line, Withybed and Wimperhill Woods, back to the mills and then take the path past Dowles Manor to return to the road. Dowles, like Bewdley, was once a busy place, with thriving mills, clay-mining, charcoal-burning and bark-stripping for the tanneries in Bewdley. The hill on the south side of the brook, opposite Dowles, is marked as Tanners' Hill on the map, though it is Bark Hill on the road sign. (Bark provided the tannin used to convert hides into leather).

The church at Dowles, dating from the tenth century, was re-built in the eighteenth century, but when work ceased in the forest, the parishioners gradually left the district, the church decayed and was eventually demolished.

The churchyard is now overgrown with a great variety of wild flowers, which also grow in profusion along the sides of the brook.

Dowles Manor is privately owned but there is a good view of this exceptional Elizabethan timber-framed house from the forest walk. I was privileged to visit the house with an art society to see the amazingly well preserved wall paintings, which are in all the main rooms. Unlike Tickenhill, the façade has not been altered out of all recognition.

Much of the forest is owned by the Forestry Commission, which provides a car park on Callow Hill, on the A4117 to Cleobury Mortimer. It also provides a leaflet which contains a plan of the many public walks, together with interesting descriptions of the whys and wherefores of its tree planting. The commission preserve specimens of the Whitty pear, found in the forest in the mid-seventeenth century and ancestor of those in the modern Evesham orchards.

The forest deer are hard to find, but a likely place is on walk No. 4, where the Ranger has his lookout by the edge of the beechwood and a salt lick is kept for the deer.

When the area was re-planted, around Walk No. 8, the Commission left some of the dead timber for nesting sites for owls and woodpeckers. The Wyre Forest warrants many visits to savour its infinite variety.

For another good walk and a wonderful view, climb Stagborough Hill, lower down the river, before visiting Arley Kings, the home of Layamon, priest of the church on the hill. He it was who wrote the first poem in English, 150 years before Chaucer.

The church, high on the hill at Areley Kings, stands by the village green and the half-timbered church house. The group which includes the church, its handsome Georgian vicarage and the buildings opposite, is completely unspoiled. The surrounding steep hillside offers a splendid view across Shropshire.

In the church, there is a modern memorial window to Layamon and an old inscription in the stone of the base of the font. The bowl is modern but the base of the font was unearthed during the restoration of the church. Its Latin inscription, translated, reads—"In the time of St Layamon". There seems little doubt that the place he refers to in his poem, is Areley Kings—"Ernley, a noble church on Severn's bank."

More modern benefactors at Areley Kings are the Lloyds, another branch of the Lloyd family which settled in Birmingham in the eighteenth century and founded Lloyd's Bank. There is a memorial in the church to Sampson Zachary Lloyd, and Mrs Zachary Lloyd presented 246 acres of land alongside the left bank of the river to the National Trust. This will protect some of the river bank from the encroachment of Stourport, which, away from the river, sprawls, with many small works of varying trades, until it joins Kidderminster. But despite this there is much beautiful country surrounding Kidderminster. Bewdley and the Severn are only three miles away, with the charming villages of Wolverley, Churchill and Bellbroughton close by and there are numerous walks along the Stour and the canal to Stourport. These natural rural beauties compensate for the haphazard siting of industry.

North of Kidderminster, leading out of the village of Wolverley, with its traces of rock dwellings cut in the steep sandstone rock below the church, is a lane leading up to Kingsford Park. This is Worcestershire's most recent country park, a 200-acre extension to the National Trust lands of Kinver Edge.

When completed, it is to be a park for pedestrians and equestrians to go their separate ways along paths clearly defined. The ground is mostly covered with silver birch and there are outcrops of the red sandstone rock which forms Kinver Edge. The woods are the haunt of a great variety of the smaller birds, a joy during the week. At weekends, since humans tend to walk in family groups, their chatter as they tramp along the paths, sends the birds, particularly the yellow hammers, out of sight. The chaffinches seem more accustomed to the human voice.

In the car park, a large scale map shows good circular walks and others which lead up to Kinver Edge, which has been the wind-swept property of the National Trust since the first world war. Here, the heather and gorse attract many butterflies and moths, and for those with the knowledge to recognise the species, many varieties of insects and snails.

Much of the Trusts 200 acres covers the long high ridge of Kinver Edge. Here the air is fresh and the views long. On one side is the valley of the Stour, so closely followed by the Staffordshire and Worcestershire Canal into Kidderminster, on the other, the farmlands and the woods by Enville Hall and the Common. These 400 acres in total, provide a stretch of woodland country and high ridge walks, and a sanctuary for birds and small mammals less then five miles from the centre of Stourbridge or Kidderminster.

The land for Kidderminster's park was presented by John Brinton, a member of one of the oldest carpet

Kidderminster Locks on the Staffordshire and Worcestershire Canal.

weaving firms. The weaving of carpets was developed in the district in the eighteenth century, to replace the declining trade of the cloth weavers, who had been established in the town as early as the thirteenth century.

There are a few Georgian buildings in Church Street, leading up to St Mary's Church, which has recently been isolated by the new ring road, but what is interesting about Kidderminster is its famous people.

John Baskerville, the printer and type-cutter, was born at Sion House at Wolverley. Sir Rowland Hill, who introduced the penny post, was born in Blackwell Street. Sir Josiah Mason, who endowed Birmingham's Josiah Mason College, came from Mill Street and, if it had not been for Thomas Foley, one of Kidderminster's industrialists, the beautiful church at Great Witley would not exist. Richard Baxter, who could not get on with the people of Bridgnorth, settled as a minister in Kidderminster and preached nonconformity throughout the Civil War and the regime of Cromwell. There is a statue of him in front of St Mary's and his oak chair is kept in the sanctuary.

Stourport is James Brindley's town. When Bewdley would have none of his canal scheme, he decided to follow the Stour Valley and join the Severn near a country inn. From that time, Stourport sprang up like magic. Its quays and warehouses replaced the inland port of Bewdley higher up the river. Now, the commercial traffic by canal has gone. But the riverside at Stourport and the canal basins at Mart Lane are ablaze with colourful pleasure boats. The long frontage of the central warehouse, with its nineteenth century brick and its elegant cupula, forms a quiet background to the gay marina.

The Tontine Inn backs on to the basin. A large garden in front slopes down to the river walk. This inn, originally in the centre of the building, was opened in 1788 by the Canal Company and now occupies five houses—those on either side of the original having been used formerly by hop merchants. The name Tontine refers to a financial scheme by which subscribers to the canal received annuities out of profits.

To the south of Stourport is Hartlebury Common, which despite its fringe of houses and small works, still offers walks along sandy paths. One of these leads to Hartlebury Castle, which for centuries was the home of the Bishops of Worcester. The present building dates from the seventeenth and eighteenth centuries and is in a variety of styles with battlements, lantern, sandstone wings, spacious outbuildings, cupula and lodges.

Only a small section of the moat remains to remind us of its military past. The castle, or fortified house, was begun about 1255 by Bishop Walter de Cantilupe and completed in the same century by Bishop Gieffard. It remained more or less undisturbed until it was destroyed during the Civil War, after being used as a prison by Cromwell.

The rebuilding has left us a conglomeration of styles of no great beauty; nevertheless, what the building lacks in beauty externally is compensated for by its interest within. The Worcestershire County Museum occupies the entire north wing. Interest is immediately aroused by the collection of hanging signs over the main entrance. These signs were hung outside craftsmens' shops, so that a glance along a street could quickly indicate the whereabouts and occupation of the various traders. No one would be likely to miss the handsome brass glove of the Worcestershire glove makers.

The museum is essentially a folk museum, built up originally from the collection made by Mr and Mrs J. F. Parker, who lived for many years at Tickenhill. Every year, the museum expands into the grounds, where a large hall has been built to house the collection of rare vehicles. It contains a great variety of bicycles, a decorative hearse, farm carts, carriages and early gypsy caravans. There is a blacksmith's shop, a wheelwright's shop, both equipped with tools ranging over many periods. There is also a cider mill dated about 1700. This is a recent acquisition, which was removed, complete with its half-timbered building and great stone press, from a Worcestershire farm and re-erected at Hartlebury. The walks in the grounds pass through beautiful avenues of chestnuts and beeches and a small nature reserve has been started—this already contains some rare wild flowers.

This part of Worcestershire is good walking country and there are many well-signposted public footpaths. At Chaddesley Corbett, a large-scale map of the district is posted in the lych-gate of the church. It shows all the rights of way in the district and gives an encouragingly detailed list of recommended walks and their attractions.

Chaddesley Corbett has one of the most beautiful village streets in the county. Beside the church is Lych-gate House. Its fine early Georgian façade faces the Talbot Inn, now handsomely restored in all its timber-framed glory. Elsewhere along the street are half-timbered yeoman's cottages and farmhouses. Part of the attraction of the street is the absence of that manifestation of Victorian respectability, the front garden.

The village was important in Saxon times and was one of the few places to be retained by its Saxon owner after the Conquest. The Corbetts were connected with Chaddesley throughout the centuries, until the death of the last member of the family in 1964.

In the church there is a brass to a Keeper and his family from Dunclent Park, which was at one time part of the great Feckenham Forest. The Keeper, who died in 1511, was appropriately named, Thomas Forest.

The two Scratch Dials on the south wall of the church are difficult to find, as they are barely visible in the crumbling stone, but one of them is more elaborate than

Hartlebury. Types of gypsy caravans may be seen in the Worcestershire Museum.

usual, with traces of numerals to indicate the time.

The carving on the font is thought to be about 1160. Although not considered by some to be the best work of the Hereford carvers, it is intriguing to try to unravel the complicated design of strange dragons with unicorn's horns. Or are they nor-whales?

One of the short walks recommended in the lych-gate leads to Harvington Hall. This picturesque Elizabethan house, surrounded by a large moat, was a Catholic stronghold for centuries. Now, with its acre of garden, it belongs to the National Trust. In the early sixteenth century, the house belonged to Humphrey Pakington, a lawyer, who is thought to have re-built the previous medieval building. There are memorials to the Pakingtons in St Cassian's Church at Chaddesley. Several of the Catholic priests who officiated at Harvington are buried in the chapel vault.

The Hall is riddled with ingenious 'priest holes' or hiding places, exciting for young visitors, who are allowed to climb in and out, but which were terrifying places for the many priests who were hidden by Mary Yates, the Lady of the Manor during the times of religious persecution.

I visited Harvington several times with fellow artists, when the Elizabethan wall paintings were being restored. Considered to be some of the best in Worces-

tershire, they show a Flemish influence in the arabesques and lush foliage and the elegant nudes with leafy tails.

The Hall belonged in the eighteenth and nineteenth centuries to the Throckmortons, who removed the original staircase to Coughton Court their house in Warwickshire.

Harvington Hall, where many Catholic priests were safely hidden in the ingenious priest holes.

CHAPTER TEN

Salute to Shakespeare

The Catholic Throckmortons, who lived at Coughton in Queen Elizabeth's reign, suffered, with many local families, from Protestant domination. They looked forward to the tolerance promised by James I, but finding this was not forthcoming, they became involved in the Gunpowder Plot, intended to destroy both King and Parliament.

Robert Catesby, chief instigator of the plot, was related to the Throckmortons, to the Leighs at Stoneleigh and the Wintours at Huddington.

Huddington Court, a sixteenth-century timber-framed house, surrounded by a moat and trim lawns, is one of the most picturesque houses in Worcestershire. It was here that the Catholic plotters met before leaving for London and it was here they rested for a short time after the failure of the plot, before continuing their flight into Wales.

Huddington is privately owned but a view of its architectural beauties, its gables, its slightly projecting oriel windows and its dovecots, may be enjoyed from the lane and from the lawn, which must be crossed in order to visit the small parish church of St James.

This simple grey stone Norman church complements the elaborate timbering of the house. The handsome marble tomb in the church is that of a later Wintour, not the unlucky Thomas, who was wounded when his cousin Robert Catesby was killed.

The arms of Thomas Wintour's father can be seen in one of the windows in part of the Raven Hotel in Droitwich, which, 400 years ago, was the Manor House of the Wintours.

An overall picture of the present town of Droitwich can be seen from the churchyard of St Augustine's at Dodderhill. This church, used as a barracks in 1646 by Cromwell's soldiers, is a fine vantage point. It stands high above what was the old town, which, before subsidence took place, was on the banks of the River Salwarpe and beside the once busy Droitwich canal. Little of the old lower town remains. What few buildings there are lean at strange angles around the thirteenth-century church of St Andrew itself struggling to remain vertical. Part of the old industrial waste land has been landscaped into walks beside the Salwarpe, leading

Stratford-upon-Avon. The fifteenth-century Guild Chapel, built by Sir Hugh Clopton, who also built the present stone bridge across the Avon.

to a statue of St Richard de Wyche, the town's patron saint, whose small chapel is in St Andrew's church.

The Roman name for Droitwich was Salinae (Salt Springs) and in the past, salt provided a livelihood for its people, though the subsidence, caused by draining the brine from the underground salt deposits into pits, was responsible for the downfall of its old buildings.

Many of the Salt Ways radiated from Droitwich and in Henry VIII's time, more than 300 furnaces were busy evaporating brine from the brine pits. The wet salt was first drained into baskets and then dried in ovens, to form salt loaves. From pre-Roman times, these loaves were transported along the Salt Ways by pack mule. One of these Saltways went past Romsley to supply the large requirements of the Abbey at Hales.

Before the days of refrigeration, salt was the main food preservative and was used in great quantities for packing meat and fish for winter use—especially when cattle had to be slaughtered for lack of winter fodder.

The modern salt works were at Stoke Prior, about four miles from Droitwich, but have recently been closed by Imperial Chemical Industries. The brine here was pumped to the surface from 1,000 feet below. It was at this works that John Corbett of Brierley Hill made his fortune. With the coming of the railways, he foresaw the decline in canal traffic, sold his fleet of barges and bought

Huddington Court. Owned by the Wintour family from the mid-fifteenth century. Here Thomas, his brother Robert and his cousin Robert Catesby planned the Gunpowder Plot.

the salt works. A trained engineer, he was able to bring up the brine from great depths and exploit the deposits of salt to greater advantage.

As a Member of Parliament, he was responsible for the introduction of many reforms and devoted much of his

202

wealth to good works. He gave Droitwich its brine baths and the Salters' Hall and was largely responsible for its development as a Spa town. The baths are beside the Winter Gardens in the town centre and the brine, which is far stronger than sea water, is used for remedial purposes. The baths also house a large heated swimming pool, open to the general public—a splendid place in which to learn to swim, as one immediately gains confidence from the extraordinary buoyancy of the water.

John Corbett married a French wife and built for her the Chateau Impney, in extensive parklands beside the Salwarpe. This vast brick and stone chateau in the Louis XIII manner, utterly divorced from the surrounding countryside, was designed by the Paris architect Tronguois. For many years now it has been a red-brick white elephant of a country hotel, since Droitwich has gradually declined as a Spa town, but the Chateau has just received an internal face lift in preparation for Common Market visitors and a hoped-for influx of tourism.

Far removed from the simple grey stone walls of St Andrew's, built after the fire which largely destroyed Droitwich in 1290, are the elaborate mosaics of the Roman Catholic church of the Sacred Heart. This red brick church in the Italian style, was consecrated in 1932. Except for the stone columns and the marble facing on the lower part of the walls, the interior is entirely covered with mosaic pictures. The small squares are cut from fine Venetian glass, and laid by skilled craftsmen to elaborate designs. The overall effect is overpowering.

According to Pevsner, "The most Italian ecclesiastic space in the whole of England" is not far away from Droitwich, at Great Witley. This superbly beautiful church, planned by the first Lord Foley, adjoins the ruins of Great Witley Court (burnt out in 1937) and is the parish church. It replaced the one existing at the beginning of the eighteenth century.

Between Droitwich and Great Witley, the banks of the Severn at Holt Fleet are crowded with caravans but it is possible to take a more peaceful view of the Severn from the Norman church at Holt, which stands high above the river, together with the remains of the Norman castle.

Continue on the A423 and the first entrance to the grounds of Witley Court (unsignposted), is at the lodge, just beyond the village of Little Witley. Even in ruins, with a colony of jack-daws as its only inhabitants, Witley Court is a handsome shell. The small church beside it is a pre-Rococo gem in white and gold. The magnificent oil paintings are by Antonio Bellucci. The painted glass, designed by Francisco Slater and painted by Joshua Price, is dated 1719–1721. The papier mâché work is by Henry Clay of Birmingham. All these treasures came to the church from Canons, the manor house built by the Duke of Chandos near Edgware, which was demolished in 1747. The paintings and glass were bought by the second Lord Foley and fitted into this small parish church with consummate skill, by the architect Gibbs.

It is extraordinary to walk from what is now a deserted but very English parkland, into a completely unexpected Italian church.

Witley Court, with its views across to the Abberley Hills, where Henry IV and Owen Glendower played cat and mouse, was a Jacobean house. It was bought in 1655 by Thomas Foley, son of the Kidderminster industrialist. Later, it was bought by the eleventh Lord Ward, first Earl of Dudley and rebuilt into a regal palace in 1860 by Samuel Dawkes.

This was burnt out in 1937 and the problem of what to do with the stately ruins has increased, since much of the beautiful stonework of the terraces, the orangery and the fountains which adorned the gardens, was sold some years ago.

One of the Salt Ways out of Droitwich passed through Bromsgrove, a small country town which recently lost many of its old buildings in a road widening scheme. What it lost in the cause of progress, is compensated for by its open air museum of buildings at Avoncroft, Stoke Heath.

This museum was begun by a group of enthusiasts, who, being unable to prevent the destruction of one of Bromsgrove's earliest timber-framed buildings in the main street, transported the timbers to the grounds of Avon Croft College and by 1967, had reconstructed it and in so doing started what was to prove to be a unique museum.

It is a struggling enterprise, with the usual lack of funds, but already these eager volunteers, having acquired some 10 acres of land, have, with the help of some of the country's leading architects, rescued and re-erected on this site a great variety of buildings, from the humble nailers' and chainmakers' workshops, to the handsome fourteenth-century roof from Gueston Hall at Worcester.

Wherever possible, the buildings are used for lectures, concerts and the occasional medieval feast. Part of the land has been set aside for the reconstruction of Iron-Age huts, with a view to showing the development through the ages of building and architecture. The aims of the museum are to stimulate public interest in historic buildings and, where possible, to prevent their total destruction. Each visit reveals further progress and the site, high up above Bromsgrove, by Stoke Heath, offers a

Bromsgrove. A Midland type post-mill from Dansey Green, Tanworth-in-Arden, reconstructed at the Avoncroft Museum of Buildings.

stimulating walk.

It is good walking country between the museum and Feckenham. Feckenham Forest once covered nearly 200 square miles across Worcestershire, from the Severn to the Warwickshire border. It was largely destroyed to supply fuel for the Droitwich salt works and had practically disappeared by the end of the seventeenth century.

Some idea of the great trees which grew there can be found on the walks which cross Pipers Hill and Dodderhill Common. Here, the giant oaks, the beeches and the swirling trunks of the great Spanish chestnuts, with their age-old carpet of leafmould, flaming with colour in the autumn, are reminders of the former glory of the forest.

Feckenham village still boasts a village green and in the church is a relic of John de Feckenham, the wood-cutter's boy, an unbending Roman Catholic, who became the last Abbot of Westminster.

From Feckenham, it is only a few miles to Coughton Park, with its fine avenue of elms, which one hopes will not fall prey to the Dutch Elm disease.

Coughton Court was given to the National Trust by Sir Robert Throckmorton, in 1946, so it is possible to enter by the great gateway built in 1509, to visit the room where some of the wives of the Gunpowder Plotters waited anxiously for news, and to see the Jacobean

Coughton Court. Inherited by the Throckmorton family in 1409. The central gate house was added in 1509.

staircase in the ballroom, which was removed from Harvington Hall.

At the back of the house, which now has its gateway flanked by Georgian Gothic wings is an Elizabethan courtyard. The parish church stands beside the house and contains the Throckmorton tombs and also some handsome brasses. In the churchyard is a sundial on an old preaching cross and the green of the ancient yews is enhanced by the dark red foliage of the recently planted prunus.

The lane beside the park leads down to a wide but shallow ford across the Arrow, where the banks are overgrown with wild balsam and young willow. From here, there is a choice of footpaths leading to Alcester.

The lane leads through Kinwarton past the old rectory and the small church with its wooden tower. Inside the church, there is a rare fifteenth-century alabaster carving, thought to be part of a reredos, which was discovered a hundred years ago among some rubbish, at Binton, a village four miles away. A large, circular dovecot, preserved by the National Trust, stands in a field nearby. It is thought to be about 600 years old and to have been part of a moated grange which once belonged to Evesham Abbey.

Both the footpaths and the lane bring one into Alcester at the quiet end, where the Arrow is joined by the Alne. The main road from Stratford to Evesham is at right angles to the main street, leaving a wide, peaceful approach to the church, round which it winds its way to the seventeenth-century Town Hall. The street has a variety of building styles—there are fine Georgian façades, half-timbered gables above the shops, and a number of attractive small cottages. Particularly charming are Butter Street, a stone-paved passageway round one side of the churchyard, and Malt Mill Lane, with its overhanging upper storeys and gardens which back on to the river.

Alcester has been a quiet place since its once thriving needlemaking industry moved to Redditch in the early nineteenth century and its mills fell into decay. The church contains the tomb of one of Warwick's Fulke Grevilles, who died in 1560. He was the grandfather of the more famous Fulke Greville, the friend of Sir Philip Sidney. There is also an elegant Chantrey tomb of the Seymours of Ragley Hall.

Several walks from Alcester, pass through the country to the north, and above Ragley Hall, returning to Ragley Park along the Ridgeway. From this high ground is one of the best views of the hall, a large Palladian mansion, designed in 1680 for the Seymour family by Robert Hooke.

When Henry VIII married Jane Seymour, her brother was created Earl of Hertford and later became Lord Protector to his young nephew, Edward VI.

The hall has remained the home of the Seymours and is open to the public during the summer. Visitors are encouraged to use and enjoy the extensive park with its peaceful walks and there are also boating facilities and a

Alcester. A village street of many architectural variations.

J. PRIDDEY

cricket ground.

From the walks within the park, one can recognise once again the hand of Lancelot Brown and appreciate the carefully planted banks of trees, the unexpected vistas and the beautiful lake. They were designed and laid out by him at Ragley in 1750.

After the glories of the hall, with its 400-acre park, the small villages along the valley of the Arrow should not be overlooked. Wixford's church is dedicated to St Milburga, daughter of Penda, the Saxon King of Mercia. The village and much of the surrounding property belonged to the Throckmortons, who built the almshouses. Exhall and Broom are delightful villages and so at the moment, are the Graftons, which are being defended by the conservationists against the threat of a new town development.

The Avon villages between Bidford and Stratford are in danger of river development, in the form of pleasure-boat moorings and the vexed question arises —by whom and how shall the countryside be enjoyed?

The narrow seven-arch bridge at Bidford-on-Avon, which for centuries has carried the section of Roman Icknield Street called Buckle Street, across to the Cotswolds, is in no danger, as it is one of Bidford's tourist attractions. The Romans used the ford here and Bidford is one of the few places where a Saxon cemetery has been found near a Roman road, although it conformed with the general Saxon practice of burying their dead near a river. The relics which were found may be seen at the New Place Museum in Stratford.

At Welford, where the Avon loops its way round the old part of the village, there is a maypole on the village green. A street of thatched cottages leads down to the weir. Beside the bridge, which spans two arms of the Avon, is a pub called 'The Four Alls', named after the old jingle—

> King rules over all,
> Parson prays for all,
> Soldier fights for all,
> Farmer pays for all.

A field path from Welford leads to the small village of Weston, where the church contains the tombs of the Warwickshire Grevilles, who at one time owned a castle on the hill commanding a view across to Clifford Chambers on the River Stour.

The town of Stratford-upon-Avon is expanding rapidly. The footpaths to Anne Hathaway's cottage at Shottery, the girlhood home of Shakespeare's wife, are a more pleasant route than the road, which cuts through the new housing estates. These unfortunately encircle the

Welford-on-Avon. Here the maypole dance is a living tradition.

small conservation area which has been reserved at Shottery. But the home of Shakespeare's mother, the Ardens' farm at Wilmcote, is however still surrounded by agricultural land.

The Ardens lived in this large timber-framed house in the sixteenth century, when their daughter married John Shakespeare of Snitterfield. The house has survived in such excellent condition largely because it was lived in until 1930, when it was acquired by the Shakespeare Birthday Trust. There has been no fundamental change in the structure or layout of the house and farm premises since Shakespeare's time.

They are open to the public as a period museum, which includes the dovecot, the cider mill, the stables, the dairy and the barns. Since 1930, the Trust has gathered together an extensive collection of items illustrating every aspect of country life. Each out-building contains a varied assortment of bygone tools, implements and equipment. It is a pleasure after touring such a comprehensive exhibition, to be able to sit quietly in the well kept garden, listening to the birds and absorbing the atmosphere of past centuries.

The stones for the foundations of the house and farm buildings, came from a local quarry at Wilmcote—the Forest of Arden provided the timber for the framing.

Wilmcote. Here, Shakespeare's mother, Mary Arden, spent her girlhood. Now a museum.

The centre of life in the forest was Henley-in-Arden. In the twelfth century, the clearing in the forest was dominated by the castle at Beaudesert.

O Beaudesert! Old Mountfort's lofty seat.
Haunt of my youthful steps.

wrote Richard Jago, the poet, to his friend William Shenstone, at Halesowen. (They both attended the Grammar school at Solihull.) Mountfort's seat is certainly lofty, but worth the steep climb for walks and views. The mound which towers above Beaudesert Church and the vicarage, where Richard Jago was born, was probably a fortified site before Thurston de Mountfort built his castle in the early twelfth century. Because of the protection Thurston's fortification gave to traders, and as a result of the plentiful supply of timber in the surrounding Forest of Arden, the village of Henley-in-Arden developed around the main highway between Birmingham and Oxford. By the Middle Ages, it was a busy market town.

It must have been a popular place for travellers in the coaching days, for at one time, it had more than a dozen inns. The 'Blue Bell' is a good example of fifteenth-century half-timbering, with its overhanging upper storey and its high gateway. Much of the 'Three Tuns' is seventeenth-century and the 'White Swan' is mainly sixteenth. Since the latter is the largest inn, it claims to have housed Dr Samuel Johnson on his return from Scotland, as Boswell recorded that they "... happened to lie at *the* Inn at Henley."

Many of the picturesque houses along the main street were once inns. The 'Cross Keys', the 'Bear and Ragged Staff', the 'George and Dragon' and the 'King's Head', have all been converted into private houses.

In the nineteenth century, exposed half-timbering was not the fashion. My grandfather lived at the White House and family photographs show it with a simple plastered Georgian façade. Many other buildings were the same, including the 'White Swan'. With the dawn of tourism, the fashion for half-timbering returned—every beam was exposed and many new ones added during the restoration of the original façades.

The Guild Hall, in the centre of the village, stands beside St John's Church and was built for the Guild, a social and religious order, which among other good works, presented Miracle and Mystery plays. The building was known as early as 1408 but after the dissolution of the Guilds, it was used for a variety of domestic purposes. Before it was restored in 1915, it had been a butcher's shop.

The ground floor room is now the public library and the Hall above is approached by a flight of stone steps from the delightful Garden of Rest at the rear. The civic treasures on display in the Hall include the charter granted by Henry VI in 1449, and a rare oak pitch-pipe used for pitching the voice in Beaudesert Church.

The tall stone house behind the Cross, the only building of its kind in the variety of period houses in Henley's

*Henley-in-Arden.
Many of the houses are
built with oak from the
Forest of Arden.*

wide main street, was once the asylum. My mother used to tell us gruesome stories of how the village boys of her youth taunted the chained inmates.

At that time, the vicar of St John's Church, beside the Guild Hall, was G. E. Bell, several of whose twelve children were authors. The best known, perhaps, is John Keeble Bell (Keeble Howard) whose plays were popular in the early 1920s. His farce, *Lord Babs*, was playing in London at the time of his death in 1928. There is a memorial to him in the church, the fabric of which was extensively restored in 1856.

Very different is the Saxon sanctuary at St Peter's Church at Wooton Wawen, the oldest church in Warwickshire. Wahen the Saxon gave the settlement its name and built his cruciform church on the rising ground about 1045.

When the Normans spread out over Britain, the manor of Wooton was granted to Thurston de Mountfort and St Peter's Church was enlarged to become the mother church of Henley-in-Arden and Ullenhall. During the first 400 years of its existence, the church was enlarged to almost three times the size of Wahen's building but the sanctuary remained virtually untouched.

The mechanism of an early tower clock, with good examples of hand-forged iron cogwheels, has been preserved.

According to Dugdale, the windows in his time contained the arms of many local families—the Catesbys, Harewells, Staffords, Beauchamps and the Hastings, and also the arms of the Abbey of Conchis in Normandy. The church was given to the monks of Conchis shortly after the Conquest by Robert de Stafford. Papers in the record office show that Sir George Throckmorton was commissioned in Edward VI's time to take an inventory of items in the ecclesiastic buildings in Warwickshire.

There are half-timbered cottages along the bend in the road, where the Bull's Head Inn, well prepared for tourism, with its secondary title, La Tête de Boeuf, presents a Tudor façade.

Wooton Hall stands in a wooded park beside the church. The River Alne flows through the grounds and splashes down a large curved weir, beside the roadside mill. The house was built in the Italian style about 1687, for the Smythe family. Maria Ann Smythe, who spent her childhood there, was the great love of George IV. As the widowed Mrs Fitzherbert, her beauty and charm fascinated him and she became his morganatic wife in 1785.

On the hill, just after the road passes under the aqueduct, is the Navigation Inn. This used to serve the bargees from the busy Stratford canal, but now has a large car park, a wharf for the touring long boats and a hiring office. In spring, the canal banks are covered with primroses and violets, which as children, we picked while listening to my mother's stories about the maypole dances and the wakes, which were held on the green, outside the Bull's Head, and the annual donkey race from the 'Navigation' to the 'Bull'.

Behind the 'Bull', a lane winds round the foot of the low Alne Hills, crosses the River Alne and leads to Aston Cantlow. The village is famous for its Shakespeare connections. John Shakespeare from Snitterfield and Mary Arden from Wilmcote, the poet's parents, are reputed to have been married in the church and to have taken their wedding breakfast at the 'King's Head'. The clock in the church tower, by a fourteenth-century smith, and one of the oldest in England, no doubt ticked the time away that day, but the church register of the memorable marriage is missing.

At the end of the lane, between the church and the inn, is the site of the castle of the de Cantilupes. The last of the line was killed at the battle of Evesham and the castle was demolished. Walter de Cantilupe, one of the foremost ecclesiastics of his time, became Bishop of Worcester, was a friend and adviser of Simon de Montfort and openly defied the King. He joined the Barons and fortified his manor house at Hartlebury, but was

Aston Cantlow, once owned by the medieval de Cantilupe family, remembered as the wedding place of Shakespeare's parents.

forced to retire after the battle of Evesham.

The site of the de Cantilupes castle has been repeatedly ploughed, over the centuries and there is little to remind us of its existence except perhaps for the name, Castle Farm, on the gate.

After their marriage, the young Shakespeares lived in

Stratford-upon-Avon and their famous son William, was born at a house in Henley Street.

Stratford has developed into a Mecca for international tourists. With the completion of the new Hilton Hotel and the possibility, after nearly 150 years of wrangling, of a good road bridge across the Avon, the town seems to be set fair to continue selling its postcards, souvenirs and theatre tickets for a long time to come.

The planning authorities have at last obtained a conservation order for the centre of the town, and many of the buildings, especially those with half-timbering, are being most carefully restored. This follows a lead given in 1910 by Stratford's much maligned and rather unwelcome citizen, Marie Corelli, who spent £200 on the restoration of the Tudor House, on the corner of Ely Street and High Street. When the plaster was removed from this corner shop, elaborate half-timbering was disclosed, which had remained covered for 200 years.

The people of Stratford did not appreciate their Shakespeare until a growing interest in his works began to develop in the early eighteenth century. Many provincial towns held puritanical views about the 'wicked London theatre' and Stratford-upon-Avon was no exception. In 1622, the King's Players were paid six shillings from the borough funds NOT to perform in the town. It was not until 1746 that the first Shakespearean productions were allowed into Stratford and only then on condition that the strolling players gave five shillings to the poor of Stratford.

The first Shakespearean Festival was organised by David Garrick in 1769, after the corporation had persuaded him to present a bust of Shakespeare for their new Town Hall.

An elaborate octagonal amphitheatre, to seat 1,000 and to accommodate an orchestra, was erected on the Bancroft, beside the Avon. This time, the citizens joined whole-heartedly in the preparations for the festival. Shops, houses and inns were decorated, masquerade costumes and favours were imported and sedan chairs procured to convey the gentry around the town. This proved to be a popular innovation as the weather was far from good, but the rain did not dampen the firework pictures nor detract from the brilliantly lit transparences which lined the opposite bank.

The festival lasted three days. There were banquets, balls and concerts. Music composed by Dr Arne and Odes to Shakespeare written by David Garrick, yet Shakespeare's own words remained unheard throughout the entire festivities.

The festival brought heavy financial losses for Garrick but nationwide publicity for Stratford-upon-Avon and this, together with improved means of transport, has brought visitors flocking to see the birthplace and the poet's tomb.

In 1824, the Shakespeare Club (which still exists) was founded to arrange periodic festivals in honour of the poet.

About the same time, a Mrs Hornby lived at the Birthplace. She was described by Washington Irving as— "a garrulous old lady in a frosty red face . . . garnished with artificial locks of flaxen hair, curling from under an exceedingly dirty cap. She was particularly assiduous in exhibiting the relics, with which this, like all other celebrated shrines abounds." For a considerable consideration, Mrs Hornby could be persuaded to part with her precious relics.

When the house came on the market in 1847, it was purchased as a national memorial and it was that decision which was the genesis of Stratford as a tourist centre.

The Trustees and Guardians of the Birthplace were formally incorporated by a special Act of Parliament in 1891. Ever since, they have taken into their care all the historic buildings which have had any connection with Shakespeare and his family.

As the poet observed—"The play's the thing". Where could one be seen? Visiting companies during the second half of the eighteenth century played in theatres in Greenhall Street, Henley Street and Rother Market. The first theatre to be specially built for a Shakespeare festival, was planned by members of the Shakespeare Club in 1827. It stood in Chapel Lane for nearly fifty years, in what is now the Greater Garden of New Place.

But this was not enough for that great Shakespeare enthusiast Charles Edward Flower, who inaugurated the Shakespeare Memorial Association, with the object of building a theatre for the performance of Shakespeare's plays, the founding of a library of dramatic literature and a Shakespeare Museum.

Persistent, despite the scorn of London's critics and the apathy of the townsfolk, he pressed on, providing the land, near to the site where Garrick's Rotunda had stood a century earlier, and succeeded, largely at his own expense, in seeing a theatre built.

"A piece of pinchbeck nineteenth-century medievalism" is how one critic described the theatre. But for all its turrets, gables and fussy timbering, it was loved by many famous actors.

The first performance took place on Shakespeare's birthday in 1879. The unhappy choice, *Much Ado About Nothing,* gave the London critics another chance to mock, to deride the building, the Festival and even the audience.

"The whole business of the Memorial Theatre at

217

Stratford Memorial Theatre Museum. Part of the old building saved from the fire in 1926.

Stratford-upon-Avon is a solemn farce"; if Shakespeare was to be performed, it should be in London. If the critics were alive today, they would have to admit "the solemn farce" is having a very long run.

Charles Flower's much maligned theatre was burned down in 1926 and when Mr (later Sir) Archibald Flower

assumed responsibility for raising the money for a new theatre, it flowed in from all parts of England, America, the Dominions and, in fact, the whole of the civilised world.

Bernard Shaw greeted the news of the fire typically: "Stratford-upon-Avon is to be congratulated on the fire . . ." He welcomed the proposal for a new theatre with "It shows theatre sense." But as all who have presented plays there know, it was years before the stage was cleared of a surfeit of mechanical devices and the theatre provided with adequate front of house lighting, more seats, and box-office telephones sufficient to cope with the ever increasing demand for tickets.

A later production of *Much Ado* was my first experience of Shakespeare and was my first visit to a theatre —the trip being a special treat for my seventh birthday. I did not understand one word of the play, despite my mother's efforts to explain it to me on the train journey home. She eventually gave up in despair but hoped at least that I would never forget Frank Benson's wonderful performance as Benedick. What I never forgot was the magic of the scenery and the costumes, of people walking around creating beautiful pictures, and the vague, childish desire this gave me to create this kind of picture myself.

I don't remember whether my mother was best pleased

to see her favourite actor, Frank Benson, or her favourite novelist, Miss Marie Corelli, whom we saw during the afternoon driving along Church Street in her small pony chaise. I was delighted with the two small Shetland ponies, if unimpressed by the fat little lady whose novels had broken 'best seller' records. At the height of her fame, she was a friend of the King and of many of the great people of her time, and was the only literary personality invited to attend the coronation.

Two wars and hundreds of productions later, I was designing the costumes in which members of 'The Crazy Gang' were to drive round the Coliseum stage in that selfsame chaise.

Mason Croft, Marie Corelli's house in Church Street, where crowds waited for a sight of her, was at that time covered with creeper and gay with window boxes. It had a porch and a small front garden. Today, the façade has been stripped bare, and the house is used as a Shakespeare Institute by the University of Birmingham. A small plaque records the tenure by Marie Corelli from 1901 to 1924.

The comparison is odious, but Shakespeare's plays waited two centuries for the recognition they deserved; from then on, their popularity has increased year by year, whereas Marie Corelli's works sold in thousands on publication. *The Sorrows of Satan* and *The Mighty Atom* were household and palace words, yet the author and her works were almost forgotten before she died in 1924.

By 1943, there was no money left for the upkeep of Mason Croft, which she had left as her personal museum. It was a case of 'Going-going-gone!' for the house and contents and all her personal treasures, were sold by auction.

Feckenham. Once the centre of the great Worcestershire Forest and the home of Mary Tudor's chaplain, John of Feckenham, the last Abbot of Westminster.

CHAPTER ELEVEN

Chapels and Castles

A bold scheme for a navigable circular cruise of the south Midlands is being completed by the Inland Waterways Association. It includes Birmingham, Worcester, Tewkesbury, Evesham and Stratford-upon-Avon—the Birmingham Worcester Canal is already open. At Worcester, boats join the Severn and proceed to Tewkesbury—here they join the Avon to travel up to Evesham.

Work on the canal from Birmingham to Stratford was completed by voluntary labour, with financial help from the National Trust. The last lock on this section of the canal is in the Bancroft Gardens at Stratford and lowers the level of the canal water to that of the Avon—it was officially opened by the Queen Mother in 1964.

On the Upper Avon, between Evesham and Stratford, the work of dredging, lock-building and restoration, has gone on steadily and the opening of an extra 17 miles of the Upper Avon is within sight. The nine miles from Evesham to Barton are well used and four locks between Stratford and Barton will shortly be in use.

When the dredging work is completed, it is hoped to extend the popular river walks. The walk from Stratford through Weston-on-Avon to Welford, is clearly defined, as is the one to Clifford Chambers, a charming village on the Stour. Here, the path leaves the river and continues across meadows to re-join the Stour at Preston.

By alternating between field paths and lanes, the Stour can be closely followed until it flows under the main road into the grounds of the hotel at Ettington Park.

On the upper reaches of the Avon above Stratford is the village of Alveston, with elegant houses bordering the village green. Beyond the weir at Alveston, the river is suitable for small boats as far as Charlecote and from the river is one of the loveliest views of the stone bridge at Charlecote Park, in which the deer may sometimes be seen at the water's edge.

Shakespeare is supposed to have been caught poaching deer in Charlecote Park, though some say that there were no deer in the park in Shakespeare's time. There are so few authentic records of the 52 years of Shakespeare's life that fancy out-weighs fact. One story has it that he was reprimanded by Sir Thomas Lucy at Charlecote and in revenge, caricatured him in the plays

Warwick. The Lord Leycester Hospital and the chapel built over Westgate.

as Justice Shallow. Yet another maintains that Shallow was based on the character of a London magistrate William Gardner, whom the poet particularly disliked. And of course, there is the school of thought which declares that Francis Bacon and many others wrote the plays anyway.

The present house in Charlecote park was built for Thomas Lucy in 1558, built in the form of an E, as a compliment to his Queen, who knighted him in 1566 and paid a visit to his new house six years later. The Tudor gateway and the brewhouse are much as they were in the time of Elizabeth I.

The family took the name of Fairfax Lucy in 1892, when the Lucy heiress married Sir Henry William Ramsey Fairfax, Bart. In the early 1920s, Marie Corelli was a frequent visitor at Charlecote, and was presented with a Lucy heirloom, a carved oak chair, inscribed "Richard, Viscount Lumley of Waterford. 1675." This intriguing inscription was traced back to Lady Elizabeth Lucy, who bore several children to Edward IV, surnamed Plantagenet. One of the Lumleys married Lady Lucy's daughter, Elizabeth Plantagenet.

Charlecote was handed over to the National Trust by Sir Montgomerie Fairfax Lucy in 1946.

Barford, which is a village mainly of brick cottages,

Hampton Lucy. A village near Charlecote Park named after the Lucy family. The nineteenth-century church was designed by Thomas Rickman.

redeemed by a few Georgian houses, seems a homely place after the elegance of Charlecote. It is the centre of a farming community and was the birthplace of Joseph Arch, the farm labourer, born in a cottage opposite the church, who founded the Agricultural Workers' Union and fought, as an M.P., for the rights of farm workers, at the end of the nineteenth century.

A stone bridge of five arches crosses the Avon at Barford, and across the fields, can be seen the graceful spire of Sherbourne Church, designed by Sir Gilbert Scott, which, with a small group of cottages, hardly constitute a village. There is no pub and no shop and, when I lived at Sherbourne some two miles from the church we had to cross the fields to Barford to do the shopping. But during 20 years connection with Sherbourne, I never once regretted the isolation.

I came to know intimately its fields, woods, lanes and streams. I was able to walk for miles on an estate around the cottage, without crossing a road. I could follow a fox along a path in a larch wood or sit down-wind of a vixen on a summer evening and watch her playing with her cubs.

The chimney in the cottage by Sherbourne Brook was simple, square and open to the sky. Rain spluttered down on to the logs on a stormy night. Bats found their way down at first light and slept during the day in the hollow of a cast-iron fender. Nightingales sang in a larch wood, which in the spring was carpeted with white violets, followed by heartsease and a succession of summer flowers. Wild orchids grew in the boggy land beside the stream and a pair of otters played in its clear water, until the village boys discovered them and frightened them away. But a pair of kingfishers brought up their family successfully in a hole in its sandy bank.

There is nothing quite so wonderful as sleeping out, not in a stuffy tent on the ground, but on a cut rick, under the shelter of a high open Dutch barn, able to watch the comings and goings of the night creatures. A white barn owl lived in a brick and stone barn in my favourite rickyard. Each night, it flew low along the hedges, in search of food. I watched it come in and go out but never found its sleeping place. The small Spanish owls were not so shy—they flew in and out of the Dutch barn and often spent the day there. All kinds of small birds slept in the rick and after dark, it was possible to put a hand in the barely visible holes and touch their warm feathers.

When the wind was right, the chimes of the clock in St Mary's tower in Warwick could be heard above the hoot of the owls. Then, with the light of day, the Warwick skyline appeared in the distance, dominated by the pinnacled church tower, rising 175 feet above the town.

The castle was built on an escarpment above the River Avon and the town on the rising rock beyond —consequently the tower of St Mary's is a landmark for miles around. In 1694, the centre of Warwick was de-

Barford. Joseph Arch, the agricultural labourers' friend, is not forgotten.

stroyed by fire and the oldest buildings are to be found on what was the periphery of the old town. Mill Street, separated from the town by the castle, escaped destruction. Oken's House and neighbouring half-timbered houses close by the castle wall in Castle Street were not destroyed, nor were the two remaining gates with their adjacent buildings at the East and West ends of the main street.

Today's visitors to Warwick and Stratford, with coach-parks packed and streets crowded with tourists, may not realise how good it was to have known both towns in the days of petrol rationing. Then, they were more ordinary country towns and the theatre audience at Stratford was composed of local people, evacuees and occasional airmen. The few Red buses in Warwick drove slowly up Jury Street, prepared to stop for the castle peacocks to make their lordly way back to the park. Nowadays the peacocks wisely confine their contact with the town to an occasional perch on the park walls.

The present castle walls form an irregular quadrangle. First came Caesar's Tower and then Guy's Tower and later, two smaller towers were added by Richard III and his brother Clarence, both sons-in-law of Warwick the King-Maker, who was more kingly in both possessions and renown, than the king himself. But it was King Alfred's Æthelfleda, in 914, who first made and fortified the mound on which Henry de Newburgh later erected his Norman castle.

The impressive state apartments, which were added in the reign of James I and have since been modernised and enlarged, give this feudal fortress the appearance of a palatial country house, with gigantic 'follies' in the grounds.

The castle park was laid out in 1749 by Lancelot Brown, but it was a difficult site, even for his genius. Restricted by the Avon on the south and the town on the north, he managed to give an illusion of length to the entrance carriage-way, by taking it in a great curve, through a cutting in the rock, and by planting banks of trees.

He isolated the park from Castle Lane and the town by a long belt of trees and then had to content himself with steep lawns sloping down to the Avon.

From the windows of the state rooms in the castle, one looks down on the remains of the old bridge, which connected Mill Street with the coach road to Banbury until some of its seven arches were washed away in a flood towards the end of the eighteenth century. It had served the people of Warwick well, since 1375, but the loss was not serious, since the handsome single-span bridge, designed by William Eborall and sited to give a magnificent view of the castle, had already been provided by the reigning Earl, George Greville.

As there are no trees in the streets of Warwick, the two small gardens hidden away between the buildings in the town centre offer a welcome respite from sightseeing. The smaller, but none the less charming one, is the Quakers' garden, opposite the Leycester Hospital. From the top of the garden steps, above the road traffic, it is possible to appreciate the gables and half-timbered front of the Hospital, which otherwise can only be viewed at an angle from High Street, as the road drops steeply downhill.

The Pageant Garden in Castle Street is protected by a high wall. It is an unexpected and a peaceful place, with its large Spanish-chestnut tree and seats from which the façade of the Courthouse with the long windows of the elegant upstairs ballroom can be seen. This building dates from 1725.

Beside St Mary's Church, there is a narrow pathway called Tink-a-Tank, which passes between the churchyard and the high stone wall of the Priest's House. The only explanation I could find for the unusual name was given to me by inhabitants, who said it had always been the children's name for the strange echoing sound their feet made as they skipped along the stone flags.

There is no echo in Mill Street, which since the destruction of the old bridge has become a quiet cul-de-sac; the Tudor buildings are beautifully preserved converted into houses, and their gardens slope down to the Avon.

Another building to escape the fire was the Guildhall beside the West Gate, founded by Richard II but acquired and endowed by the Earl of Leicester in 1571 as a hospital for a Master and twelve Brethren.

One of the brethren is usually available to conduct visitors round this old building. Its small chapel is built over Westgate, which was hollowed out of the original sandstone cliff when the town was built.

The seventeenth-century Market Hall, in the centre of the road, at the end of Market Place, was in danger of destruction to make way for bus stops, but was rescued and is used as a County Museum, as is St John's House, at the east end of the town. This is a Jacobean house built by Anthony Staughton on the site of the Hospital of St John, founded by William de Newburgh in the reign of Henry II. The Newburghs were the first family to hold the castle after the Conquest. Since then it has passed by marriage to the famous families of Beauchamp, Neville, Dudley and Greville.

The parish church of St Mary was destroyed in the fire, with the exception of the Chancel, the Chapter House and the Chapel of our Lady, better known now as the Beauchamp Chapel. In the church, are the tombs of the various families who owned the castle—an alabaster monument to Thomas Beauchamp, builder of Caesar's Tower, a medieval brass in the Chapter House to a later Thomas Beauchamp who built Guy's Tower, a monument to Fulke Greville, who served Queen Elizabeth I and King James, and in the Chapel is all the golden splendour of Richard Beauchamp's tomb.

Landor House, by East-gate, built in 1692, was the birthplace of that explosive personality and poet, Walter Savage Landor. He fought Napoleon in Spain at his own expense at the head of his own regiment and returned, a sadder, if not wiser man, to write his poem 'Count Julian'. He was befriended by Southey in his youth and was cared for by Browning in his poverty-stricken old age. His works were in our school curriculum before we were old enough to appreciate the subtlety of his epigrams and satire. We preferred the rousing poems of John Masefield, whom Warwick claims as one of her famous men, as he attended the old Grammar School. A friend of Sir Barry Jackson, he was another of the personalities we were allowed to meet in our student days, when we were given crowd work in his production of *The Faithful*.

Another early seventeenth-century house, its future use as yet undecided, is Marble House. It is a typical wealthy merchant's house of the period, and stood outside the town in a country lane called The Jitty, but has now been surrounded by a housing estate. The Jitty crossed the end of Theatre Street, which once boasted a playhouse. Here, William Charles Macready played, after a triumph at the old Stratford theatre in Chapel Street.

In a house in Linen Street, close to Theatre Street, a girl cried bitterly, as she left her beloved Warwick to emigrate with her family to the United States. In 1888, in Michigan, her daughter, Clara Bryant, married the neighbour's son, Henry Ford. When he was a millionaire, he brought Clara and his children to visit the old house in Linen Street. A keen collector of period engines, he discovered Warwick's horse-drawn steam fire engine, which was eventually shipped to his museum in America.

The engine was a 400-gallon 'Double Vertical', made by Shand, Mason and Co. This intricate machine in shining brass, with its twin cylinders, gauges, steam valves and levers all exposed to view, was the delight of the small boys of Warwick, who raced along beside it to fires in order to see it working.

One of the last fires attended by the engine was the one at the Memorial Theatre at Stratford in 1926. As the horses struggled up Sherbourne Hill, they were overtaken by the motor-driven engine from Leamington, but once at the fire, the crew regained their morale when the

227

Warwick's horse-drawn fire engine, now in the Henry Ford Museum, U.S.A.

jet of water from their steam-driven pump rose far higher than that of any from the seven motor engines in attendance.

Another delight of Warwick children was to ride on the horsedrawn trams between Warwick and Leamington. Even the young Grevilles from the castle joined in the fun of jumping off the tram at the humped canal bridge to help push the tram over the hump.

During the last war, we could have used some help at the East Gate. Cars used to drive down Jury Street, straight under the East Gate arch and only lorry traffic took the road round it. One freezing Sunday dawn, I left the Memorial Theatre, driving my car in front of the last load of scenery, already late for the opening in Coventry because the intense cold of the January night had frozen the radiators.

Automatically, I drove through the arch and the sleepy lorry driver followed into but not through it—he was stopped as if by some unseen hand. The engine was all right, the sides of the lorry just cleared the walls of the arch, but the lorry could only move backwards or forwards a few feet. The windows of the chapel above the arch rattled their protest—an ancient monument disturbed by Cinderella's ballroom as the lorry revved up and lurched to and fro, It was of no avail. The driver's mate had to skid up the hoar-frosted scenery to try to unload it piece by piece. After the first few pieces were at last levered slowly from under the tight securing rope, the gremlin was disclosed. The iron hook which once held the town gate's arch lantern, was hooked securely round the load rope. An hour later and numb with cold, we left East Gate and the sleeping town of Warwick.

Today, the town of Warwick is well supplied on the fringe with open spaces. St Nicholas Park stretches along the Avon from Castle Bridge to an entrance on the Leamington Road, and Priory Park from the railway to Northgate.

Westward of the Rock, lie the common and the racecourse—an ideal green belt, now in jeopardy owing to the conflict over the siting of the relief road. There is also the paramount question of the future of Warwick —should it develop its tourist trade or become a light industry and shopping centre? It is difficult for the visitor, enjoying the magnificent castle and traces of the medieval walled town and the remaining Georgian buildings, to appreciate fully the traffic problems of the people living and working in the town.

Looking at the long term building plans, it is not easy for a lover of the lanes and field paths around this part of Warwickshire to look forward to the time when Warwick, Leamington, Kenilworth and Barford may be one vast conurbation—eventually linked up with Stratford and Coventry.

Country parks as fresh-air centres are excellent, but not quite the same as favourite field paths, walks along a hedgerow, across a brook and through a wood. The car left behind, and only an occasional walker to disturb bird-watching and observation of the tracks of small creatures and the occasional sighting of the rarer wild flowers. Then the private rewards of the countryside are at their best.

At Sherbourne, there was 'First and Last', a magnificent chestnut in a hedgerow, always the first tree to show its sticky buds and the last to shed its yellowing leaves. The road builders who had to cut it down, would not have heard the locals' nostalgic remark, "First and Last's gone, then. What's next?"

With this in mind, I enquired about the historic site at Guy's Cliff. The chantry chapel is graded as a No. 2 Building and scheduled as an ancient monument. There is hope for its ultimate preservation, although at the time of writing it is in a sorry state. The house, a toppling ruin, has been empty since the first world war and, like Great Witley Court, is home for many jackdaws.

Adjoining the back of the house is the chapel of St Mary Magdalen, dating from the reign of Henry VI (1422-61). John Rous, the historian, a native of Warwick, was one of the two chantry priests who lived at the Hermitage. The windows of the chapel are boarded up and it is impossible to go inside as it is used as a store.

The original Hermitage is said to have been set up by St Dubritius in the sixth century. The cells are clearly visible, hollowed out of the rock, but the cave, the resort of the hermit Guhthi in the tenth century and later of Guy of Warwick, after a surfeit of Crusades, is unapproachable.

A new housing estate has already reached Guy's Cliff on the Warwick side and the grounds of the ruined home of the Greatheeds is occupied by huts and engineers' equipment.

Bertie Greatheed, the dramatist, was the son of Samuel Greatheed (1710–1765) and his wife, Lady Mary Bertie, was the daughter of the Duke of Ancaster. When Sarah Kemble fell in love with William Siddons, whom her father considered a poor actor and unsuitable husband, she was sent from her father's touring company to a post as maid to Lady Mary. The servants' hall rang with her recitations from Shakespeare and Milton and occasionally, she was invited upstairs to entertain the guests. After two years, she ran away to marry her William Siddons in Coventry but remained a friend of the Greatheeds. When she and her brother John Kemble were famous, they played in Bertie Greatheed's ill-fated production of *The Regent* at Drury Lane in 1788.

Samuel Greatheed added the Saxon mill to his estate in 1780. Now used as a restaurant, it remains in good repair. The mill wheel is flood-lit at night and kept in running order so that it can be seen by the diners through the plate glass floor above it.

The mill was given to the Austin canons at Kenilworth by Geoffrey de Clinton, whose father had founded the abbey in 1122. The date of the present mill building is uncertain and at one time it was two mills under one roof, using the central driving power. The building beyond the wheel has an old timber balcony, favoured by many Midland artists, including David Cox. From this balcony there is a good view downstream across the foaming waters of the weir and along the river as it bends out of sight around the high sandstone cliff.

The field walk over the weir bridge, up the hill to Old Milverton Church, is particularly rewarding. On the way back, from the height of the path, there is a dramatic view of the cliff, rising sheer from the river. Towering above the trees, are the ruins of the house with the small chapel clinging precariously to the edge of the cliff.

After Warwick, it is interesting to visit Leamington, a complete contrast in town planning. Whereas Warwick is an example of a medieval plan, Leamington has an early nineteenth-century grid-iron plan. There are wide streets, avenues of trees and elegant Regency terraces, squares and crescents. As yet, it does not suffer from Warwick's traffic problems, though there are too many minor crossroads.

As a Spa town, it is not so historic as Bath or as large as Cheltenham, but it has much to offer. The residential

Guy's Cliff. The bridge path over the weir, which leads to Old Milverton.

part of the town was designed for the land north of the River Leam, while the canal, railway, commercial section and artisan dwellings were kept, where possible, to the south of the river. The town owes much to the good taste of Edward Willes, on whose estate most of it was built. He had the foresight to preserve the banks of the

Leam for parks and gardens, unlike Warwick, where so much of the Avon is hidden from the public, despite persistent pressure for river walks.

Edward Willes presented his Newbold Meadows to the town and their 13 acres and large lake now provide an ornamental garden of outstanding beauty—named the Jephson Gardens, in memory of Dr Henry Jephson, who was largely responsible for the Spa's medical reputation.

Although the fashion for 'taking the waters' had declined by 1860, the Pump Room, with its baths and medical facilities has survived and today thousands of National Health patients benefit from the variety of treatments available. A very different clientèle from the gentry who made the Pump Room so popular when Queen Victoria graciously allowed Leamington Spa to be called Royal in 1838.

Another name was changed by gracious permission. William's Hotel, opened in 1819 by a former butler of the Greatheed family of Guy's Cliff, was re-named The Regent, after the Prince visited the Spa while staying at Warwick Castle.

Leamington's houses have a variety of particularly beautiful ironwork in their balconies, railings and verandah supports. A walk round Lansdowne Circus, the full beauty of which cannot be otherwise appreciated due to

Leamington. Lansdowne Crescent, one example of the town's elegant Georgian buildings.

the wealth of greenery in the centre garden, will disclose a splendid variety of intricate patterns.

Although many of the large houses, some of which housed the exiled Napoleon III and his friends, have been turned into flats, preservation orders and the co-operation between the County Planning Officer and the tenants have saved the buildings from deterioration.

Two plans are under way for the future. One is a continuation of the riverside walk beside the Leam from Victoria Park to its confluence with the Avon; the other is the proposed Newbold Comyn Park, with 200 acres of open country watered by the Leam. When complete this will offer facilities for sailing, camping, riding and walking, as well as organised sports.

Leamington claims to have the oldest lawn tennis club in England. The game was developed there from the Spanish game of pelota, introduced by J.B.A. Pereira, a resident Spanish merchant. It was played with friends of Dr Haynes, on the lawn of the Manor House, and the game gradually developed into lawn tennis. A plaque in the grounds of the Manor House, now a hotel, records its origin in 1872.

The Theatre in Leamington has had a chequered career. There was the Royal Music Hall and the Temple of Drama, which, in its heyday in 1828, attracted packed houses to see William Charles Macready, who had lived as a boy near the Old Bowling Green Inn. The Clement Street theatre was opened by Mr and Mrs Charles Kean in 1848 and before the last war, a repertory company was struggling along at the Regent Theatre. Today the torch is carried by the Loft Theatre Players, an amateur company blessed with a newly built, intimate little theatre on the bank of the Leam, facing the pleasure grounds.

The village of Stoneleigh and the country town of Kenilworth lie between Leamington and Coventry. Stoneleigh Park, and the house where Jane Austin was a guest of the Leighs, provides a view of the winding Avon with its beautiful bridges. The park now accommodates a permanent agricultural show ground and also the School of Farm Mechanisation. Seasonal visitors and the exhibitors arrive by the thousand and many of the surrounding lanes have of necessity become main roads, though the village of Stoneleigh has been by-passed. The small group of cottages, with the forge on the green, are peaceful enough. In the stone church along the lane by the Avon are the vaults of the Lords Leigh and the black and white tomb of Lady Alice Leigh. Her father was Lord Mayor of London and attended the coronation of Elizabeth I. Alice married Sir Robert Dudley, son of the Queen's favourite, the Earl of Leicester. When her father-in-law died, Alice became mistress of Kenilworth

Castle. Her errant husband eloped to Italy with Lady Sheffield—never to return to his sorrowing wife and children.

Kenilworth is developing rapidly but has little to recommend it other than the history of the castle ruins. To the west of the spreading town is a pleasant green, backed by a row of brick and stone cottages which face the ruins of the once magnificent castle, founded originally about 1120 by Geoffrey de Clinton. From then onwards, it was used, improved and enlarged by successive owners. It reverted to the Crown when Robert Dudley was hanged for treason, but was returned by Elizabeth I to Dudley's son Robert, whom she created Earl of Leicester in 1564.

After the Dissolution, the site of Kenilworth Abbey had been granted to Robert Dudley's father and the young Robert was able to use much of the Abbey material for the extensive new building, which he had carried out at the castle.

When the Queen visited him in 1575, Leicester entertained her there for nineteen days, with a display of pageantry and splendour which has rarely been equalled, each day's entertainment costing £1,000.

After the Civil War, much of the castle was destroyed, though Leicester's Gatehouse and barn survived and were used as dwellings until after the last war.

On 17th November 1958 Lord Kenilworth presented the castle to the people of Kenilworth—it was an appropriate date, as it commemorated the four-hundredth anniversary of Queen Elizabeth's accession.

The ruins are in the care of the Ministry of Works and it is a delight to walk on the well kept lawns under the tall beech trees and think on the famous people, some sad, some gay, who walked within its walls. When Roger Mortimer had charge of the castle, a splendid tourney was held on the causeway for Henry III's son, Edmund Crouchback. It was at Kenilworth that Edward II signed his abdication, before he went to his death at Berkeley Castle and John of Gaunt, fourth son of Edward III, lavished money on the building of the Great Hall and private apartments. Henry V had a romantic summer lodge built on the far side of the Mere. Henry VIII spent considerable sums on the upkeep of the castle but it was Leicester who was the last great builder. He added a block at the south west corner of the inner ward, a gatehouse on the north side, and modernised the Keep and John of Gaunt's apartments until he had a castle his beloved Queen delighted to visit.

It was a pity that after destroying the castle, the Parliamentarian officers, headed by Colonel Hawkesworth, drained both the Mere, which formed an extensive lake on the south of the castle walls and a moat on the north

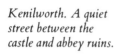

Kenilworth. A quiet street between the castle and abbey ruins.

side. A wide expanse of water would enhance the ruins and add considerably to the amenities of suburban Kenilworth.

Part of the Abbey lands is reserved as a park, on the banks of the small Finham Brook and some of the foundations of the Abbey and a gateway, can be seen in the churchyard of the parish church of St Nicholas. The magnificent Norman doorway of St Nicholas came from the Abbey and in the church, there is a ten-hundredweight pig of lead which was made from the Abbey roof.

After Robert Dudley had finished with the carefully dressed stone of the Abbey, the remainder was carted away for the building of the neighbouring farms and cottages; this accounts for their solid, sturdy appearance.

The castle ruins have been described as ugly, stark—a Victorian factory. But sit on the green opposite on a moonlit night, when the coach loads of visitors have gone, and then the ruins make a rare pattern against the sky and history becomes alive.

Kenilworth Castle." . . . in 1815, these trophies of time were quite neglected. Now . . . they are preserved and protected.". (Sir Walter Scott.)

236

CHAPTER TWELVE

Weavers, Watchmakers and Wars

The tall spires of three churches are clearly visible from Gibbet Hill when approaching Coventry along the Kenilworth Road. This pleasant road, with wide grass verges and protected woodlands, leads to Stivichal Common. The common adjoins the War Memorial Park, where a great variety of trees has been planted and the park extends across one hundred acres to Cheylesmore, the former estate of the Earls of Coventry.

The road continues towards the city centre, through Grey Friars Green, passing the elegant houses of Warwick Row, where George Eliot attended school. But beyond the Green, the main stream of one-way traffic is racing along and harassed visitors to the city seek a place in one of the crowded car parks within the circle of the Ring Road. This road surrounds the city centre, just as the great walls once encircled the old city of Coventry. Twentieth-century Coventry is the home of the

motorcar and Coventry people own the largest number of cars per head in the country, so it is recommended to explore the city centre on foot.

Old and new! There is so much to see—all of it huddled together in a relatively small area, with little room to spare for open spaces. Undoubtedly, the new cathedral is the focal point of the city centre. The beautifully dressed pink and blue stone rises beside the dark sandstone ruins of the old cathedral, where perhaps a more suitable positioning might be found for Epstein's powerful sculpture of the Struggling Christ.

It is amazing that the three tall spires or any of the city's timber-framed buildings, survived the bomb blast and the great fire of 1940. Survive they did and there are many historic buildings in Coventry if you know where to look. The direction signs point to the cathedral or to the shopping precincts.

I knew the town before the war, when the Repertory Theatre stood beside the old Grammar School on the corner of Hales Street and Bishop Street, but the once familiar haunts are hard to find. It is wise to start from the excellent Information Office in Broadgate and set out, armed with an up-to-date street map and a pocketful of free pamphlets.

The growth and development of Coventry was very different from that of Birmingham. Coventry was a

*Coventry. Bayley
Lane, beside the ruins
of St Michael's Cathe-
dral.*

small place, with a circumference of barely 2½ miles and was enclosed within a stout wall, 12 feet high. A good hound could have run across the town from Grey Friars to Swanswell Gate in less than five minutes. The wall was built in the 40 years following 1355 and had 12 gates and 32 towers. Charles II had the wall destroyed in 1662, because the Parliamentarians of Coventry had refused entry to his father.

Birmingham was surrounded by large family estates, belonging to the Colmores, the Goughs and the Holtes. These families sold their land for development. As a result, Birmingham became an important centre of the industrial revolution, whereas Coventry remained restricted.

Extensive commons, linked by Cheylesmore Park and the meadows of the Lammas and Michaelmas lands, surrounded Coventry, until eventually, after many years of dispute, enclosure came as a consequence of Acts of Parliament in 1860 and 1875. Meanwhile, Birmingham had been expanding rapidly for more than a hundred years.

The Marquis of Hertford sold the Cheylesmore estate in 1871. By the beginning of the twentieth century, Coventry's expansion was under way and the subsequent growth absorbed outlying manufacturing villages, in which craftsmen had settled when space within the city became too limited.

Ribbon weavers had set up at Hillfields. The villages of Chapelfields and Earlsdon were developed by the watchmakers, who had become overcrowded in Spon Street. As far out as Kingfield, the Quaker brothers, John and Joseph Cash, established a settlement of cottage homes, each provided with a powered workshop above.

In Birmingham, the metal trades have had their ups and downs since the first smiths settled by the River Rea, but the city's basic trades were always concerned with metals.

In Coventry on the contrary, the workers had to change from one trade to another—from being cloth weavers and cap-makers, using wool supplied by the Abbey's flocks; skinners, tanners and curriers, who worked on the raw hides for harness, shoe and glove making to becoming watch-makers, ribbon weavers, bicycle makers, and in more recent times, manufacturers of the latest models in cars and aero-engines.

Coventry workers have become accustomed over the centuries to depressions and the dying out of their trades. Their wool supplies dwindled after the Dissolution. Their hand-made watches could not compete with the Swiss imports, which were allowed into this country at the end of the nineteenth century. The ribbon trade declined owing to a change in fashion and the competition from France and Switzerland, when the import duty was removed by Mr Gladstone in 1860.

With the declining fashion in ribbons, the Coventry workers with their usual resilience turned to the rising popularity of the bicycle for their living. In 1940 came the biggest blow of all—the destruction by German bombs of much of their historic city, and many of their bicycle and developing motor car factories.

Fifteen years later, in spite of a shortage of money and materials, they were re-building their city and creating one of the first pedestrian shopping centres, a covered market, the Belgrave Repertory Theatre, the Lanchester Technical College, swimming baths, a library, the Herbert Museum and Art Gallery, hotels and their magnificent Cathedral—all alas within the boundary of the old city walls.

Small wonder there is no open space, only the small gardens left here and there. The largest of these is the Lady Herbert Garden of $1\frac{3}{4}$ acres in Hales Street. At the garden entrance is the Swanswell Gate and through the garden, a section of the city wall leads up to the Cook Street Gate. These are the only remaining city gates and both are well preserved. The gardens are a horticulturalists' delight, with their flowering shrubs, climbers and well planted borders. There are plenty of seats and a seated shelter from which to enjoy the colour of the flowers, the sandstone walls and the construction of the

Coventry. Lady Herbert's Garden alongside the old city wall between the Swanswell and Cook Street Gates.

old gateways.

Owing to the lack of any directional signs, the remaining section of wall, showing the base of one of the wall's 32 towers, is hard to locate. It lies between the Bishop Street and the Well Street gates and can be found on the rising ground behind the garage in Lamb Street, where

240

the old wall is cut off by the new wall of the Ring Road. A stepped footpath has been made beside it. On the other side of Lamb Street, the path follows a section of wall with a ruined round tower, between commercial buildings, to the backs of premises in Upper Well Street.

Looking across Well Street, down the open wastes on either side of Bond Street, is a group of buildings which escaped the blitz. The long gabled frontage of Bond's Hospital, with richly carved barge-boards, occupies one side of a quadrangle. The hospital, founded in 1506 and named after Thomas Bond, one of Coventry's drapers is Home, as it always has been, for 12 aged men, who have their own bed-sitting rooms and share a common room.

To the left of the imposing stone archway is the early Tudor building of Bablake School. The school was moved to larger premises at the end of the nineteenth century and the premises are now used by the Council. In the quadrangle beyond the archway, there is a shady seat in the small garden, from which can be seen the cloistered walk of the school under the overhang of the first storey. Opposite, there is another section of the city wall. The buildings stand on land given in 1344 by Queen Isabella, the scheming wife of Edward II, who, after his murder, tried to salve her conscience with pious deeds.

St John's Church forms the other side of the quad-rangle. The original building was a guild chapel, despoiled after the Dissolution and most of the present church is part of the restoration of 1875. The church is only separated from the Ring Road traffic by a narrow pavement. The door faces across the road to one of the entrances to the Precincts, thronged with shoppers, and offers—"A Welcome to All, at any hour of any day—a seat in the quiet reposeful interior"—according to the notice I saw, but alas, the door was firmly locked and there was no indication as to where the key might be obtained.

Around the other side of the church is Spon Street, where the city's watchmakers had their workshops and where they drank their ale at the Windmill Inn, next to Rotherham's.

Rotherham's no longer make watches but the Rotherham family house still forms part of the Spon Street frontage and Spon Street is now a conservation area. Here, the old buildings are being restored and others in the city which cannot remain on their original sites, are being removed and re-erected in Spon Street. Two workshop-houses are already completed and in time, it is hoped the whole street will be a record of the city's industrial history.

One of the many advantages of the Ring Road is the number of streets which have become relatively traffic-free culs-de-sac. There are only six exit streets from the

Coventry. **The garden of Bond's Hospital and Bablake School, dating from the early sixteenth century.**

city centre to the Ring Road.

Spon Street and its neighbour, Holyhead Road, are both *culs-de-sac*, and at the far end of Holyhead Road is one of the few remaining blocks of 'Top Shops'. These cottage shops were built in many parts of Coventry in the nineteenth century, with workshops on the second floor powered by a central steam engine. The men paid for the power they used, and wives and children could take their turn at the looms. In this way the families were able to keep their cherished independence and were not classed as factory workers.

Much of the new city centre has been designed for 'pedestrian circulation'. Walking through the shopping precincts, the first of which was opened in 1955, it is interesting to see how they have weathered. 'SEE' is the operative word. The present population of developing Coventry is approximately 350,000 and it seemed as if all the wives and children, prams, baskets and dogs surge ceaselessly through the shopping areas. The flock of pigeons, which rivals that of Trafalgar Square, walk unconcerned through the army of feet.

But the buildings are undistinguished—there is little to commend in them, the lettering of the shop names and the standard of the window dressing lack taste or style. True, the monotonous first floors of the buildings will be less obvious when the trees have grown, but it is doubt-

Coventry. Spon Street, the nineteenth-century watchmakers' quarter, where old workshops are being re-erected.

ful if the pools and fountains will ever be free of sodden litter and plastic containers.

In open markets, the combination of smells from the variety of goods on the stalls and the sweating humanity surrounding them, floats upwards into the open air.

A breath of fresh air would be welcome in Coventry's

243

Coventry. The old and the new.

household goods on sale and also for some of the sculptures in the Precincts. Presumably, the three-dimensional and relief work on display is for the cultural benefit of the busy shoppers who have little time to spare for art galleries. Or are they placed there to whet their appetite for more? Either way, surely they should be of the highest possible artistic merit. Why are works of the stature of Epstein and Hepworth confined to the Cathedral Precincts?

Looking down one of the Precinct arcades, with ghostly daylight coming through the blue fibreglass roof, there is a long view of Ford's Hospital. This handsomely gabled, half-timbered building, its daub and wattle painted a warm cream, its timbers a weathered brown, was built on the Grey Friars Monastery ground about 1512. Since then, it has been used continuously to house old people, except for the war years, when it was damaged in 1940 and not fully restored until 13 years later.

Behind and beside Ford's is one of the city's delightful small gardens, reached either through the archway which leads between the apartments or by the gate in Grey Friars Lane. Much loving care and labour have been expended on landscaping this garden, with its roses, shrubs and small pool, its rockeries and its neat paved walks. The evident thought behind this, makes it all the

covered market. Under the shallow market dome, ingeniously designed to serve as a first storey carpark, the air is thick with an indescribable mixture of smells—fish, meat, flowers, leather and humanity.

Plastic! Polythene! Polystyrene! words of the twentieth century. These are the materials used for most of the

244

more regrettable that the designers provided no shield for an unsightly row of dustbins.

At the end of Grey Friars Lane, on busy Union Street, stands the tower and steeple of Christ Church. This was built in the fourteenth century by the Grey Friars and was part of the large church adjoining the Friary. Their church was destroyed at the Dissolution and the later church, destroyed in 1940, was a much smaller one built in the 1830s.

Walking around the city centre, where efforts have been and still are being made to preserve the historic buildings which survived the war, it is obvious that these would have been much more effective if more land had been available. Christchurch steeple, one of Coventry's Three Spires, is easily seen from a distance but the four supporting arches of the tower, on the footpath below the carpark, with the Union Street shops meeting them on either side, are difficult to appreciate. Surrounded by a little space even on three sides, the beauty of the sandstone arches would have been enhanced.

Once again, there are no directional signs to the gateway of the Cheylesmore Manor House, which has been most carefully restored. It lies behind the new shops in Union Street, almost opposite the Christchurch arches. A low archway between the shops leads into Manor Yard, a pleasant, paved, tree-planted area, with a

seat from which to look up at the gateway. Little is known of the medieval manor house built behind the gateway in Cheylesmore Park. The parklands which stretched southwards for nearly two miles between Whitely and Stivichall Commons, are now occupied by motor-car factories and a maze of tightly packed streets; in the centre is the small open space surrounding Quinton pool.

The Black Prince was one of the Lords of the Manor of Cheylesmore. His exploits are recorded in the east window and tapestry in the Guildhall—a splendid hall in Bayley Lane, built for the Merchant Guild of St Mary in 1342. Despite the treatment it received after the suppression of the guilds, and the damage caused by incendiary bombs in 1940, it is now one of the finest examples of a medieval Guildhall in England.

On the other side of the Cathedral ruins, facing the small green planted with prunus trees, is Priory Row. At the end, near the new Cathedral, are the best examples of Coventry's Georgian houses.

No. 11 was built in the reign of George II (1727–60) and in 1849 it was the home of Dr Nathaniel Troughton. Dr Troughton was the senior partner in the firm of solicitors, Troughton, Lee and Kirby, who had their offices in Kirby House, Little Park Street. Nathaniel Troughton was a meticulous and prolific artist. Coventry City

Council are fortunate in having inherited at least a thousand of his water-colours and drawings, depicting the city of his time. These are an invaluable record of many of the streets and buildings which were reduced to rubble in 1940.

At the Trinity Street end of Priory Row are three half-timbered buildings built in the sixteenth century. These at one time formed Lych Gate House, built for John Bryan, Vicar of Holy Trinity. Between these houses and the later buildings in Priory Row are the ruins of the Priory, founded by the Mercian Earl Leofric and his wife Lady Godiva. This Priory was built in the thirteenth century to replace the smaller church on which Lady Godiva had lavished so much of her wealth before the building was destroyed by the Danes.

The most extensive survival of Coventry's early monastic buildings is part of the friary, built in 1342 for the Carmelite order, the White Friars. It is Coventry's one ancient building which, at the moment at least, can be viewed from a reasonable distance—across the waste land beside White Friar Lane and from the White Friar Gate House in Much Park Street.

The restored Gate House is occupied by a potter. A first class craftsman producing excellent work, he has converted the ground floor into a showroom with an art gallery where he shows contemporary European art. A

visit to the gallery is a chance to see the interior of this historic building, enhanced by the contents.

All that remains of the monastic buildings which occupied a large corner of the city between the New Gate and Gosford Gate is the east side of the cloisters, with the dormitory above. It is hoped, when the Ring Road is completed, that the waste land behind the building will be a garden.

After the suppression of the monastery, the house and its land were acquired by John Hales and it remained in his family until the eighteenth century, when it became a workhouse. A large Salvation Army Hostel is built on to the present Gulson Road frontage. As a result of several bequests, the old buildings were restored and opened in 1970 as a local history museum.

What a joy it is to walk in this fine old building, passing under the massive timber roof of the dormitory or under the groined vaulting of the cloister walk, with its nine bays. Along this walk, friars enjoyed quiet contemplation for nearly 200 years following the foundation of the friary in 1342.

Whether or not you believe the legend of Lady Godiva's ride, she was undoubtedly a kind and generous woman, Coventry's first famous lady.

In the fourteenth century, the churches of Holy Trinity and St Michael's were built. Holy Trinity, (now fully

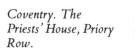

Coventry. The
Priests' House, Priory
Row.

restored after its bomb damage), was built for the tenants of the Prior's half of the town and St Michael's for those of the Earl. These rival churches were separated by a narrow roadway, appropriately named Cuckoo Lane.

According to an old rhyme, the two ladies of the Botoner family gave generously towards the building of St Michael's.

> William and Adam built the tower,
> Ann and Mary built the spire,
> William and Adam built the church,
> Ann and Mary built the quire.

Although she was not born in Coventry, Sarah Kemble's romantic marriage to William Siddons took place at St Michael's in 1773. Nearly a hundred years later, in a small house in Smithford Street, Ellen Terry was born. Daughter of well-known provincial actors, she is considered by many to have been England's finest actress.

She was an old lady before I saw her in a film. In my student days her grandson, John Gielgud, was playing his first Romeo at the Birmingham Repertory Theatre.

George Eliot spent her youth in Coventry, attending school in Warwick Row and keeping house for her father when he moved to Bird Grove—a house still standing with an entrance on to a side road appropriately named George Eliot Road.

All her novels, so many with a Warwickshire and Coventry background, were written after her father's death, when she lived in London with G. H. Lewes, the author of many philosophical books.

Warwick Row was a select district in George Eliot's youth. By 1911, the professional classes lived in the large houses in the Quadrant, on the other side of Grey Friars' Green. Here, at No. 1 Dr Walter Brazil was joined by his two sisters, Amy and Angela, two widely-travelled ladies. They settled happily enough in Coventry and filled their home with friends for musical evenings. Both sisters had studied art in Europe, and Amy became one of the distinguished members of the Warwickshire Society of Artists. One of their friends was Mary Dormer Harris, a farmer's daughter from Stoneleigh and a scholar of Lady Margaret Hall, Oxford. Her book on Warwickshire, illustrated with her own water-colours, is a charming record of the local villages between the wars. She also made a transcription of the Coventry Leet Book and, with the Brazils, was a prominent member of the City Guild and Museum Society, formed in 1914.

Angela Brazil's books about girls' schools were read avidly by my generation, as each one appeared. Angela died in 1947.

Although the total area covered by Coventry's parks and open spaces is over 1,200 acres, it seems woefully inadequate. Between the crowded housing estates and industrial sites from Tile Hill to Binley or Cheylesmore to Bedworth, the public parks are small and far apart. For fresh air or a walk in the wind, it is necessary to go to the city boundary—to the 100 acres of War Memorial Park or further out to Coombe Park.

The Corporation have acquired the Coombe Abbey Estate, barely two miles beyond the city boundary, for use as a country park. The Abbey was founded in 1150 on the banks of the River Smite, by Cistercian monks, who used the abundant grazing land for raising sheep. Together with their neighbours at Stoneleigh Abbey, they were the principal suppliers of wool to the Coventry weavers.

Today's motor manufacturers are concerned with export but so were their forbears, the Coventry weavers. Coventry cloth was well known when Edward III came to the throne in 1327 and the trade flourished until Tudor times. Their chief port of export, Bristol, was reached by road to the Avon and thence by boat to the Severn. Records show a steady trade with Ireland, and bolts of Coventry cloth went as far afield as the Baltic port of Stralsund.

After the Dissolution, most of the Abbey buildings were demolished but one wall of twelfth century construction, with three arches, originally the entrance to the Chapter House, now forms part of the courtyard of the present house.

One of the first owners of the Coombe estate was Sir John Harrington, who had in his care, Princess Elizabeth, daughter of James I. In 1605, the Gunpowder plotters tried to kidnap her but failed, and after remaining for three years in the comparative safety of the walled city of Coventry, she returned to Coombe.

Coombe belonged to the Craven family until the estate was sold in 1923. The Coventry Corporation were unable to purchase the house and the surrounding 279 acres until 1964, but two years later, it was opened as a natural park. With grants from the Countryside Commission, there are plans for its future development.

The approach to the house is magnificent. A drive between wide lawns, flanked on either side by fine avenues of lime trees, leads down a slight incline to the house. This is not open to the public, and is a jumble of architectural styles, but the vista across the formal garden and ornamental lake with its elegant stone balustrade, to the long lake beyond, demonstrates once more the master hand of 'Capability' Brown. Giant oaks, tall firs, pines and spreading beeches, are massed together on rising ground, forming a wonderful background to the gardens. Nature trails have already been set out in the woods and fields. There is an excellent small museum at the entrance to the trails, showing the types of birds, animals, butterflies and insects to be found.

Many types of waterfowl can be seen on the lake, and reeds have been allowed to grow as a habitat for reed buntings. In the tall trees beside the end of the lake, a heronry is already well established.

One of the factors in favour of Coventry's early weavers was the accessibility of the Roman Watling Street and the Fosse Way—trade routes well-established centuries before Coventry's walls were built.

At Baginton, which lies beyond the city boundary and north of the Fosse Way, a Roman fort known as the Lunt is being excavated. The interesting thing about this fort is the discovery of a weapon-training ground or *lundus*. This circular arena may also have been used for training horses by a method which was recommended as early as the fourth century, B.C. Another suggested possibility is that it was a *vivarium*—a place where wild animals were kept. Some Roman soldiers served as huntsmen and the forests around Baginton may well have contained wild animals, particularly bears. These animals were keenly hunted, not only for the sport itself and for eventual bear-baiting, but also for their pelts.

The Lunt excavations are on land scheduled for recreation. It has been possible to reconstruct one of the fort's wooden entrance gates and look-out tower with a section of the ramparts on either side. The walk on the top of the ramparts, a wall of earth reinforced with heavy timber palisades, affords a view of the lay-out of the whole fort. With the aid of the printed leaflet and the excellent large scale plan at the entrance, it is easy to visualise the buildings which surrounded the *gyrus* or training circle.

The village of Allesley, which used to be a bottle-neck on the old Birmingham road, is now part of a conservation area and is by-passed by the Dunchurch Highway.

The village street, which seemed so narrow when full of traffic, is pleasantly wide. The buildings on either side are typical of a small Midlands village. The cottages are separated by larger Georgian houses and the Stone House on the corner is largely sixteenth century.

Narrow Rectory Lane winds steeply up the hill to the church car park, which on my visit, was screened by tall rhododendrons in full bloom. High above the village street, thrushes and blackbirds were busy in the large churchyard. Further along, Rectory Lane crosses the River Sherbourne, which used to be a much larger river when it flowed through the walled city of Coventry.

One of the welcome open-space plans for the future is the development of land alongside the river and the brooks, including floodlands unsuitable for building.

Allesley, A quiet village atmosphere has returned since the construction of the Allesley by-pass.

Layouts for part of the scheme have already commenced at Bell Green and Canley.

The city lost a great potential asset when the River Sherbourne was directed underground at Spon End, not to emerge again until it flows under the Gulson Road.

There are by-roads out of Allesley to the pleasant acres of Coundon Park, up Wall Hill to Corley Moor, a favourite drive in George Eliot's day; also to Green End and on to Shustoke, where William Dugdale was born in 1605 and from which he attended the Free Grammar School in Coventry.

Across the fields, is the tall spire of Coleshill Church, a place deeply involved in the history of Warwickshire. The manor was held by Edward the Confessor and later by those master builders, the de Clintons and then the de Mountforts, whose castle stood to the south west of the town. It was here Robert Dudley, Earl of Leicester, crossed the moat on his clandestine visits to Lettice, Countess of Essex.

In coaching days, Coleshill was on the main route north from London to Chester, and was the place where the mail was off-loaded for—'Birmingham, near Coleshill'. Now, it is busy again on the route of the new road which connects with Stonebridge and the M1. A little further on between the new housing estates and the

mining villages around Nuneaton, stand the cooling towers of Hams Hall Power Station. It was from here, reluctantly, we followed a main road back to Birmingham.

Coleshill, which has Norman building, ancient family tombs, and a modern power station.

252

Index